T0274203

Data Mining

Data Mining

Edited by
Julio Bolton

Larsen & Keller
www.larsen-keller.com

Data Mining
Edited by Julio Bolton
ISBN: 978-1-63549-301-6 (Hardback)

© 2017 Larsen & Keller

 Larsen & Keller

Published by Larsen and Keller Education,
5 Penn Plaza,
19th Floor,
New York, NY 10001, USA

Cataloging-in-Publication Data

Data mining / edited by Julio Bolton.
      p. cm.
Includes bibliographical references and index.
ISBN 978-1-63549-301-6
    1. Data mining. 2. Electronic information resources.
I. Bolton, Julio.
QA76.9.D343 D38 2017
006.312--dc23

The publisher's policy is to use permanent paper from mills that operate a sustainable forestry policy. Furthermore, the publisher ensures that the text paper and cover boards used have met acceptable environmental accreditation standards.

Printed and bound in the United States of America.

For more information regarding Larsen and Keller Education and its products, please visit the publisher's website www.larsen-keller.com

Table of Contents

           • H2O (Software)   177
           • SAS (Software)   180
           • Orange (Software)   184
           • Massive Online Analysis   187
           • Natural Language Toolkit   189
           • OpenNN   190
           • General Architecture for Text Engineering   191

Chapter 8 **Applications of Data Mining**   **194**
           • Predictive Analytics   194
           • Decision Support System   208
           • Web Mining   213

Chapter 9 **Allied Fields of Data Mining**   **218**
           • Artificial Intelligence   218
           • Machine Learning   241
           • Statistics   252
           • Database   268

           Permissions

           Index

Preface

Data mining refers to that field of information technology, which deals with the extraction of useful information from various data sets and their transformation into an understandable structure. It consists of elements of machine learning, database systems, artificial intelligence, statistics, etc. This book unfolds the innovative aspects of data mining, which will be crucial for the holistic understanding of the subject matter. Selected concepts that redefine this field have been presented in the text. For someone with an interest and eye for detail, this textbook covers the most significant topics of this field. The textbook covers the fundamental components and practices that make up the data mining. It will serve as a reference to a broad spectrum of readers.

A foreword of all chapters of the book is provided below:

Chapter 1 - Data mining is a field in the subject of computer science. It helps in discovering and classification of data sets. It is associated with the processes of machine learning, artificial intelligence and database systems. This chapter will provide an integrated understanding of data mining; **Chapter 2** - Data is a set of information that is characterized in a particular manner. Data quality, data set, data management, data wrangling and data integration are some of the aspects that have been elucidated in the chapter. The section on data offers an insightful focus, keeping in mind the subject matter; **Chapter 3** - Analysis of data is the process that is used in altering and demonstrating data and it helps in discovering useful information and assists decision-making. Data analysis has aspects such as regression analysis, data cleaning, data transformation and data fusion. This chapter is a compilation of the concepts and processes of data mining that form an integral part of the broader subject matter; **Chapter 4** - The various data mining techniques are sequential pattern mining, process mining, text mining, data stream mining, bibliomining etc. Sequential pattern mining is concerned with searching for relevant patterns between data examples. The section serves as a source to understand the various data mining techniques; **Chapter 5** - The data mining algorithms are alpha algorithm, apriori algorithm, GSP algorithm and Teiresias algorithm. Alpha algorithm is an algorithm that is aimed at reconstructing causality while Teiresias algorithm enables the discovery of rigidity in biological sequences. The topics discussed in the chapter are of great importance to broaden the existing knowledge on data mining algorithms; **Chapter 6** - Cluster analysis is the task of grouping objects in a manner where the same group is more similar to other groups in some manner. Cluster analysis is used in many fields such as pattern recognition, image analysis, bioinformatics, information retrieval and computer graphics. The aspects explained in the following section are of vital importance and provide a better understanding of cluster analysis and examples of its algorithms; **Chapter 7** - The common data mining software are H2O, SAS, Orange, Massive Online Analysis, Natural Language Toolkit and General Architecture for Text Engineering. H2O is a software that is used for analysis of data. The speed of H2O allows users to fit thousands of models in order to discover patterns in data. This section is an overview of the subject matter, incorporating all the aspects of common data mining software; **Chapter 8** - Predictive analytics is a technique that helps in analyzing current and historical facts. These facts help in making predictions for unknown events. Decision support system and web mining are the other applications of data mining. Data mining can best be understood in confluence with the major applications listed in the following chapter; **Chapter 9** - Data mining is an interdisciplinary subject. It is a part of other fields as well. Fields such as artificial intelligence, machine learning, statistics and database make use of data mining. This subject helps in discovering patterns in the data sets and these data sets are involved in the joining of subjects such as artificial intelligence, statistics and database. This section will provide a glimpse of the related fields of data mining.

At the end, I would like to thank all the people associated with this book devoting their precious time and providing their valuable contributions to this book. I would also like to express my gratitude to my fellow colleagues who encouraged me

Editor

1

Introduction to Data Mining

Data mining is a field in the subject of computer science. It helps in discovering and classification of data sets. It is associated with the processes of machine learning, artificial intelligence and database systems. This chapter will provide an integrated understanding of data mining.

Data mining is an interdisciplinary subfield of computer science. It is the computational process of discovering patterns in large data sets involving methods at the intersection of artificial intelligence, machine learning, statistics, and database systems. The overall goal of the data mining process is to extract information from a data set and transform it into an understandable structure for further use. Aside from the raw analysis step, it involves database and data management aspects, data pre-processing, model and inference considerations, interestingness metrics, complexity considerations, post-processing of discovered structures, visualization, and online updating. Data mining is the analysis step of the "knowledge discovery in databases" process, or KDD.

The term is a misnomer, because the goal is the extraction of patterns and knowledge from large amounts of data, not the extraction (mining) of data itself. It also is a buzzword and is frequently applied to any form of large-scale data or information processing (collection, extraction, warehousing, analysis, and statistics) as well as any application of computer decision support system, including artificial intelligence, machine learning, and business intelligence. The book Data mining: Practical machine learning tools and techniques with Java (which covers mostly machine learning material) was originally to be named just Practical machine learning, and the term data mining was only added for marketing reasons. Often the more general terms (large scale) data analysis and analytics – or, when referring to actual methods, artificial intelligence and machine learning – are more appropriate.

The actual data mining task is the automatic or semi-automatic analysis of large quantities of data to extract previously unknown, interesting patterns such as groups of data records (cluster analysis), unusual records (anomaly detection), and dependencies (association rule mining). This usually involves using database techniques such as spatial indices. These patterns can then be seen as a kind of summary of the input data, and may be used in further analysis or, for example, in machine learning and predictive analytics. For example, the data mining step might identify multiple groups in the data, which can then be used to obtain more accurate prediction results by a decision support system. Neither the data collection, data preparation, nor result interpretation and reporting is part of the data mining step, but do belong to the overall KDD process as additional steps.

The related terms data dredging, data fishing, and data snooping refer to the use of data mining methods to sample parts of a larger population data set that are (or may be) too small for reliable statistical inferences to be made about the validity of any patterns discovered. These methods can, however, be used in creating new hypotheses to test against the larger data populations.

Etymology

In the 1960s, statisticians used terms like "Data Fishing" or "Data Dredging" to refer to what they considered the bad practice of analyzing data without an a-priori hypothesis. The term "Data Mining" appeared around 1990 in the database community. For a short time in 1980s, a phrase "database mining"™, was used, but since it was trademarked by HNC, a San Diego-based company, to pitch their Database Mining Workstation; researchers consequently turned to "data mining". Other terms used include Data Archaeology, Information Harvesting, Information Discovery, Knowledge Extraction, etc. Gregory Piatetsky-Shapiro coined the term "Knowledge Discovery in Databases" for the first workshop on the same topic (KDD-1989) and this term became more popular in AI and Machine Learning Community. However, the term data mining became more popular in the business and press communities. Currently, Data Mining and Knowledge Discovery are used interchangeably. Since about 2007, "Predictive Analytics" and since 2011, "Data Science" terms were also used to describe this field.

In the Academic community, the major forums for research started in 1995 when the First International Conference on Data Mining and Knowledge Discovery (KDD-95) was started in Montreal under AAAI sponsorship. It was co-chaired by Usama Fayyad and Ramasamy Uthurusamy. A year later, in 1996, Usama Fayyad launched the journal by Kluwer called Data Mining and Knowledge Discovery as its founding Editor-in-Chief. Later he started the SIGKDDD Newsletter SIGKDD Explorations. The KDD International conference became the primary highest quality conference in Data Mining with an acceptance rate of research paper submissions below 18%. The Journal Data Mining and Knowledge Discovery is the primary research journal of the field.

Background

The manual extraction of patterns from data has occurred for centuries. Early methods of identifying patterns in data include Bayes' theorem (1700s) and regression analysis (1800s). The proliferation, ubiquity and increasing power of computer technology has dramatically increased data collection, storage, and manipulation ability. As data sets have grown in size and complexity, direct "hands-on" data analysis has increasingly been augmented with indirect, automated data processing, aided by other discoveries in computer science, such as neural networks, cluster analysis, genetic algorithms (1950s), decision trees and decision rules (1960s), and support vector machines (1990s). Data mining is the process of applying these methods with the intention of uncovering hidden patterns in large data sets. It bridges the gap from applied statistics and artificial intelligence (which usually provide the mathematical background) to database management by exploiting the way data is stored and indexed in databases to execute the actual learning and discovery algorithms more efficiently, allowing such methods to be applied to ever larger data sets.

Process

The Knowledge Discovery in Databases (KDD) process is commonly defined with the stages:

> (1) Selection

> (2) Pre-processing

> (3) Transformation

(4) Data Mining

(5) Interpretation/Evaluation.

It exists, however, in many variations on this theme, such as the Cross Industry Standard Process for Data Mining (CRISP-DM) which defines six phases:

(1) Business Understanding

(2) Data Understanding

(3) Data Preparation

(4) Modeling

(5) Evaluation

(6) Deployment

or a simplified process such as (1) pre-processing, (2) data mining, and (3) results validation.

Polls conducted in 2002, 2004, 2007 and 2014 show that the CRISP-DM methodology is the leading methodology used by data miners. The only other data mining standard named in these polls was SEMMA. However, 3–4 times as many people reported using CRISP-DM. Several teams of researchers have published reviews of data mining process models, and Azevedo and Santos conducted a comparison of CRISP-DM and SEMMA in 2008.

Pre-processing

Before data mining algorithms can be used, a target data set must be assembled. As data mining can only uncover patterns actually present in the data, the target data set must be large enough to contain these patterns while remaining concise enough to be mined within an acceptable time limit. A common source for data is a data mart or data warehouse. Pre-processing is essential to analyze the multivariate data sets before data mining. The target set is then cleaned. Data cleaning removes the observations containing noise and those with missing data.

Data Mining

Data mining involves six common classes of tasks:

- Anomaly detection (Outlier/change/deviation detection) – The identification of unusual data records, that might be interesting or data errors that require further investigation.

- Association rule learning (Dependency modelling) – Searches for relationships between variables. For example, a supermarket might gather data on customer purchasing habits. Using association rule learning, the supermarket can determine which products are frequently bought together and use this information for marketing purposes. This is sometimes referred to as market basket analysis.

- Clustering – is the task of discovering groups and structures in the data that are in some way or another "similar", without using known structures in the data.

- Classification – is the task of generalizing known structure to apply to new data. For example, an e-mail program might attempt to classify an e-mail as "legitimate" or as "spam".

- Regression – attempts to find a function which models the data with the least error.

- Summarization – providing a more compact representation of the data set, including visualization and report generation.

Results Validation

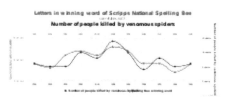

An example of data produced by data dredging through a bot operated by statistician Tyler Viglen, apparently showing a close link between the best word winning a spelling bee competition and the number of people in the United States killed by venomous spiders. The similarity in trends is obviously a coincidence.

Data mining can unintentionally be misused, and can then produce results which appear to be significant; but which do not actually predict future behaviour and cannot be reproduced on a new sample of data and bear little use. Often this results from investigating too many hypotheses and not performing proper statistical hypothesis testing. A simple version of this problem in machine learning is known as overfitting, but the same problem can arise at different phases of the process and thus a train/test split - when applicable at all - may not be sufficient to prevent this from happening.

The final step of knowledge discovery from data is to verify that the patterns produced by the data mining algorithms occur in the wider data set. Not all patterns found by the data mining algorithms are necessarily valid. It is common for the data mining algorithms to find patterns in the training set which are not present in the general data set. This is called overfitting. To overcome this, the evaluation uses a test set of data on which the data mining algorithm was not trained. The learned patterns are applied to this test set, and the resulting output is compared to the desired output. For example, a data mining algorithm trying to distinguish "spam" from "legitimate" emails would be trained on a training set of sample e-mails. Once trained, the learned patterns would be applied to the test set of e-mails on which it had not been trained. The accuracy of the patterns can then be measured from how many e-mails they correctly classify. A number of statistical methods may be used to evaluate the algorithm, such as ROC curves.

If the learned patterns do not meet the desired standards, subsequently it is necessary to re-evaluate and change the pre-processing and data mining steps. If the learned patterns do meet the desired standards, then the final step is to interpret the learned patterns and turn them into knowledge.

Research

The premier professional body in the field is the Association for Computing Machinery's (ACM) Special Interest Group (SIG) on Knowledge Discovery and Data Mining (SIGKDD). Since 1989 this

ACM SIG has hosted an annual international conference and published its proceedings, and since 1999 it has published a biannual academic journal titled "SIGKDD Explorations".

Computer science conferences on data mining include:

- CIKM Conference – ACM Conference on Information and Knowledge Management

- DMIN Conference – International Conference on Data Mining

- DMKD Conference – Research Issues on Data Mining and Knowledge Discovery

- DSAA Conference – IEEE International Conference on Data Science and Advanced Analytics

- ECDM Conference – European Conference on Data Mining

- ECML-PKDD Conference – European Conference on Machine Learning and Principles and Practice of Knowledge Discovery in Databases

- EDM Conference – International Conference on Educational Data Mining

- INFOCOM Conference – IEEE INFOCOM

- ICDM Conference – IEEE International Conference on Data Mining

- KDD Conference – ACM SIGKDD Conference on Knowledge Discovery and Data Mining

- MLDM Conference – Machine Learning and Data Mining in Pattern Recognition

- PAKDD Conference – The annual Pacific-Asia Conference on Knowledge Discovery and Data Mining

- PAW Conference – Predictive Analytics World

- SDM Conference – SIAM International Conference on Data Mining (SIAM)

- SSTD Symposium – Symposium on Spatial and Temporal Databases

- WSDM Conference – ACM Conference on Web Search and Data Mining

Data mining topics are also present on many data management/database conferences such as the ICDE Conference, SIGMOD Conference and International Conference on Very Large Data Bases

Standards

There have been some efforts to define standards for the data mining process, for example the 1999 European Cross Industry Standard Process for Data Mining (CRISP-DM 1.0) and the 2004 Java Data Mining standard (JDM 1.0). Development on successors to these processes (CRISP-DM 2.0 and JDM 2.0) was active in 2006, but has stalled since. JDM 2.0 was withdrawn without reaching a final draft.

For exchanging the extracted models – in particular for use in predictive analytics – the key standard is the Predictive Model Markup Language (PMML), which is an XML-based language developed by the Data Mining Group (DMG) and supported as exchange format by many data mining applications. As the name suggests, it only covers prediction models, a particular data mining task of high importance to business applications. However, extensions to cover (for example) subspace clustering have been proposed independently of the DMG.

Notable Uses

Data mining is used wherever there is digital data available today. Notable examples of data mining can be found throughout business, medicine, science, and surveillance.

Privacy Concerns and Ethics

While the term "data mining" itself has no ethical implications, it is often associated with the mining of information in relation to peoples' behavior (ethical and otherwise).

The ways in which data mining can be used can in some cases and contexts raise questions regarding privacy, legality, and ethics. In particular, data mining government or commercial data sets for national security or law enforcement purposes, such as in the Total Information Awareness Program or in ADVISE, has raised privacy concerns.

Data mining requires data preparation which can uncover information or patterns which may compromise confidentiality and privacy obligations. A common way for this to occur is through data aggregation. Data aggregation involves combining data together (possibly from various sources) in a way that facilitates analysis (but that also might make identification of private, individual-level data deducible or otherwise apparent). This is not data mining per se, but a result of the preparation of data before – and for the purposes of – the analysis. The threat to an individual's privacy comes into play when the data, once compiled, cause the data miner, or anyone who has access to the newly compiled data set, to be able to identify specific individuals, especially when the data were originally anonymous.

It is recommended that an individual is made aware of the following before data are collected:

- the purpose of the data collection and any (known) data mining projects;
- how the data will be used;
- who will be able to mine the data and use the data and their derivatives;
- the status of security surrounding access to the data;
- how collected data can be updated.

Data may also be modified so as to become anonymous, so that individuals may not readily be identified. However, even "de-identified"/"anonymized" data sets can potentially contain enough information to allow identification of individuals, as occurred when journalists were able to find several individuals based on a set of search histories that were inadvertently released by AOL.

The inadvertent revelation of personally identifiable information leading to the provider violates Fair Information Practices. This indiscretion can cause financial, emotional, or bodily harm to the indicated individual. In one instance of privacy violation, the patrons of Walgreens filed a lawsuit against the company in 2011 for selling prescription information to data mining companies who in turn provided the data to pharmaceutical companies.

Situation in Europe

Europe has rather strong privacy laws, and efforts are underway to further strengthen the rights of the consumers. However, the U.S.-E.U. Safe Harbor Principles currently effectively expose European users to privacy exploitation by U.S. companies. As a consequence of Edward Snowden's Global surveillance disclosure, there has been increased discussion to revoke this agreement, as in particular the data will be fully exposed to the National Security Agency, and attempts to reach an agreement have failed.

Situation in the United States

In the United States, privacy concerns have been addressed by the US Congress via the passage of regulatory controls such as the Health Insurance Portability and Accountability Act (HIPAA). The HIPAA requires individuals to give their "informed consent" regarding information they provide and its intended present and future uses. According to an article in Biotech Business Week', "'[i] n practice, HIPAA may not offer any greater protection than the longstanding regulations in the research arena,' says the AAHC. More importantly, the rule's goal of protection through informed consent is undermined by the complexity of consent forms that are required of patients and participants, which approach a level of incomprehensibility to average individuals." This underscores the necessity for data anonymity in data aggregation and mining practices.

U.S. information privacy legislation such as HIPAA and the Family Educational Rights and Privacy Act (FERPA) applies only to the specific areas that each such law addresses. Use of data mining by the majority of businesses in the U.S. is not controlled by any legislation.

Copyright Law

Situation in Europe

Due to a lack of flexibilities in European copyright and database law, the mining of in-copyright works such as web mining without the permission of the copyright owner is not legal. Where a database is pure data in Europe there is likely to be no copyright, but database rights may exist so data mining becomes subject to regulations by the Database Directive. On the recommendation of the Hargreaves review this led to the UK government to amend its copyright law in 2014 to allow content mining as a limitation and exception. Only the second country in the world to do so after Japan, which introduced an exception in 2009 for data mining. However, due to the restriction of the Copyright Directive, the UK exception only allows content mining for non-commercial purposes. UK copyright law also does not allow this provision to be overridden by contractual terms and conditions. The European Commission facilitated stakeholder discussion on text and data mining in 2013, under the title of Licences for Europe. The focus on the solution to this legal issue being licences and not limitations and exceptions led to representatives of universities, researchers, libraries, civil society groups and open access publishers to leave the stakeholder dialogue in May 2013.

Situation in the United States

By contrast to Europe, the flexible nature of US copyright law, and in particular fair use means that content mining in America, as well as other fair use countries such as Israel, Taiwan and South Korea is viewed as being legal. As content mining is transformative, that is it does not supplant the original work, it is viewed as being lawful under fair use. For example, as part of the Google Book settlement the presiding judge on the case ruled that Google's digitisation project of in-copyright books was lawful, in part because of the transformative uses that the digitisation project displayed - one being text and data mining.

Software

Free Open-source Data Mining Software and Applications

The following applications are available under free/open source licenses. Public access to application sourcecode is also available.

- Carrot2: Text and search results clustering framework.

- Chemicalize.org: A chemical structure miner and web search engine.

- ELKI: A university research project with advanced cluster analysis and outlier detection methods written in the Java language.

- GATE: a natural language processing and language engineering tool.

- KNIME: The Konstanz Information Miner, a user friendly and comprehensive data analytics framework.

- Massive Online Analysis (MOA): a real-time big data stream mining with concept drift tool in the Java programming language.

- ML-Flex: A software package that enables users to integrate with third-party machine-learning packages written in any programming language, execute classification analyses in parallel across multiple computing nodes, and produce HTML reports of classification results.

- MLPACK library: a collection of ready-to-use machine learning algorithms written in the C++ language.

- MEPX - cross platform tool for regression and classification problems based on a Genetic Programming variant.

- NLTK (Natural Language Toolkit): A suite of libraries and programs for symbolic and statistical natural language processing (NLP) for the Python language.

- OpenNN: Open neural networks library.

- Orange: A component-based data mining and machine learning software suite written in the Python language.

- R: A programming language and software environment for statistical computing, data mining, and graphics. It is part of the GNU Project.

- scikit-learn is an open source machine learning library for the Python programming language

- Torch: An open source deep learning library for the Lua programming language and scientific computing framework with wide support for machine learning algorithms.

- UIMA: The UIMA (Unstructured Information Management Architecture) is a component framework for analyzing unstructured content such as text, audio and video – originally developed by IBM.

- Weka: A suite of machine learning software applications written in the Java programming language.

Proprietary Data-mining Software and Applications

The following applications are available under proprietary licenses.

- Angoss KnowledgeSTUDIO: data mining tool provided by Angoss.

- Clarabridge: enterprise class text analytics solution.

- HP Vertica Analytics Platform: data mining software provided by HP.

- IBM SPSS Modeler: data mining software provided by IBM.

- KXEN Modeler: data mining tool provided by KXEN.

- LIONsolver: an integrated software application for data mining, business intelligence, and modeling that implements the Learning and Intelligent OptimizatioN (LION) approach.

- Megaputer Intelligence: data and text mining software is called PolyAnalyst.

- Microsoft Analysis Services: data mining software provided by Microsoft.

- NetOwl: suite of multilingual text and entity analytics products that enable data mining.

- OpenText™ Big Data Analytics: Visual Data Mining & Predictive Analysis by Open Text Corporation

- Oracle Data Mining: data mining software by Oracle.

- PSeven: platform for automation of engineering simulation and analysis, multidisciplinary optimization and data mining provided by DATADVANCE.

- Qlucore Omics Explorer: data mining software provided by Qlucore.

- RapidMiner: An environment for machine learning and data mining experiments.

- SAS Enterprise Miner: data mining software provided by the SAS Institute.

- STATISTICA Data Miner: data mining software provided by StatSoft.

- Tanagra: A visualisation-oriented data mining software, also for teaching.

Marketplace Surveys

Several researchers and organizations have conducted reviews of data mining tools and surveys of data miners. These identify some of the strengths and weaknesses of the software packages. They also provide an overview of the behaviors, preferences and views of data miners. Some of these reports include:

- Hurwitz Victory Index: Report for Advanced Analytics as a market research assessment tool, it highlights both the diverse uses for advanced analytics technology and the vendors who make those applications possible.Recent-research

- 2011 Wiley Interdisciplinary Reviews: Data Mining and Knowledge Discovery

- Rexer Analytics Data Miner Surveys (2007–2013)

- Forrester Research 2010 Predictive Analytics and Data Mining Solutions report

- Gartner 2008 "Magic Quadrant" report

- Robert A. Nisbet's 2006 Three Part Series of articles "Data Mining Tools: Which One is Best For CRM?"

- Haughton et al.'s 2003 Review of Data Mining Software Packages in The American Statistician

- Goebel & Gruenwald 1999 "A Survey of Data Mining a Knowledge Discovery Software Tools" in SIGKDD Explorations

References

- Witten, Ian H.; Frank, Eibe; Hall, Mark A. (30 January 2011). Data Mining: Practical Machine Learning Tools and Techniques (3 ed.). Elsevier. ISBN 978-0-12-374856-0.

- Mena, Jesús (2011). Machine Learning Forensics for Law Enforcement, Security, and Intelligence. Boca Raton, FL: CRC Press (Taylor & Francis Group). ISBN 978-1-4398-6069-4.

- Kantardzic, Mehmed (2003). Data Mining: Concepts, Models, Methods, and Algorithms. John Wiley & Sons. ISBN 0-471-22852-4. OCLC 50055336.

- UK Researchers Given Data Mining Right Under New UK Copyright Laws. Archived June 9, 2014, at the Wayback Machine. Out-Law.com. Retrieved 14 November 2014

- "Text and Data Mining:Its importance and the need for change in Europe". Association of European Research Libraries. Retrieved 14 November 2014.

- "Judge grants summary judgment in favor of Google Books — a fair use victory". Lexology.com. Antonelli Law Ltd. Retrieved 14 November 2014.

- Hastie, Trevor; Tibshirani, Robert; Friedman, Jerome (2009). "The Elements of Statistical Learning: Data Mining, Inference, and Prediction". Retrieved 2012-08-07.

- Piatetsky-Shapiro, Gregory; Parker, Gary (2011). "Lesson: Data Mining, and Knowledge Discovery: An Introduction". Introduction to Data Mining. KD Nuggets. Retrieved 30 August 2012.

- Mikut, Ralf; Reischl, Markus (September–October 2011). "Data Mining Tools". Wiley Interdisciplinary Reviews: Data Mining and Knowledge Discovery. 1 (5): 431–445. doi:10.1002/widm.24. Retrieved October 21, 2011.

- Kobielus, James; The Forrester Wave: Predictive Analytics and Data Mining Solutions, Q1 2010, Forrester Research, 1 July 2008

- Fayyad, Usama (15 June 1999). "First Editorial by Editor-in-Chief". SIGKDD Explorations. 1 (1): 1. doi:10.1145/2207243.2207269. Retrieved 27 December 2010.

2

Data: Quality, Set and Management

Data is a set of information that is characterized in a particular manner. Data quality, data set, data management, data wrangling and data integration are some of the aspects that have been elucidated in the chapter. The section on data offers an insightful focus, keeping in mind the subject matter.

Data

Data is a set of values of qualitative or quantitative variables. An example of qualitative data would be an anthropologist's handwritten notes about her interviews with people of an Indigenous tribe. Pieces of data are individual pieces of information. While the concept of data is commonly associated with scientific research, data is collected by a huge range of organizations and institutions, including businesses (e.g., sales data, revenue, profits, stock price), governments (e.g., crime rates, unemployment rates, literacy rates) and non-governmental organizations (e.g., censuses of the number of homeless people by non-profit organizations).

Some of the different types of data.

Data is measured, collected and reported, and analyzed, whereupon it can be visualized using graphs, images or other analysis tools. Data as a general concept refers to the fact that some existing information or knowledge is *represented* or *coded* in some form suitable for better usage or processing. *Raw data* ("unprocessed data") is a collection of numbers or characters before it has been "cleaned" and corrected by researchers. Raw data needs to be corrected to remove outliers or obvious instrument or data entry errors (e.g., a thermometer reading from an outdoor Arctic location recording a tropical temperature). Data processing commonly occurs by stages, and the "processed data" from one stage may be considered the "raw data" of the next stage. Field data is raw data that is collected in an uncontrolled "in situ" environment. Experimental data is data that is generated within the context of a scientific investigation by observation and recording.

Etymology and Terminology

The first English use of the word "data" is from the 1640s. Using the word "data" to mean "transmittable and storable computer information" was first done in 1946. The expression "data processing" was first used in 1954.

The Latin word *data* is the plural of *datum*, "(thing) given," neuter past participle of *dare* "to give". Data may be used as a plural noun in this sense, with some writers in the 2010s using *datum* in the singular and *data* for plural. In the 2010s, though, in non-specialist, everyday writing, "data" is most commonly used in the singular, as a mass noun (like "information", "sand" or "rain").

Meaning

Data, information, knowledge and wisdom are closely related concepts, but each has its own role in relation to the other, and each term has its own meaning. Data is collected and analyzed; data only becomes information suitable for making decisions once it has been analyzed in some fashion. Knowledge is derived from extensive amounts of experience dealing with information on a subject. For example, the height of Mt. Everest is generally considered data. The height can be recorded precisely with an altimeter and entered into a database. This data may be included in a book along with other data on Mt. Everest to describe the mountain in a manner useful for those who wish to make a decision about the best method to climb it. Using an understanding based on experience climbing mountains to advise persons on the way to reach Mt. Everest's peak may be seen as "knowledge". Some complement the series "data", "information" and "knowledge" with "wisdom", which would mean the status of a person in possession of a certain "knowledge" who also knows under which circumstances is good to use it.

That is to say, data is the least abstract, information the next least, and knowledge the most abstract. Data becomes information by interpretation; e.g., the height of Mt. Everest is generally considered "data", a book on Mt. Everest geological characteristics may be considered "information", and a climber's guidebook containing practical information on the best way to reach Mt. Everest's peak may be considered "knowledge". "Information" bears a diversity of meanings that ranges from everyday usage to technical use. Generally speaking, the concept of information is closely related to notions of constraint, communication, control, data, form, instruction, knowledge, meaning, mental stimulus, pattern, perception, and representation. Beynon-Davies uses the concept of a sign to differentiate between data and information; data is a series of symbols, while information occurs when the symbols are used to refer to something.

Before the development of computing devices and machines, only people could collect data and impose patterns on it. Since the development of computing devices and machines, these devices can also collect data. In the 2010s, computers are widely used in many fields to collect data and sort or process it, in disciplines ranging from marketing, analysis of social services usage by citizens to scientific research. These patterns in data are seen as information which can be used to enhance knowledge. These patterns may be interpreted as "truth" (though "truth" can be a subjective concept), and may be authorized as aesthetic and ethical criteria in some disciplines or cultures. Events that leave behind perceivable physical or virtual remains can be traced back through data. Marks are no longer considered data once the link between the mark and observation is broken.

Mechanical computing devices are classified according to the means by which they represent data. An analog computer represents a datum as a voltage, distance, position, or other physical quantity. A digital computer represents a piece of data as a sequence of symbols drawn from a fixed alphabet. The most common digital computers use a binary alphabet, that is, an alphabet of two characters, typically denoted "0" and "1". More familiar representations, such as numbers or letters, are then constructed from the binary alphabet. Some special forms of data are distinguished. A computer program is a collection of data, which can be interpreted as instructions. Most computer languages make a distinction between programs and the other data on which programs operate, but in some languages, notably Lisp and similar languages, programs are essentially indistinguishable from other data. It is also useful to distinguish metadata, that is, a description of other data. A similar yet earlier term for metadata is "ancillary data." The prototypical example of metadata is the library catalog, which is a description of the contents of books.

In Other Fields

Though data is also increasingly used in other fields, it has been suggested that the highly interpretive nature of them might be at odds with the ethos of data as "given". Peter Checkland introduced the term *capta* (from the Latin *capered*, "to take") to distinguish between an immense number of possible data and a sub-set of them, to which attention is oriented. Johanna Drucker has argued that since the humanities affirm knowledge production as "situated, partial, and constitutive," using *data* may introduce assumptions that are counterproductive, for example that phenomena are discrete or are observer-independent. The term *capta*, which emphasizes the act of observation as constitutive, is offered as an alternative to *data* for visual representations in the humanities.

Data Quality

Data quality refers to the condition of a set of values of qualitative or quantitative variables. There are many definitions of data quality but data is generally considered high quality if it is "fit for [its] intended uses in operations, decision making and planning." (Tom Redman<Redman, T.C. (2008). Data driven: Profiting from your most important business asset (p. 56). Boston, Mass.: Harvard Business Press.>). Alternatively, data is deemed of high quality if it correctly represents the real-world construct to which it refers. Furthermore, apart from these definitions, as data volume increases, the question of internal consistency within data becomes significant, regardless of fitness for use for any particular external purpose. People's views on data quality can often be in disagreement, even when discussing the same set of data used for the same purpose.

Definitions

This list is taken from the online book "Data Quality: High-impact Strategies".

- Degree of excellence exhibited by the data in relation to the portrayal of the actual scenario.
- The state of completeness, validity, consistency, timeliness and accuracy that makes data appropriate for a specific use.

- The totality of features and characteristics of data that bears on its ability to satisfy a given purpose; the sum of the degrees of excellence for factors related to data.

- The processes and technologies involved in ensuring the conformance of data values to business requirements and acceptance criteria.

- Complete, standards based, consistent, accurate and time stamped.

If the ISO 9000:2015 definition of quality is applied, data quality can be defined as the degree to which a set of characteristics of data fulfills requirements. Examples of characteristics are: completeness, validity, accuracy, consistency, availability and timeliness. Requirements are defined as the need or expectation that is stated, generally implied or obligatory.

History

Before the rise of the inexpensive computer data storage, massive mainframe computers were used to maintain name and address data for delivery services. This was so that mail could be properly routed to its destination. The mainframes used business rules to correct common misspellings and typographical errors in name and address data, as well as to track customers who had moved, died, gone to prison, married, divorced, or experienced other life-changing events. Government agencies began to make postal data available to a few service companies to cross-reference customer data with the National Change of Address registry (NCOA). This technology saved large companies millions of dollars in comparison to manual correction of customer data. Large companies saved on postage, as bills and direct marketing materials made their way to the intended customer more accurately. Initially sold as a service, data quality moved inside the walls of corporations, as low-cost and powerful server technology became available.

Companies with an emphasis on marketing often focused their quality efforts on name and address information, but data quality is recognized as an important property of all types of data. Principles of data quality can be applied to supply chain data, transactional data, and nearly every other category of data found. For example, making supply chain data conform to a certain standard has value to an organization by: 1) avoiding overstocking of similar but slightly different stock; 2) avoiding false stock-out; 3) improving the understanding of vendor purchases to negotiate volume discounts; and 4) avoiding logistics costs in stocking and shipping parts across a large organization.

For companies with significant research efforts, data quality can include developing protocols for research methods, reducing measurement error, bounds checking of data, cross tabulation, modeling and outlier detection, verifying data integrity, etc.

Overview

There are a number of theoretical frameworks for understanding data quality. A systems-theoretical approach influenced by American pragmatism expands the definition of data quality to include information quality, and emphasizes the inclusiveness of the fundamental dimensions of accuracy and precision on the basis of the theory of science (Ivanov, 1972). One framework, dubbed "Zero Defect Data" (Hansen, 1991) adapts the principles of statistical process control to data quality. Another framework seeks to integrate the product perspective (conformance to specifications) and the service perspective (meeting consumers' expectations) (Kahn et al. 2002). Another framework is based in semiotics to evaluate the quality of the form, meaning and use of the data (Price and Shanks, 2004). One highly theoretical approach analyzes the ontological nature of information systems to define data quality rigorously (Wand and Wang, 1996).

A considerable amount of data quality research involves investigating and describing various categories of desirable attributes (or dimensions) of data. These dimensions commonly include accuracy, correctness, currency, completeness and relevance. Nearly 200 such terms have been identified and there is little agreement in their nature (are these concepts, goals or criteria?), their definitions or measures (Wang et al., 1993). Software engineers may recognize this as a similar problem to "ilities".

MIT has a Total Data Quality Management program, led by Professor Richard Wang, which produces a large number of publications and hosts a significant international conference in this field (International Conference on Information Quality, ICIQ). This program grew out of the work done by Hansen on the "Zero Defect Data" framework (Hansen, 1991).

In practice, data quality is a concern for professionals involved with a wide range of information systems, ranging from data warehousing and business intelligence to customer relationship management and supply chain management. One industry study estimated the total cost to the U.S. economy of data quality problems at over U.S. $600 billion per annum (Eckerson, 2002). Incorrect data – which includes invalid and outdated information – can originate from different data sources – through data entry, or data migration and conversion projects.

In 2002, the USPS and PricewaterhouseCoopers released a report stating that 23.6 percent of all U.S. mail sent is incorrectly addressed.

One reason contact data becomes stale very quickly in the average database – more than 45 million Americans change their address every year.

In fact, the problem is such a concern that companies are beginning to set up a data governance team whose sole role in the corporation is to be responsible for data quality. In some[who?] organizations, this data governance function has been established as part of a larger Regulatory Compliance function - a recognition of the importance of Data/Information Quality to organizations.

Problems with data quality don't only arise from *incorrect* data; *inconsistent* data is a problem as well. Eliminating data shadow systems and centralizing data in a warehouse is one of the initiatives a company can take to ensure data consistency.

Enterprises, scientists, and researchers are starting to participate within data curation communities to improve the quality of their common data.

The market is going some way to providing data quality assurance. A number of vendors make tools for analyzing and repairing poor quality data *in situ," service providers can clean the data on a contract basis and consultants can advise on fixing processes or systems to avoid data quality problems in the first place. Most data quality tools offer a series of tools for improving data, which may include some or all of the following:*

1. Data profiling - initially assessing the data to understand its quality challenges.

2. Data standardization - a business rules engine that ensures that data conforms to quality rules.

3. Geocoding - for name and address data. Corrects data to U.S. and Worldwide postal standards.

4. Matching or Linking - a way to compare data so that similar, but slightly different records can be aligned. Matching may use "fuzzy logic" to find duplicates in the data. It often recognizes that "Bob" and "Robert" may be the same individual. It might be able to manage "householding", or finding links between spouses at the same address, for example. Finally, it often can build a "best of breed" record, taking the best components from multiple data sources and building a single super-record.

5. Monitoring - keeping track of data quality over time and reporting variations in the quality of data. Software can also auto-correct the variations based on pre-defined business rules.

6. Batch and Real time - Once the data is initially cleansed (batch), companies often want to build the processes into enterprise applications to keep it clean.

There are several well-known authors and self-styled experts, with Larry English perhaps the most popular guru. In addition, IQ International - the International Association for Information and Data Quality was established in 2004 to provide a focal point for professionals and researchers in this field.

ISO 8000 is an international standard for data quality.

Data Quality Assurance

Data quality assurance is the process of profiling the data to discover inconsistencies and other anomalies in the data, as well as performing data cleansing activities (e.g. removing outliers, missing data interpolation) to improve the data quality.

These activities can be undertaken as part of data warehousing or as part of the database administration of an existing piece of applications software.

Data Quality Control

Data quality control is the process of controlling the usage of data with known quality measurements for an application or a process. This process is usually done after a Data Quality Assurance (QA) process, which consists of discovery of data inconsistency and correction.

Data QA processes provides following information to Data Quality Control (QC):

*   Severity of inconsistency

*   Incompleteness

*   Accuracy

*   Precision

*   Missing / Unknown

The Data QC process uses the information from the QA process to decide to use the data for analysis or in an application or business process. For example, if a Data QC process finds that the data contains too many errors or inconsistencies, then it prevents that data from being used for its intended process which could cause disruption. For example, providing invalid measurements from several sensors to the automatic pilot feature on an aircraft could cause it to crash. Thus, establishing data QC process provides the protection of usage of data control and establishes safe information usage.

Optimum use of Data Quality

Data Quality (DQ) is a niche area required for the integrity of the data management by covering gaps of data issues. This is one of the key functions that aid data governance by monitoring data to find exceptions undiscovered by current data management operations. Data Quality checks may be defined at attribute level to have full control on its remediation steps.

DQ checks and business rules may easily overlap if an organization is not attentive of its DQ scope. Business teams should understand the DQ scope thoroughly in order to avoid overlap. Data quality checks are redundant if business logic covers the same functionality and fulfills the same purpose as DQ. The DQ scope of an organization should be defined in DQ strategy and well implemented. Some data quality checks may be translated into business rules after repeated instances of exceptions in the past.

Below are a few areas of data flows that may need perennial DQ checks:

Completeness and precision DQ checks on all data may be performed at the point of entry for each mandatory attribute from each source system. Few attribute values are created way after the initial creation of the transaction; in such cases, administering these checks becomes tricky and should be done immediately after the defined event of that attribute's source and the transaction's other core attribute conditions are met.

All data having attributes referring to *Reference Data* in the organization may be validated against the set of well-defined valid values of Reference Data to discover new or discrepant values through the validity DQ check. Results may be used to update *Reference Data* administered under *Master Data Management (MDM).*

All data sourced from a *third party* to organization's internal teams may undergo accuracy (DQ) check against the third party data. These DQ check results are valuable when administered on data that made multiple hops after the point of entry of that data but before that data becomes authorized or stored for enterprise intelligence.

All data columns that refer to *Master Data* may be validated for its consistency check. A DQ check administered on the data at the point of entry discovers new data for the MDM process, but a DQ check administered after the point of entry discovers the failure (not exceptions) of consistency.

As data transforms, multiple timestamps and the positions of that timestamps are captured and may be compared against each other and its leeway to validate its value, decay, operational significance against a defined SLA (service level agreement). This timeliness DQ check can be utilized to decrease data value decay rate and optimize the policies of data movement timeline.

In an organization complex logic is usually segregated into simpler logic across multiple processes.

Reasonableness DQ checks on such complex logic yielding to a logical result within a specific range of values or static interrelationships (aggregated business rules) may be validated to discover complicated but crucial business processes and outliers of the data, its drift from BAU (business as usual) expectations, and may provide possible exceptions eventually resulting into data issues. This check may be a simple generic aggregation rule engulfed by large chunk of data or it can be a complicated logic on a group of attributes of a transaction pertaining to the core business of the organization. This DQ check requires high degree of business knowledge and acumen. Discovery of reasonableness issues may aid for policy and strategy changes by either business or data governance or both.

Conformity checks and integrity checks need not covered in all business needs, it's strictly under the database architecture's discretion.

There are many places in the data movement where DQ checks may not be required. For instance, DQ check for completeness and precision on not–null columns is redundant for the data sourced from database. Similarly, data should be validated for its accuracy with respect to time when the data is stitched across disparate sources. However, that is a business rule and should not be in the DQ scope.

Regretfully, from a software development perspective, Data Quality is often seen as a non functional requirement. And as such, key data quality checks/processes are not factored into the final software solution. Within Healthcare, wearable technologies or Body Area Networks, generate large volumes of data. The level of detail required to ensure data quality is extremely high and is often under estimated. This is also true for the vast majority of mHealth apps, EHRs and other health related software solutions. The primary reason for this, stems from the extra cost involved is added a higher degree of rigor within the software architecture.

Criticism of Existing Tools and Processes

The main reasons cited are:

- Project costs: costs are typically in the hundreds of thousands of dollars
- Time: lack of enough time to deal with large-scale data-cleansing software
- Security: concerns over sharing information, giving an application access across systems, and effects on legacy systems

Professional Associations

IQ International—the International Association for Information and Data Quality

IQ International is a not-for-profit, vendor neutral, professional association formed in 2004, dedicated to building the information and data quality profession.

Data Set

A data set (or dataset, although this spelling is not present in many contemporary dictionaries) is a collection of data.

Most commonly a data set corresponds to the contents of a single database table, or a single statistical data matrix, where every column of the table represents a particular variable, and each row corresponds to a given member of the data set in question. The data set lists values for each of the variables, such as height and weight of an object, for each member of the data set. Each value is known as a datum. The data set may comprise data for one or more members, corresponding to the number of rows.

The term data set may also be used more loosely, to refer to the data in a collection of closely related tables, corresponding to a particular experiment or event. An example of this type is the data sets collected by space agencies performing experiments with instruments aboard space probes.

In the open data discipline, dataset is the unit to measure the information released in a public open data repository. The European Open Data portal aggregates more than half a million datasets. In this field other definitions have been proposed but currently there is not an official one. Some other issues (real-time data sources, non-relational datasets, etc.) increases the difficulty to reach a consensus about it.

History

Historically, the term originated in the mainframe field, where it had a well-defined meaning, very close to the contemporary *computer file*.

Properties

Several characteristics define a data set's structure and properties. These include the number and types of the attributes or variables, and various statistical measures applicable to them, such as standard deviation and kurtosis.

The values may be numbers, such as real numbers or integers, for example representing a person's height in centimeters, but may also be nominal data (i.e., not consisting of numerical values), for example representing a person's ethnicity. More generally, values may be of any of the kinds described as a level of measurement. For each variable, the values are normally all of the same kind. However, there may also be *missing values*, which must be indicated in some way.

In statistics, data sets usually come from actual observations obtained by sampling a statistical population, and each row corresponds to the observations on one element of that population. Data sets may further be generated by algorithms for the purpose of testing certain kinds of software. Some modern statistical analysis software such as SPSS still present their data in the classical data set fashion. If data is missing or suspicious an imputation method may be used to complete a data set.

Classic Data Sets

Several classic data sets have been used extensively in the statistical literature:

- Iris flower data set – Multivariate data set introduced by Ronald Fisher (1936).
- MNIST database – Images of handwritten digits commonly used to test classification, clustering, and image processing algorithms

- *Categorical data analysis* – Data sets used in the book, *An Introduction to Categorical Data Analysis*.

- *Robust statistics* – Data sets used in *Robust Regression and Outlier Detection* (Rousseeuw and Leroy, 1986). Provided on-line at the University of Cologne.

- *Time series* – Data used in Chatfield's book, *The Analysis of Time Series*, are provided on-line by StatLib.

- *Extreme values* – Data used in the book, *An Introduction to the Statistical Modeling of Extreme Values* are a snapshot of the data as it was provided on-line by Stuart Coles, the book's author.

- *Bayesian Data Analysis* – Data used in the book are provided on-line by Andrew Gelman, one of the book's authors.

- The Bupa liver data – Used in several papers in the machine learning (data mining) literature.

- Anscombe's quartet – Small data set illustrating the importance of graphing the data to avoid statistical fallacies

Data Collection

Adélie penguins are identified and weighed each time they cross the automated weighbridge on their way to or from the sea.

Data collection is the process of gathering and measuring information on targeted variables in an established systematic fashion, which then enables one to answer relevant questions and evaluate outcomes. The data collection component of research is common to all fields of study including physical and social sciences, humanities and business.It help us to collect the main points as gathered information. While methods vary by discipline, the emphasis on ensuring accurate and honest collection remains the same. The goal for all data collection is to capture quality evidence that then translates to rich data analysis and allows the building of a convincing and credible answer to questions that have been posed.

Importance

Regardless of the field of study or preference for defining data (quantitative or qualitative), accurate data collection is essential to maintaining the integrity of research. Both the selection of appropriate data collection instruments (existing, modified, or newly developed) and clearly delineated instructions for their correct use reduce the likelihood of errors occurring.

A formal data collection process is necessary as it ensures that the data gathered are both defined and accurate and that subsequent decisions based on arguments embodied in the findings are valid. The process provides both a baseline from which to measure and in certain cases a target on what to improve.

Types

Generally there are three types of data collection and they are:

1. Surveys: Standardized paper-and-pencil or phone questionnaires that ask predetermined questions.

2. Interviews: Structured or unstructured one-on-one directed conversations with key individuals or leaders in a community.

3. Focus groups: Structured interviews with small groups of like individuals using standardized questions, follow-up questions, and exploration of other topics that arise to better understand participants.

Consequences from improperly collected data include:

- Inability to answer research questions accurately;

- Inability to repeat and validate the study.

Impact of Faulty Data

Distorted findings result in wasted resources and can mislead other researchers to pursue fruitless avenues of investigation. This compromises decisions for public policy.

While the degree of impact from faulty data collection may vary by discipline and the nature of investigation, there is the potential to cause disproportionate harm when these research results are used to support public policy recommendations.

Anomaly Detection

In data mining, anomaly detection (also outlier detection) is the identification of items, events or observations which do not conform to an expected pattern or other items in a dataset. Typically the anomalous items will translate to some kind of problem such as bank fraud, a structural defect, medical problems or errors in a text. Anomalies are also referred to as outliers, novelties, noise, deviations and exceptions.

In particular, in the context of abuse and network intrusion detection, the interesting objects are often not *rare* objects, but unexpected *bursts* in activity. This pattern does not adhere to the common statistical definition of an outlier as a rare object, and many outlier detection methods (in particular unsupervised methods) will fail on such data, unless it has been aggregated appropriately. Instead, a cluster analysis algorithm may be able to detect the micro clusters formed by these patterns.

Three broad categories of anomaly detection techniques exist. Unsupervised anomaly detection techniques detect anomalies in an unlabeled test data set under the assumption that the majority of the instances in the data set are normal by looking for instances that seem to fit least to the remainder of the data set. Supervised anomaly detection techniques require a data set that has been labeled as "normal" and "abnormal" and involves training a classifier (the key difference to many other statistical classification problems is the inherent unbalanced nature of outlier detection). Semi-supervised anomaly detection techniques construct a model representing normal behavior from a given *normal* training data set, and then testing the likelihood of a test instance to be generated by the learnt model.

Applications

Anomaly detection is applicable in a variety of domains, such as intrusion detection, fraud detection, fault detection, system health monitoring, event detection in sensor networks, and detecting Eco-system disturbances. It is often used in preprocessing to remove anomalous data from the dataset. In supervised learning, removing the anomalous data from the dataset often results in a statistically significant increase in accuracy.

Popular Techniques

Several anomaly detection techniques have been proposed in literature. Some of the popular techniques are:

- Density-based techniques (k-nearest neighbor, local outlier factor, and many more variations of this concept).

- Subspace- and correlation-based outlier detection for high-dimensional data.

- One class support vector machines.

- Replicator neural networks.

- Cluster analysis-based outlier detection.

- Deviations from association rules and frequent itemsets.

- Fuzzy logic based outlier detection.

- Ensemble techniques, using feature bagging, score normalization and different sources of diversity.

The performance of different methods depends a lot on the data set and parameters, and methods have little systematic advantages over another when compared across many data sets and parameters.

Application to Data Security

Anomaly detection was proposed for intrusion detection systems (IDS) by Dorothy Denning in 1986. Anomaly detection for IDS is normally accomplished with thresholds and statistics, but can also be done with soft computing, and inductive learning. Types of statistics proposed by 1999 included profiles of users, workstations, networks, remote hosts, groups of users, and programs based on frequencies, means, variances, covariances, and standard deviations. The counterpart of anomaly detection in intrusion detection is misuse detection.

Software

- ELKI is an open-source Java data mining toolkit that contains several anomaly detection algorithms, as well as index acceleration for them.

Statistical Classification

In machine learning and statistics, classification is the problem of identifying to which of a set of categories (sub-populations) a new observation belongs, on the basis of a training set of data containing observations (or instances) whose category membership is known. An example would be assigning a given email into "spam" or "non-spam" classes or assigning a diagnosis to a given patient as described by observed characteristics of the patient (gender, blood pressure, presence or absence of certain symptoms, etc.). Classification is an example of pattern recognition.

In the terminology of machine learning, classification is considered an instance of supervised learning, i.e. learning where a training set of correctly identified observations is available. The corresponding unsupervised procedure is known as clustering, and involves grouping data into categories based on some measure of inherent similarity or distance.

Often, the individual observations are analyzed into a set of quantifiable properties, known variously as explanatory variables or *features*. These properties may variously be categorical (e.g. "A", "B", "AB" or "O", for blood type), ordinal (e.g. "large", "medium" or "small"), integer-valued (e.g. the number of occurrences of a particular word in an email) or real-valued (e.g. a measurement of blood pressure). Other classifiers work by comparing observations to previous observations by means of a similarity or distance function.

An algorithm that implements classification, especially in a concrete implementation, is known as a classifier. The term "classifier" sometimes also refers to the mathematical function, implemented by a classification algorithm, that maps input data to a category.

Terminology across fields is quite varied. In statistics, where classification is often done with logistic regression or a similar procedure, the properties of observations are termed explanatory variables (or independent variables, regressors, etc.), and the categories to be predicted are known as outcomes, which are considered to be possible values of the dependent variable. In machine learning, the observations are often known as *instances*, the explanatory variables are termed *features* (grouped into a feature vector), and the possible categories to be predicted are *classes*. Other fields may use different terminology: e.g. in community ecology, the term "classification" normally refers to cluster analysis, i.e. a type of unsupervised learning, rather than the supervised learning described in this article.

Relation to Other Problems

Classification and clustering are examples of the more general problem of pattern recognition, which is the assignment of some sort of output value to a given input value. Other examples are regression, which assigns a real-valued output to each input; sequence labeling, which assigns a class to each member of a sequence of values (for example, part of speech tagging, which assigns a part of speech to each word in an input sentence); parsing, which assigns a parse tree to an input sentence, describing the syntactic structure of the sentence; etc.

A common subclass of classification is probabilistic classification. Algorithms of this nature use statistical inference to find the best class for a given instance. Unlike other algorithms, which simply output a "best" class, probabilistic algorithms output a probability of the instance being a member of each of the possible classes. The best class is normally then selected as the one with the highest probability. However, such an algorithm has numerous advantages over non-probabilistic classifiers:

- It can output a confidence value associated with its choice (in general, a classifier that can do this is known as a *confidence-weighted classifier*).

- Correspondingly, it can *abstain* when its confidence of choosing any particular output is too low.

- Because of the probabilities which are generated, probabilistic classifiers can be more effectively incorporated into larger machine-learning tasks, in a way that partially or completely avoids the problem of *error propagation*.

Frequentist Procedures

Early work on statistical classification was undertaken by Fisher, in the context of two-group problems, leading to Fisher's linear discriminant function as the rule for assigning a group to a new observation. This early work assumed that data-values within each of the two groups had a multivariate normal distribution. The extension of this same context to more than two-groups has also been considered with a restriction imposed that the classification rule should be linear. Later work for the multivariate normal distribution allowed the classifier to be nonlinear: several classification rules can be derived based on slight different adjustments of the Mahalanobis distance, with a new observation being assigned to the group whose centre has the lowest adjusted distance from the observation.

Bayesian Procedures

Unlike frequentist procedures, Bayesian classification procedures provide a natural way of taking into account any available information about the relative sizes of the sub-populations associated with the different groups within the overall population. Bayesian procedures tend to be computationally expensive and, in the days before Markov chain Monte Carlo computations were developed, approximations for Bayesian clustering rules were devised.

Some Bayesian procedures involve the calculation of group membership probabilities: these can be viewed as providing a more informative outcome of a data analysis than a simple attribution of a single group-label to each new observation.

Binary and Multiclass Classification

Classification can be thought of as two separate problems – binary classification and multiclass classification. In binary classification, a better understood task, only two classes are involved, whereas multiclass classification involves assigning an object to one of several classes. Since many classification methods have been developed specifically for binary classification, multiclass classification often requires the combined use of multiple binary classifiers.

Feature Vectors

Most algorithms describe an individual instance whose category is to be predicted using a feature vector of individual, measurable properties of the instance. Each property is termed a feature, also known in statistics as an explanatory variable (or independent variable, although features may or may not be statistically independent). Features may variously be binary (e.g. "male" or "female"); categorical (e.g. "A", "B", "AB" or "O", for blood type); ordinal (e.g. "large", "medium" or "small"); integer-valued (e.g. the number of occurrences of a particular word in an email); or real-valued (e.g. a measurement of blood pressure). If the instance is an image, the feature values might correspond to the pixels of an image; if the instance is a piece of text, the feature values might be occurrence frequencies of different words. Some algorithms work only in terms of discrete data and require that real-valued or integer-valued data be *discretized* into groups (e.g. less than 5, between 5 and 10, or greater than 10)

Linear Classifiers

A large number of algorithms for classification can be phrased in terms of a linear function that assigns a score to each possible category k by combining the feature vector of an instance with a vector of weights, using a dot product. The predicted category is the one with the highest score. This type of score function is known as a linear predictor function and has the following general form:

$$\text{score}(X_i, k) = \beta_k X_i,$$

where X_i is the feature vector for instance i, β_k is the vector of weights corresponding to category k, and score(X_i, k) is the score associated with assigning instance i to category k. In discrete choice theory, where instances represent people and categories represent choices, the score is considered the utility associated with person i choosing category k.

Algorithms with this basic setup are known as linear classifiers. What distinguishes them is the procedure for determining (training) the optimal weights/coefficients and the way that the score is interpreted.

Examples of such algorithms are

- Logistic regression and Multinomial logistic regression
- Probit regression
- The perceptron algorithm
- Support vector machines
- Linear discriminant analysis.

Algorithms

Examples of classification algorithms include:

- Linear classifiers

- o Fisher's linear discriminant
- o Logistic regression
- o Naive Bayes classifier
- o Perceptron
- Support vector machines
  - o Least squares support vector machines
- Quadratic classifiers
- Kernel estimation
  - o k-nearest neighbor
- Boosting (meta-algorithm)
- Decision trees
  - o Random forests
- Neural networks
- FMM Neural Networks
- Learning vector quantization

Evaluation

Classifier performance depends greatly on the characteristics of the data to be classified. There is no single classifier that works best on all given problems (a phenomenon that may be explained by the no-free-lunch theorem). Various empirical tests have been performed to compare classifier performance and to find the characteristics of data that determine classifier performance. Determining a suitable classifier for a given problem is however still more an art than a science.

The measures precision and recall are popular metrics used to evaluate the quality of a classification system. More recently, receiver operating characteristic (ROC) curves have been used to evaluate the tradeoff between true- and false-positive rates of classification algorithms.

As a performance metric, the uncertainty coefficient has the advantage over simple accuracy in that it is not affected by the relative sizes of the different classes. Further, it will not penalize an algorithm for simply *rearranging* the classes.

Application Domains

Classification has many applications. In some of these it is employed as a data mining procedure, while in others more detailed statistical modeling is undertaken.

- Computer vision
  - o Medical imaging and medical image analysis

- o   Optical character recognition

- o   Video tracking

- Drug discovery and development

  - o   Toxicogenomics

  - o   Quantitative structure-activity relationship

- Geostatistics

- Speech recognition

- Handwriting recognition

- Biometric identification

- Biological classification

- Statistical natural language processing

- Document classification

- Internet search engines

- Credit scoring

- Pattern recognition

- Micro-array classification

Data Curation

Data curation is a broad term used to indicate processes and activities related to the organization and integration of data collected from various sources, annotation of the data, and publication and presentation of the data such that the value of the data is maintained over time, and the data remains available for reuse and preservation. Data curation includes "all the processes needed for principled and controlled data creation, maintenance, and management, together with the capacity to add value to data". In science, data curation may indicate the process of extraction of important information from scientific texts, such as research articles by experts, to be converted into an electronic format, such as an entry of a biological database.

In the modern era of big data the curation of data has become more prominent, particularly for software processing high volume and complex data systems. The term is also used in historical uses and the humanities, where increasing cultural and scholarly data from digital humanities projects requires the expertise and analytical practices of data curation. In broad terms, curation means a range of activities and processes done to create, manage, maintain, and validate a component.

Definition and Practice

Data curation is typically user initiated and maintains metadata rather than the database itself. According to the University of Illinois' Graduate School of Library and Information Science, "Data curation is the active and on-going management of data through its lifecycle of interest and usefulness to scholarship, science, and education; curation activities enable data discovery and retrieval, maintain quality, add value, and provide for re-use over time." The data curation workflow is distinct from data quality management, data protection, lifecycle management and data movement.

Deep background on data libraries appeared in a 1982 issue of the Illinois journal, *Library Trends*. For historical background on the data archive movement, "Social Scientific Information Needs for Numeric Data: The Evolution of the International Data Archive Infrastructure." The exact curation process undertaken within any organisation depends on the volume of data, how much noise the data contains and what the expected future use of the data means to its dissemination.

This term is sometimes used in context of biological databases, where specific biological information is firstly obtained from a range of research articles and then stored within a specific category of database. For instance, information about anti-depressant drugs can be obtained from various sources and, after checking whether they are available as a database or not, they are saved under a drug's database's anti-depressive category. Enterprises are also utilizing data curation within their operational and strategic processes to ensure data quality and accuracy.

Projects and Studies

The Dissemination Information Packages (DIPS) for Information Reuse (DIPIR) project is studying research data produced and used by quantitative social scientists, archaeologists, and zoologists. The intended audience is researchers who use secondary data and the digital curators, digital repository managers, data center staff, and others who collect, manage, and store digital information.

Data Management

Data management comprises all the disciplines related to managing data as a valuable resource.

Overview

The official definition provided by DAMA International, the professional organization for those in the data management profession, is: "Data Resource Management is the development and execution of architectures, policies, practices and procedures that properly manage the full data lifecycle needs of an enterprise." This definition is fairly broad and encompasses a number of professions which may not have direct technical contact with lower-level aspects of data management, such as relational database management.

The data lifecycle

Alternatively, the definition provided in the DAMA Data Management Body of Knowledge is: "Data management is the development, execution and supervision of plans, policies, programs and practices that control, protect, deliver and enhance the value of data and information assets."

The concept of "Data Management" arose in the 1980s as technology moved from sequential processing (first cards, then tape) to random access processing. Since it was now technically possible to store a single fact in a single place and access that using random access disk, those suggesting that "Data Management" was more important than "Process Management" used arguments such as "a customer's home address is stored in 75 (or some other large number) places in our computer systems." During this period, random access processing was not competitively fast, so those suggesting "Process Management" was more important than "Data Management" used batch processing time as their primary argument. As applications moved into real-time, interactive applications, it became obvious to most practitioners that both management processes were important. If the data was not well defined, the data would be mis-used in applications. If the process wasn't well defined, it was impossible to meet user needs.

Corporate Data Quality Management

Corporate Data Quality Management (CDQM) is, according to the European Foundation for Quality Management and the Competence Center Corporate Data Quality (CC CDQ, University of St. Gallen), the whole set of activities intended to improve corporate data quality (both reactive and preventive). Main premise of CDQM is the business relevance of high-quality corporate data. CDQM comprises with following activity areas:.

- Strategy for Corporate Data Quality: As CDQM is affected by various business drivers and requires involvement of multiple divisions in an organization; it must be considered a company-wide endeavor.

- Corporate Data Quality Controlling: Effective CDQM requires compliance with standards, policies, and procedures. Compliance is monitored according to previously defined metrics and performance indicators and reported to stakeholders.

- Corporate Data Quality Organization: CDQM requires clear roles and responsibilities for the use of corporate data. The CDQM organization defines tasks and privileges for decision making for CDQM.

- Corporate Data Quality Processes and Methods: In order to handle corporate data properly and in a standardized way across the entire organization and to ensure corporate data quality, standard procedures and guidelines must be embedded in company's daily processes.

- Data Architecture for Corporate Data Quality: The data architecture consists of the data object model - which comprises the unambiguous definition and the conceptual model of corporate data - and the data storage and distribution architecture.

- Applications for Corporate Data Quality: Software applications support the activities of Corporate Data Quality Management. Their use must be planned, monitored, managed and continuously improved.

Topics in Data Management

Topics in Data Management, grouped by the DAMA DMBOK Framework, include:

1. Data governance

    o   Data asset

    o   Data governance

    o   Data steward

2. Data Architecture, Analysis and Design

    o   Data analysis

    o   Data architecture

    o   Data modeling

3. Database Management

    o   Data maintenance

    o   Database administration

    o   Database management system

4. Data Security Management

    o   Data access

    o   Data erasure

    o   Data privacy

    o   Data security

5. Data Quality Management

    o   Data cleansing

    o   Data integrity

    o   Data enrichment

    o   Data quality

    o   Data quality assurance

6. Reference and Master Data Management

    o   Data integration

    o   Master data management

    o   Reference data

7. Data Warehousing and Business Intelligence Management

    o   Business intelligence

    o   Data mart

- o   Data mining
- o   Data movement (Extract, transform, load)
- o   Data warehouse

8. Document, Record and Content Management

- o   Document management system
- o   Records management

9. Meta Data Management

- o   Meta-data management
- o   Metadata
- o   Metadata discovery
- o   Metadata publishing
- o   Metadata registry

10. Contact Data Management

- o   Business continuity planning
- o   Marketing operations
- o   Customer data integration
- o   Identity management
- o   Identity theft
- o   Data theft
- o   ERP software
- o   CRM software
- o   Address (geography)
- o   Postal code
- o   Email address
- o   Telephone number

Body of Knowledge

The DAMA Guide to the Data Management Body of Knowledge" (DAMA-DMBOK Guide), under the guidance of a new DAMA-DMBOK Editorial Board. This publication is available from April 5, 2009.

Usage

In modern management usage, one can easily discern a trend away from the term "data" in composite expressions to the term "information" or even "knowledge" when talking in a non-technical context. Thus there exists not only data management, but also information management and knowledge management. This is a misleading trend as it obscures that traditional data are managed or somehow processed on second looks. The distinction between data and derived values can be seen in the information ladder. While data can exist as such, "information" and "knowledge" are always in the "eye" (or rather the brain) of the beholder and can only be measured in relative units.

Several organisations have established a data management centre (DMC) for their operations.

Integrated Data Management

Integrated data management (IDM) is a tools approach to facilitate data management and improve performance. IDM consists of an integrated, modular environment to manage enterprise application data, and optimize data-driven applications over its lifetime. IDM's purpose is to:

- Produce enterprise-ready applications faster

- Improve data access, speed iterative testing

- Empower collaboration between architects, developers and DBAs

- Consistently achieve service level targets

- Automate and simplify operations

- Provide contextual intelligence across the solution stack

- Support business growth

- Accommodate new initiatives without expanding infrastructure

- Simplify application upgrades, consolidation and retirement

- Facilitate alignment, consistency and governance

- Define business policies and standards up front; share, extend, and apply throughout the lifecycle

Data Mapping

In computing and data management, data mapping is the process of creating data element mappings between two distinct data models. Data mapping is used as a first step for a wide variety of data integration tasks including:

- Data transformation or data mediation between a data source and a destination

- Identification of data relationships as part of data lineage analysis

- Discovery of hidden sensitive data such as the last four digits of a social security number hidden in another user id as part of a data masking or de-identification project

- Consolidation of multiple databases into a single data base and identifying redundant columns of data for consolidation or elimination

For example, a company that would like to transmit and receive purchases and invoices with other companies might use data mapping to create data maps from a company's data to standardized ANSI ASC X12 messages for items such as purchase orders and invoices.

Standards

X12 standards are generic Electronic Data Interchange (EDI) standards designed to allow a company to exchange data with any other company, regardless of industry. The standards are maintained by the Accredited Standards Committee X12 (ASC X12), with the American National Standards Institute (ANSI) accredited to set standards for EDI. The X12 standards are often called ANSI ASC X12 standards.

In the future, tools based on semantic web languages such as Resource Description Framework (RDF), the Web Ontology Language (OWL) and standardized metadata registry will make data mapping a more automatic process. This process will be accelerated if each application performed metadata publishing. Full automated data mapping is a very difficult problem.

Hand-Coded, Graphical Manual

Data mappings can be done in a variety of ways using procedural code, creating XSLT transforms or by using graphical mapping tools that automatically generate executable transformation programs. These are graphical tools that allow a user to "draw" lines from fields in one set of data to fields in another. Some graphical data mapping tools allow users to "Auto-connect" a source and a destination. This feature is dependent on the source and destination data element name being the same. Transformation programs are automatically created in SQL, XSLT, Java programming language or C++. These kinds of graphical tools are found in most ETL Tools (Extract, Transform, Load Tools) as the primary means of entering data maps to support data movement. Examples include SAP BODS and Informatica PowerCenter.

Data-Driven Mapping

This is the newest approach in data mapping and involves simultaneously evaluating actual data values in two data sources using heuristics and statistics to automatically discover complex mappings between two data sets. This approach is used to find transformations between two data sets and will discover substrings, concatenations, arithmetic, case statements as well as other kinds of transformation logic. This approach also discovers data exceptions that do not follow the discovered transformation logic.

Semantic Mapping

Semantic mapping is similar to the auto-connect feature of data mappers with the exception that a metadata registry can be consulted to look up data element synonyms. For example, if the source system lists FirstName but the destination lists PersonGivenName, the mappings will still be made if these data elements are listed as synonyms in the metadata registry. Semantic mapping is only able to discover exact matches between columns of data and will not discover any transformation logic or exceptions between columns.

Data Lineage is a track of the life cycle of each piece of data as it is ingested, processed and output by the analytics system. This provides visibility into the analytics pipeline and simplifies tracing errors back to their sources. It also enables replaying specific portions or inputs of the dataflow for step-wise debugging or regenerating lost output. In fact, database systems have used such information, called data provenance, to address similar validation and debugging challenges already.

Data Wrangling

Data munging or data wrangling is loosely the process of manually converting or mapping data from one "raw" form into another format that allows for more convenient consumption of the data with the help of semi-automated tools. This may include further munging, data visualization, data aggregation, training a statistical model, as well as many other potential uses. Data munging as a process typically follows a set of general steps which begin with extracting the data in a raw form from the data source, "munging" the raw data using algorithms (e.g. sorting) or parsing the data into predefined data structures, and finally depositing the resulting content into a data sink for storage and future use. Given the rapid growth of the internet such techniques will become increasingly important in the organization of the growing amounts of data available.

A data wrangler is the person performing the wrangling. In the scientific research context, the term often refers to a person responsible for gathering and organizing disparate data sets collected by many different investigators, often as part of a field campaign. In this sense, the term could be credited to Donald Cline during the NASA/NOAA Cold Lands Processes Experiment. It specifies duties typically handled by a storage administrator for working with large amounts of data. This can occur in areas like major research projects and the making of films with a large amount of complex computer-generated imagery. In research, this involves both data transfer from research instrument to storage grid or storage facility as well as data manipulation for re-analysis via high performance computing instruments or access via cyberinfrastructure-based digital libraries.

The "wrangler" non-technical term is often said to derive from work done by the United States Library of Congress's National Digital Information Infrastructure and Preservation Program (NDIIPP) and their program partner the Emory University Libraries based MetaArchive Partnership. The term "mung" has roots in munging as described in the Jargon File. The term "Data Wrangler" was also suggested as the best analogy to coder for code for someone working with data.

On a film or television production utilizing digital cameras that are not tape based, a data wrangler is employed to manage the transfer of data from a camera to a computer and/or hard drive.

Data Integration

Data integration involves combining data residing in different sources and providing users with a unified view of these data. This process becomes significant in a variety of situations, which include both commercial (when two similar companies need to merge their databases) and scientific (combining research results from different bioinformatics repositories, for example) domains. Data integration appears with increasing frequency as the volume and the need to share existing data explodes. It has become the focus of extensive theoretical work, and numerous open problems remain unsolved.

History

Issues with combining heterogeneous data sources, often referred to as information silos, under a single query interface have existed for some time. In the early 1980s, computer scientists began designing systems for interoperability of heterogeneous databases. The first data integration system driven by structured metadata was designed at the University of Minnesota in 1991, for the Integrated Public Use Microdata Series (IPUMS). IPUMS used a data warehousing approach, which extracts, transforms, and loads data from heterogeneous sources into a single view schema so data from different sources become compatible. By making thousands of population databases interoperable, IPUMS demonstrated the feasibility of large-scale data integration. The data warehouse approach offers a tightly coupled architecture because the data are already physically reconciled in a single queryable repository, so it usually takes little time to resolve queries.

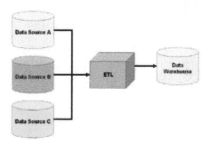

Figure : Simple schematic for a data warehouse. The ETL process extracts information from the source databases, transforms it and then loads it into the data warehouse.

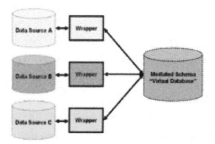

Figure : Simple schematic for a data-integration solution. A system designer constructs a mediated schema against which users can run queries. The virtual database interfaces with the source databases via wrapper code if required.

The data warehouse approach is less feasible for datasets that are frequently updated, requiring the ETL process to be continuously re-executed for synchronization. Difficulties also arise in constructing data warehouses when one has only a query interface to summary data sources and no access to the full data. This problem frequently emerges when integrating several commercial query services like travel or classified advertisement web applications.

As of 2009 the trend in data integration favored loosening the coupling between data and providing a unified query-interface to access real time data over a mediated schema, which allows information to be retrieved directly from original databases. This is consistent with the SOA approach popular in that era. This approach relies on mappings between the mediated schema and the schema of original sources, and transform a query into specialized queries to match the schema of the original databases. Such mappings can be specified in 2 ways : as a mapping from entities in the mediated schema to entities in the original sources (the "Global As View" (GAV) approach), or as a mapping from entities in the original sources to the mediated schema (the "Local As View" (LAV) approach). The latter approach requires more sophisticated inferences to resolve a query on the mediated schema, but makes it easier to add new data sources to a (stable) mediated schema.

As of 2010 some of the work in data integration research concerns the semantic integration problem. This problem addresses not the structuring of the architecture of the integration, but how to resolve semantic conflicts between heterogeneous data sources. For example, if two companies merge their databases, certain concepts and definitions in their respective schemas like "earnings" inevitably have different meanings. In one database it may mean profits in dollars (a floating-point number), while in the other it might represent the number of sales (an integer). A common strategy for the resolution of such problems involves the use of ontologies which explicitly define schema terms and thus help to resolve semantic conflicts. This approach represents ontology-based data integration. On the other hand, the problem of combining research results from different bioinformatics repositories requires bench-marking of the similarities, computed from different data sources, on a single criterion such as positive predictive value. This enables the data sources to be directly comparable and can be integrated even when the natures of experiments are distinct.

As of 2011 it was determined that current data modeling methods were imparting data isolation into every data architecture in the form of islands of disparate data and information silos. This data isolation is an unintended artifact of the data modeling methodology that results in the development of disparate data models. Disparate data models, when instantiated as databases, form disparate databases. Enhanced data model methodologies have been developed to eliminate the data isolation artifact and to promote the development of integrated data models. One enhanced data modeling method recasts data models by augmenting them with structural metadata in the form of standardized data entities. As a result of recasting multiple data models, the set of recast data models will now share one or more commonality relationships that relate the structural metadata now common to these data models. Commonality relationships are a peer-to-peer type of entity relationships that relate the standardized data entities of multiple data models. Multiple data models that contain the same standard data entity may participate in the same commonality relationship. When integrated data models are instantiated as databases and are properly populated from a common set of master data, then these databases are integrated.

Since 2011, Data hub approaches have been of greater interest than fully structured (typically relational) Enterprise Data Warehouses. Since 2013, Data lake approaches have risen to the level of Data Hubs. (These approaches combine unstructured or varied data into one location, but do not necessarily require an (often complex) master relational schema to structure and define all data in the Hub.

Example

Consider a web application where a user can query a variety of information about cities (such as crime statistics, weather, hotels, demographics, etc.). Traditionally, the information must be stored in a single database with a single schema. But any single enterprise would find information of this breadth somewhat difficult and expensive to collect. Even if the resources exist to gather the data, it would likely duplicate data in existing crime databases, weather websites, and census data.

A data-integration solution may address this problem by considering these external resources as materialized views over a virtual mediated schema, resulting in "virtual data integration". This means application-developers construct a virtual schema — the *mediated schema* — to best model the kinds of answers their users want. Next, they design «wrappers» or adapters for each data source, such as the crime database and weather website. These adapters simply transform the local query results (those returned by the respective websites or databases) into an easily processed form for the data integration solution. When an application-user queries the mediated schema, the data-integration solution transforms this query into appropriate queries over the respective data sources. Finally, the virtual database combines the results of these queries into the answer to the user›s query.

This solution offers the convenience of adding new sources by simply constructing an adapter or an application software blade for them. It contrasts with ETL systems or with a single database solution, which require manual integration of entire new dataset into the system. The virtual ETL solutions leverage virtual mediated schema to implement data harmonization; whereby the data are copied from the designated "master" source to the defined targets, field by field. Advanced Data virtualization is also built on the concept of object-oriented modeling in order to construct virtual mediated schema or virtual metadata repository, using hub and spoke architecture.

Each data source is disparate and as such is not designed to support reliable joins between data sources. Therefore, data virtualization as well as data federation depends upon accidental data commonality to support combining data and information from disparate data sets. Because of this lack of data value commonality across data sources, the return set may be inaccurate, incomplete, and impossible to validate.

One solution is to recast disparate databases to integrate these databases without the need for ETL. The recast databases support commonality constraints where referential integrity may be enforced between databases. The recast databases provide designed data access paths with data value commonality across databases.

Theory of Data Integration

The theory of data integration forms a subset of database theory and formalizes the underlying concepts of the problem in first-order logic. Applying the theories gives indications as to the feasibility and difficulty of data integration. While its definitions may appear abstract, they have sufficient generality to accommodate all manner of integration systems, including those that include nested relational / XML databases and those that treat databases as programs. Connections to particular databases systems such as Oracle or DB2 are provided by implementation-level technologies such as JDBC and are not studied at the theoretical level.

Definitions

Data integration systems are formally defined as a triple where is the global (or mediated) schema, is the heterogeneous set of source schemas, and is the mapping that maps queries between the source and the global schemas. Both and are expressed in languages over alphabets composed of symbols for each of their respective relations. The mapping consists of assertions between queries over and queries over . When users pose queries over the data integration system, they pose queries over and the mapping then asserts connections between the elements in the global schema and the source schemas.

A database over a schema is defined as a set of sets, one for each relation (in a relational database). The database corresponding to the source schema would comprise the set of sets of tuples for each of the heterogeneous data sources and is called the *source database*. Note that this single source database may actually represent a collection of disconnected databases. The database corresponding to the virtual mediated schema is called the *global database*. The global database must satisfy the mapping with respect to the source database. The legality of this mapping depends on the nature of the correspondence between and . Two popular ways to model this correspondence exist: *Global as View* or GAV and *Local as View* or LAV.

Figure 3: Illustration of tuple space of the GAV and LAV mappings. In GAV, the system is constrained to the set of tuples mapped by the mediators while the set of tuples expressible over the sources may be much larger and richer. In LAV, the system is constrained to the set of tuples in the sources while the set of tuples expressible over the global schema can be much larger. Therefore, LAV systems must often deal with incomplete answers.

GAV systems model the global database as a set of views over . In this case associates to each element of a query over . Query processing becomes a straightforward operation due to the well-defined associations between and . The burden of complexity falls on implementing mediator code instructing the data integration system exactly how to retrieve elements from the source databases. If any new sources join the system, considerable effort may be necessary to update the mediator, thus the GAV approach appears preferable when the sources seem unlikely to change.

In a GAV approach to the example data integration system above, the system designer would first develop mediators for each of the city information sources and then design the global schema around these mediators. For example, consider if one of the sources served a weather website. The designer would likely then add a corresponding element for weather to the global schema. Then the bulk of effort concentrates on writing the proper mediator code that will transform predicates on weather into a query over the weather website. This effort can become complex if some other source also relates to weather, because the designer may need to write code to properly combine the results from the two sources.

On the other hand, in LAV, the source database is modeled as a set of views over . In this case associates to each element of a query over . Here the exact associations between and are no longer well-defined. As is illustrated in the next section, the burden of determining how to retrieve elements from the sources is placed on the query processor. The benefit of an LAV modeling is that new sources can be added with far less work than in a GAV system, thus the LAV approach should be favored in cases where the mediated schema is less stable or likely to change.

In an LAV approach to the example data integration system above, the system designer designs the global schema first and then simply inputs the schemas of the respective city information sources. Consider again if one of the sources serves a weather website. The designer would add corresponding elements for weather to the global schema only if none existed already. Then programmers write an adapter or wrapper for the website and add a schema description of the website's results to the source schemas. The complexity of adding the new source moves from the designer to the query processor.

Query Processing

The theory of query processing in data integration systems is commonly expressed using conjunctive queries and Datalog, a purely declarative logic programming language. One can loosely think of a conjunctive query as a logical function applied to the relations of a database such as "where ". If a tuple or set of tuples is substituted into the rule and satisfies it (makes it true), then we consider that tuple as part of the set of answers in the query. While formal languages like Datalog express these queries concisely and without ambiguity, common SQL queries count as conjunctive queries as well.

In terms of data integration, "query containment" represents an important property of conjunctive queries. A query contains another query (denoted) if the results of applying are a subset of the results of applying for any database. The two queries are said to be equivalent if the resulting sets are equal for any database. This is important because in both GAV and LAV systems, a user poses conjunctive queries over a *virtual* schema represented by a set of views, or "materialized" conjunctive queries. Integration seeks to rewrite the queries represented by the views to make their results equivalent or maximally contained by our user's query. This corresponds to the problem of answering queries using views (AQUV).

In GAV systems, a system designer writes mediator code to define the query-rewriting. Each element in the user's query corresponds to a substitution rule just as each element in the global schema corresponds to a query over the source. Query processing simply expands the subgoals of the user's query according to the rule specified in the mediator and thus the resulting query is likely to be equivalent. While the designer does the majority of the work beforehand, some GAV systems such as Tsimmis involve simplifying the mediator description process.

In LAV systems, queries undergo a more radical process of rewriting because no mediator exists to align the user's query with a simple expansion strategy. The integration system must execute a search over the space of possible queries in order to find the best rewrite. The resulting rewrite may not be an equivalent query but maximally contained, and the resulting tuples may be incomplete. As of 2009 the MiniCon algorithm is the leading query rewriting algorithm for LAV data integration systems.

In general, the complexity of query rewriting is NP-complete. If the space of rewrites is relatively small this does not pose a problem — even for integration systems with hundreds of sources.

Data Integration Tools

- Alteryx
- Analytics Canvas
- Capsenta's Ultrawrap Platform
- Cloud Elements API Integration
- DataWatch
- Denodo Platform
- elastic.io Integration Platform
- HiperFabric
- Lavastorm
- Informatica Platform
- Oracle Data Integration Services
- ParseKit (enigma.io)
- Paxata
- RapidMiner Studio
- Red Hat JBoss Data Virtualization. Community project: teiid.
- Azure Data Factory (ADF)
- SQL Server Integration Services (SSIS)
- TMMData
- Data Ladder

Data Integration in the Life Sciences

Large-scale questions in science, such as global warming, invasive species spread, and resource depletion, are increasingly requiring the collection of disparate data sets for meta-analysis. This type of data integration is especially challenging for ecological and environmental data because metadata standards are not agreed upon and there are many different data types produced in these fields. National Science Foundation initiatives such as Datanet are intended to make data integration easier for scientists by providing cyberinfrastructure and setting standards. The five funded Datanet initiatives are DataONE, led by William Michener at the University of New Mexico; The Data Conservancy, led by Sayeed Choudhury of Johns Hopkins University; SEAD: Sustainable Environment through Actionable Data, led by Margaret Hedstrom of the University of Michigan; the DataNet Federation Consortium, led by Reagan Moore of the University of North Carolina; and *Terra Populus*, led by Steven Ruggles of the University of Minnesota. The Research Data Alliance, has more recently explored creating global data integration frameworks. The OpenPHACTS project, funded through the European Union Innovative Medicines Initiative, built a drug discovery platform by linking datasets from providers such as European Bioinformatics Institute, Royal Society of Chemistry, UniProt, WikiPathways and DrugBank.

Association Rule Learning

Association rule learning is a rule-based machine learning method for discovering interesting relations between variables in large databases. It is intended to identify strong rules discovered in databases using some measures of interestingness. Based on the concept of strong rules, Rakesh Agrawal et al. introduced association rules for discovering regularities between products in large-scale transaction data recorded by point-of-sale (POS) systems in supermarkets. For example, the rule {onions, potatoes} ⇒ {burger} found in the sales data of a supermarket would indicate that if a customer buys onions and potatoes together, they are likely to also buy hamburger meat. Such information can be used as the basis for decisions about marketing activities such as, e.g., promotional pricing or product placements. In addition to the above example from market basket analysis association rules are employed today in many application areas including Web usage mining, intrusion detection, Continuous production, and bioinformatics. In contrast with sequence mining, association rule learning typically does not consider the order of items either within a transaction or across transactions.

Definition

Example database with 5 transactions and 5 items					
transaction ID	milk	bread	butter	beer	diapers
1	1	1	0	0	0
2	0	0	1	0	0
3	0	0	0	1	1
4	1	1	1	0	0
5	0	1	0	0	0

Following the original definition by Agrawal et al. the problem of association rule mining is defined as:

Let $I = \{i_1, i_2, \ldots, i_n\}$ be a set of n binary attributes called *items*.

Let $D = \{t_1, t_2, \ldots, t_m\}$ be a set of transactions called the *database*.

Each *transaction* in D has a unique transaction ID and contains a subset of the items in I.

A *rule* is defined as an implication of the form:

$X \Rightarrow Y$

Where $X, Y \subseteq I$ and $X \cap Y = \varnothing$.

Every rule is composed by two different sets of items, also known as *itemsets*, X and Y, where X is called *antecedent* or left-hand-side (LHS) and Y *consequent* or right-hand-side (RHS).

To illustrate the concepts, we use a small example from the supermarket domain. The set of items is I = {milk, bread, butter, beer, diapers} and in the table is shown a small database containing the items, where, in each entry, the value 1 means the presence of the item in the corresponding transaction, and the value 0 represents the absence of an item in that transaction.

An example rule for the supermarket could be {butter, bread} $\Rightarrow$ {milk} meaning that if butter and bread are bought, customers also buy milk.

Note: this example is extremely small. In practical applications, a rule needs a support of several hundred transactions before it can be considered statistically significant, and data-sets often contain thousands or millions of transactions.

Useful Concepts

In order to select interesting rules from the set of all possible rules, constraints on various measures of significance and interest are used. The best-known constraints are minimum thresholds on support and confidence.

Let X be an item-set, $X \Rightarrow Y$ an association rule and T a set of transactions of a given database.

Support

Support is an indication of how frequently the item-set appears in the database.

The support value of X with respect to T is defined as the proportion of transactions in the database which contains the item-set X. In formula: $\text{supp}(X) / N$

In the example database, the item-set {beer, diapers} has a support of since it occurs in 20% of all transactions (1 out of 5 transactions). The argument of supp() is a set of preconditions, and thus becomes more restrictive as it grows (instead of more inclusive).

Confidence

Confidence is an indication of how often the rule has been found to be true.

The *confidence* value of a rule, $X \Rightarrow Y$, with respect to a set of transactions T, is the proportion of the transactions that contains X which also contains Y.

Confidence is defined as:

$$\text{conf}(X \Rightarrow Y) = \text{supp}(X \cup Y) / \text{supp}(X).$$

For example, the rule {butter, bread} $\Rightarrow$ {milk} has a confidence of $0.2 >$ in the database, which means that for 100% of the transactions containing butter and bread the rule is correct (100% of the times a customer buys butter and bread, milk is bought as well).

Note that $\text{supp}(X \cup Y)$ means the support of the union of the items in X and Y. This is somewhat confusing since we normally think in terms of probabilities of events and not sets of items. We can rewrite $\text{supp}(X \cup Y)$ as the joint probability $P(E_X \cap E_Y)$, where E_X and E_Y are the events that a transaction contains itemset X or Y, respectively.

Thus confidence can be interpreted as an estimate of the conditional probability $P(E_Y \mid E_X)$,, the probability of finding the RHS of the rule in transactions under the condition that these transactions also contain the LHS.

Lift

The *lift* of a rule is defined as:

$$\text{lift}(X \Rightarrow Y) = \frac{\text{supp}(X \cup Y)}{\text{supp}(X) \times \text{supp}(Y)}$$

or the ratio of the observed support to that expected if X and Y were independent.

For example, the rule $\{\text{milk}, \text{bread}\} \Rightarrow \{\text{butter}\}$ has a lift of $\dfrac{0.2}{0.4 \times 0.4} = 1.25$.

If the rule had a lift of 1, it would imply that the probability of occurrence of the antecedent and that of the consequent are independent of each other. When two events are independent of each other, no rule can be drawn involving those two events.

If the lift is > 1, that lets us know the degree to which those two occurrences are dependent on one another, and makes those rules potentially useful for predicting the consequent in future data sets.

The value of lift is that it considers both the confidence of the rule and the overall data set.

Conviction

The *conviction* of a rule is defined as $\text{conv}(X \Rightarrow Y) = \dfrac{1 - \text{supp}(Y)}{1 - \text{conf}(X \Rightarrow Y)}$.

For example, the rule has a conviction of , and can be interpreted as the ratio of the expected frequency that X occurs without Y (that is to say, the frequency that the rule makes an incorrect prediction) if X and Y were independent divided by the observed frequency of incorrect predictions. In this example, the conviction value of 1.2 shows that the rule would be incorrect 20% more often (1.2 times as often) if the association between X and Y was purely random chance.

Process

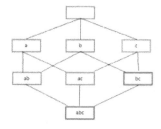

Frequent itemset lattice, where the color of the box indicates how many transactions contain the combination of items. Note that lower levels of the lattice can contain at most the minimum number of their parents' items; e.g. {ac} can have only at most items. This is called the *downward-closure property*.

Association rules are usually required to satisfy a user-specified minimum support and a user-specified minimum confidence at the same time. Association rule generation is usually split up into two separate steps:

1. A minimum support threshold is applied to find all *frequent item-sets* in a database.

2. A minimum confidence constraint is applied to these frequent item-sets in order to form rules.

While the second step is straightforward, the first step needs more attention.

Finding all frequent item-sets in a database is difficult since it involves searching all possible item-sets (item combinations). The set of possible item-sets is the power set over and has size (excluding the empty set which is not a valid item-set). Although the size of the power-set grows exponentially in the number of items in , efficient search is possible using the *downward-closure property* of support (also called *anti-monotonicity*) which guarantees that for a frequent itemset, all its subsets are also frequent and thus for an infrequent item-set, all its super-sets must also be infrequent. Exploiting this property, efficient algorithms (e.g., Apriori and Eclat) can find all frequent item-sets.

History

The concept of association rules was popularised particularly due to the 1993 article of Agrawal et al., which has acquired more than 18,000 citations according to Google Scholar, as of August 2015, and is thus one of the most cited papers in the Data Mining field. However, it is possible that what is now called "association rules" is similar to what appears in the 1966 paper on GUHA, a general data mining method developed by Petr Hájek et al.

An early (circa 1989) use of minimum support and confidence to find all association rules is the Feature Based Modeling framework, which found all rules with and greater than user defined constraints.

Alternative Measures of Interestingness

In addition to confidence, other measures of *interestingness* for rules have been proposed. Some popular measures are:

- All-confidence
- Collective strength
- Conviction
- Leverage
- Lift (originally called interest)

Several more measures are presented and compared by Tan et al. and by Hahsler. Looking for techniques that can model what the user has known (and using these models as interestingness measures) is currently an active research trend under the name of "Subjective Interestingness."

Statistically Sound Associations

One limitation of the standard approach to discovering associations is that by searching massive numbers of possible associations to look for collections of items that appear to be associated, there is a large risk of finding many spurious associations. These are collections of items that co-occur with unexpected frequency in the data, but only do so by chance. For example, suppose we are considering a collection of 10,000 items and looking for rules containing two items in the left-hand-side and 1 item in the right-hand-side. There are approximately 1,000,000,000,000 such rules. If we apply a statistical test for independence with a significance level of 0.05 it means there is only a 5% chance of accepting a rule if there is no association. If we assume there are no associations, we should nonetheless expect to find 50,000,000,000 rules. Statistically sound association discovery controls this risk, in most cases reducing the risk of finding *any* spurious associations to a user-specified significance levels.

Algorithms

Many algorithms for generating association rules were presented over time.

Some well known algorithms are Apriori, Eclat and FP-Growth, but they only do half the job, since they are algorithms for mining frequent itemsets. Another step needs to be done after to generate rules from frequent itemsets found in a database.

Apriori Algorithm

Apriori uses a breadth-first search strategy to count the support of itemsets and uses a candidate generation function which exploits the downward closure property of support.

Eclat Algorithm

Eclat (alt. ECLAT, stands for Equivalence Class Transformation) is a depth-first search algorithm using set intersection. It is a naturally elegant algorithm suitable for both sequential as well as parallel execution with locality enhancing properties. It was first introduced by Zaki, Parthasarathy, Li and Ogihara in a series of papers written in 1997.

Mohammed Javeed Zaki, Srinivasan Parthasarathy, M. Ogihara, Wei Li: New Algorithms for Fast Discovery of Association Rules. KDD 1997.

Mohammed Javeed Zaki, Srinivasan Parthasarathy, Mitsunori Ogihara, Wei Li: Parallel Algorithms for Discovery of Association Rules. Data Min. Knowl. Discov. 1(4): 343-373 (1997)

FP-growth Algorithm

FP stands for frequent pattern.

In the first pass, the algorithm counts occurrence of items (attribute-value pairs) in the dataset, and stores them to 'header table'. In the second pass, it builds the FP-tree structure by inserting instances. Items in each instance have to be sorted by descending order of their frequency in the dataset, so that the tree can be processed quickly. Items in each instance that do not meet minimum coverage threshold are discarded. If many instances share most frequent items, FP-tree provides high compression close to tree root.

Recursive processing of this compressed version of main dataset grows large item sets directly, instead of generating candidate items and testing them against the entire database. Growth starts from the bottom of the header table (having longest branches), by finding all instances matching given condition. New tree is created, with counts projected from the original tree corresponding to the set of instances that are conditional on the attribute, with each node getting sum of its children counts. Recursive growth ends when no individual items conditional on the attribute meet minimum support threshold, and processing continues on the remaining header items of the original FP-tree.

Once the recursive process has completed, all large item sets with minimum coverage have been found, and association rule creation begins.

Others

AprioriDP

AprioriDP utilizes Dynamic Programming in Frequent itemset mining. The working principle is to eliminate the candidate generation like FP-tree, but it stores support count in specialized data structure instead of tree.

Context Based Association Rule Mining Algorithm

CBPNARM is an algorithm, developed in 2013, to mine association rules on the basis of context. It uses context variable on the basis of which the support of an itemset is changed on the basis of which the rules are finally populated to the rule set.

Node-set-based Algorithms

FIN, PrePost and PPV are three algorithms based on node sets. They use nodes in a coding FP-tree to represent itemsets, and employ a depth-first search strategy to discovery frequent itemsets using "intersection" of node sets.

GUHA Procedure ASSOC

GUHA is a general method for exploratory data analysis that has theoretical foundations in observational calculi.

The ASSOC procedure is a GUHA method which mines for generalized association rules using fast bit-strings operations. The association rules mined by this method are more general than those output by apriori, for example "items" can be connected both with conjunction and disjunctions and the relation between antecedent and consequent of the rule is not restricted to setting minimum support and confidence as in apriori: an arbitrary combination of supported interest measures can be used.

OPUS Search

OPUS is an efficient algorithm for rule discovery that, in contrast to most alternatives, does not require either monotone or anti-monotone constraints such as minimum support. Initially used to find rules for a fixed consequent it has subsequently been extended to find rules with any item as a consequent. OPUS search is the core technology in the popular Magnum Opus association discovery system.

Lore

A famous story about association rule mining is the "beer and diaper" story. A purported survey of behavior of supermarket shoppers discovered that customers (presumably young men) who buy diapers tend also to buy beer. This anecdote became popular as an example of how unexpected association rules might be found from everyday data. There are varying opinions as to how much of the story is true. Daniel Powers says:

In 1992, Thomas Blischok, manager of a retail consulting group at Teradata, and his staff prepared an analysis of 1.2 million market baskets from about 25 Osco Drug stores. Database queries were developed to identify affinities. The analysis "did discover that between 5:00 and 7:00 p.m. that consumers bought beer and diapers". Osco managers did NOT exploit the beer and diapers relationship by moving the products closer together on the shelves.

Other Types of Association Mining

Multi-Relation Association Rules: Multi-Relation Association Rules (MRAR) is a new class of association rules which in contrast to primitive, simple and even multi-relational association rules (that are usually extracted from multi-relational databases), each rule item consists of one entity but several relations. These relations indicate indirect relationship between the entities. Consider the following MRAR where the first item consists of three relations *live in*, *nearby* and *humid*: "Those who *live in* a place which is *near by* a city with *humid* climate type and also are *younger* than 20 -> their *health condition* is good". Such association rules are extractable from RDBMS data or semantic web data.

Context Based Association Rules is a form of association rule. Context Based Association Rules claims more accuracy in association rule mining by considering a hidden variable named context variable which changes the final set of association rules depending upon the value of context variables. For example the baskets orientation in market basket analysis reflects an odd pattern in the early days of month.This might be because of abnormal context i.e. salary is drawn at the start of the month

Contrast set learning is a form of associative learning. Contrast set learners use rules that differ meaningfully in their distribution across subsets.

Weighted class learning is another form of associative learning in which weight may be assigned to classes to give focus to a particular issue of concern for the consumer of the data mining results.

High-order pattern discovery facilitate the capture of high-order (polythetic) patterns or event associations that are intrinsic to complex real-world data.

K-optimal pattern discovery provides an alternative to the standard approach to association rule learning that requires that each pattern appear frequently in the data.

Approximate Frequent Itemset mining is a relaxed version of Frequent Itemset mining that allows some of the items in some of the rows to be 0.

Generalized Association Rules hierarchical taxonomy (concept hierarchy)

Quantitative Association Rules categorical and quantitative data

Interval Data Association Rules e.g. partition the age into 5-year-increment ranged

Maximal Association Rules

Sequential pattern mining discovers subsequences that are common to more than minsup sequences in a sequence database, where minsup is set by the user. A sequence is an ordered list of transactions.

Sequential Rules discovering relationships between items while considering the time ordering. It is generally applied on a sequence database. For example, a sequential rule found in database of sequences of customer transactions can be that customers who bought a computer and CD-Roms, later bought a webcam, with a given confidence and support.

Subspace Clustering, a specific type of Clustering high-dimensional data, is in many variants also based on the downward-closure property for specific clustering models.

Warmr is shipped as part of the ACE data mining suite. It allows association rule learning for first order relational rules.

References

- P. Beynon-Davies (2002). Information Systems: An introduction to informatics in organisations. Basingstoke, UK: Palgrave Macmillan. ISBN 0-333-96390-3.

- P. Checkland and S. Holwell (1998). Information, Systems, and Information Systems: Making Sense of the Field. Chichester, West Sussex: John Wiley & Sons. pp. 86–89. ISBN 0-471-95820-4.

- Weimer, J. (ed.) (1995). Research Techniques in Human Engineering. Englewood Cliffs, NJ: Prentice Hall ISBN 0-13-097072-7

- Angiulli, F.; Pizzuti, C. (2002). Fast Outlier Detection in High Dimensional Spaces. Principles of Data Mining and Knowledge Discovery. Lecture Notes in Computer Science. 2431. p. 15. doi:10.1007/3-540-45681-3_2. ISBN 978-3-540-44037-6.

- Kriegel, H. P.; Kroger, P.; Schubert, E.; Zimek, A. (2012). Outlier Detection in Arbitrarily Oriented Subspaces. 2012 IEEE 12th International Conference on Data Mining. p. 379. doi:10.1109/ICDM.2012.21. ISBN 978-1-4673-4649-8.

- Furht, Borko; Armando Escalante (2011). Handbook of Data Intensive Computing. Springer Science & Business Media. p. 32. ISBN 9781461414155. Retrieved 2 October 2016.

- Sabharwal, Arjun (2015). Digital Curation in the Digital Humanities: Preserving and Promoting Archival and Special Collections. Chandos Publishing. p. 60. ISBN 9780081001783. Retrieved 2 October 2016.

- Chessell, Mandy; Nigel L Jones; Jay Limburn; David Radley; Kevin Shank (2015). Designing and Operating a Data Reservoir. IBM Redbooks. p. 111-113. ISBN 9780837440668. Retrieved 2 October 2016.

- E. Curry, A. Freitas, and S. O'Riáin, "The Role of Community-Driven Data Curation for Enterprises," in Linking Enterprise Data, D. Wood, Ed. Boston, MA: Springer US, 2010, pp. 25-47. ISBN 978-1-4419-7664-2

- Tan, Pang-Ning; Michael, Steinbach; Kumar, Vipin (2005). "Chapter 6. Association Analysis: Basic Concepts and Algorithms" (PDF). Introduction to Data Mining. Addison-Wesley. ISBN 0-321-32136-7.

- Hájek, Petr; Feglar, Tomas; Rauch, Jan; and Coufal, David; The GUHA method, data preprocessing and mining, Database Support for Data Mining Applications, Springer, 2004, ISBN 978-3-540-22479-2

- Hájek, Petr; Havránek, Tomáš (1978). Mechanizing Hypothesis Formation: Mathematical Foundations for a General Theory. Springer-Verlag. ISBN 3-540-08738-9.

- "Lecture 23 Data Quality Concepts Tutorial – Data Warehousing". Watch Free Video Training Online. Retrieved 8 December 2016.

- Atz, U (2014). "The tau of data: A new metric to assess the timeliness of data in catalogues" (PDF). CEDEM 2014 Proceedings. Retrieved 2016-08-01.

3

Data Mining: Concepts and Processes

Analysis of data is the process that is used in altering and demonstrating data and it helps in discovering useful information and assists decision-making. Data analysis has aspects such as regression analysis, data cleaning, data transformation and data fusion. This chapter is a compilation of the concepts and processes of data mining that form an integral part of the broader subject matter.

Data Analysis

Analysis of data is a process of inspecting, cleansing, transforming, and modeling data with the goal of discovering useful information, suggesting conclusions, and supporting decision-making. Data analysis has multiple facets and approaches, encompassing diverse techniques under a variety of names, in different business, science, and social science domains.

Data mining is a particular data analysis technique that focuses on modeling and knowledge discovery for predictive rather than purely descriptive purposes. Business intelligence covers data analysis that relies heavily on aggregation, focusing on business information. In statistical applications, some people divide data analysis into descriptive statistics, exploratory data analysis (EDA), and confirmatory data analysis (CDA). EDA focuses on discovering new features in the data and CDA on confirming or falsifying existing hypotheses. Predictive analytics focuses on application of statistical models for predictive forecasting or classification, while text analytics applies statistical, linguistic, and structural techniques to extract and classify information from textual sources, a species of unstructured data. All are varieties of data analysis.

Data integration is a precursor to data analysis, and data analysis is closely linked to data visualization and data dissemination. The term *data analysis* is sometimes used as a synonym for data modeling.

The Process of Data Analysis

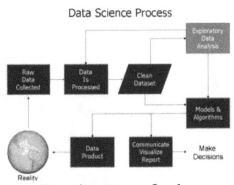

Data science process flowchart

Analysis refers to breaking a whole into its separate components for individual examination. Data analysis is a process for obtaining raw data and converting it into information useful for decision-making by users. Data is collected and analyzed to answer questions, test hypotheses or disprove theories.

Statistician John Tukey defined data analysis in 1961 as: "Procedures for analyzing data, techniques for interpreting the results of such procedures, ways of planning the gathering of data to make its analysis easier, more precise or more accurate, and all the machinery and results of (mathematical) statistics which apply to analyzing data."

There are several phases that can be distinguished, described below. The phases are iterative, in that feedback from later phases may result in additional work in earlier phases.

Data Requirements

The data necessary as inputs to the analysis are specified based upon the requirements of those directing the analysis or customers who will use the finished product of the analysis. The general type of entity upon which the data will be collected is referred to as an experimental unit (e.g., a person or population of people). Specific variables regarding a population (e.g., age and income) may be specified and obtained. Data may be numerical or categorical (i.e., a text label for numbers).

Data Collection

Data is collected from a variety of sources. The requirements may be communicated by analysts to custodians of the data, such as information technology personnel within an organization. The data may also be collected from sensors in the environment, such as traffic cameras, satellites, recording devices, etc. It may also be obtained through interviews, downloads from online sources, or reading documentation.

Data Processing

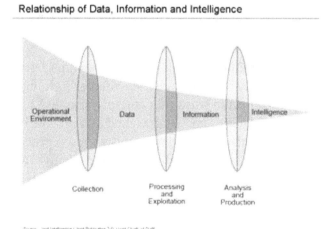

The phases of the intelligence cycle used to convert raw information into actionable intelligence or knowledge are conceptually similar to the phases in data analysis.

Data initially obtained must be processed or organized for analysis. For instance, these may involve placing data into rows and columns in a table format for further analysis, such as within a spreadsheet or statistical software.

Data Cleaning

Once processed and organized, the data may be incomplete, contain duplicates, or contain errors. The need for data cleaning will arise from problems in the way that data is entered and stored. Data cleaning is the process of preventing and correcting these errors. Common tasks include record matching, identifying inaccuracy of data, overall quality of existing data, deduplication, and column segmentation. Such data problems can also be identified through a variety of analytical techniques. For example, with financial information, the totals for particular variables may be compared against separately published numbers believed to be reliable. Unusual amounts above or below pre-determined thresholds may also be reviewed. There are several types of data cleaning that depend on the type of data such as phone numbers, email addresses, employers etc. Quantitative data methods for outlier detection can be used to get rid of likely incorrectly entered data. Textual data spellcheckers can be used to lessen the amount of mistyped words, but it is harder to tell if the words themselves are correct.

Exploratory Data Analysis

Once the data is cleaned, it can be analyzed. Analysts may apply a variety of techniques referred to as exploratory data analysis to begin understanding the messages contained in the data. The process of exploration may result in additional data cleaning or additional requests for data, so these activities may be iterative in nature. Descriptive statistics such as the average or median may be generated to help understand the data. Data visualization may also be used to examine the data in graphical format, to obtain additional insight regarding the messages within the data.

Modeling and Algorithms

Mathematical formulas or models called algorithms may be applied to the data to identify relationships among the variables, such as correlation or causation. In general terms, models may be developed to evaluate a particular variable in the data based on other variable(s) in the data, with some residual error depending on model accuracy (i.e., Data = Model + Error).

Inferential statistics includes techniques to measure relationships between particular variables. For example, regression analysis may be used to model whether a change in advertising (independent variable X) explains the variation in sales (dependent variable Y). In mathematical terms, Y (sales) is a function of X (advertising). It may be described as $Y = aX + b +$ error, where the model is designed such that a and b minimize the error when the model predicts Y for a given range of values of X. Analysts may attempt to build models that are descriptive of the data to simplify analysis and communicate results.

Data Product

A data product is a computer application that takes data inputs and generates outputs, feeding them back into the environment. It may be based on a model or algorithm. An example is an application that analyzes data about customer purchasing history and recommends other purchases the customer might enjoy.

Communication

Data visualization to understand the results of a data analysis.

Once the data is analyzed, it may be reported in many formats to the users of the analysis to support their requirements. The users may have feedback, which results in additional analysis. As such, much of the analytical cycle is iterative.

When determining how to communicate the results, the analyst may consider data visualization techniques to help clearly and efficiently communicate the message to the audience. Data visualization uses information displays such as tables and charts to help communicate key messages contained in the data. Tables are helpful to a user who might lookup specific numbers, while charts (e.g., bar charts or line charts) may help explain the quantitative messages contained in the data.

Quantitative Messages

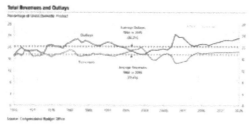

A time series illustrated with a line chart demonstrating trends in U.S. federal spending and revenue over time.

A scatterplot illustrating correlation between two variables (inflation and unemployment) measured at points in time.

Author Stephen Few described eight types of quantitative messages that users may attempt to understand or communicate from a set of data and the associated graphs used to help communicate the message. Customers specifying requirements and analysts performing the data analysis may consider these messages during the course of the process.

1. Time-series: A single variable is captured over a period of time, such as the unemployment rate over a 10-year period. A line chart may be used to demonstrate the trend.

2. Ranking: Categorical subdivisions are ranked in ascending or descending order, such as a ranking of sales performance (the *measure*) by sales persons (the *category*, with each sales person a *categorical subdivision*) during a single period. A bar chart may be used to show the comparison across the sales persons.

3. Part-to-whole: Categorical subdivisions are measured as a ratio to the whole (i.e., a percentage out of 100%). A pie chart or bar chart can show the comparison of ratios, such as the market share represented by competitors in a market.

4. Deviation: Categorical subdivisions are compared against a reference, such as a comparison of actual vs. budget expenses for several departments of a business for a given time period. A bar chart can show comparison of the actual versus the reference amount.

5. Frequency distribution: Shows the number of observations of a particular variable for given interval, such as the number of years in which the stock market return is between intervals such as 0-10%, 11-20%, etc. A histogram, a type of bar chart, may be used for this analysis.

6. Correlation: Comparison between observations represented by two variables (X,Y) to determine if they tend to move in the same or opposite directions. For example, plotting unemployment (X) and inflation (Y) for a sample of months. A scatter plot is typically used for this message.

7. Nominal comparison: Comparing categorical subdivisions in no particular order, such as the sales volume by product code. A bar chart may be used for this comparison.

8. Geographic or geospatial: Comparison of a variable across a map or layout, such as the unemployment rate by state or the number of persons on the various floors of a building. A cartogram is a typical graphic used.

Techniques for Analyzing Quantitative Data

Author Jonathan Koomey has recommended a series of best practices for understanding quantitative data. These include:

- Check raw data for anomalies prior to performing your analysis;

- Re-perform important calculations, such as verifying columns of data that are formula driven;

- Confirm main totals are the sum of subtotals;

- Check relationships between numbers that should be related in a predictable way, such as ratios over time;

- Normalize numbers to make comparisons easier, such as analyzing amounts per person or relative to GDP or as an index value relative to a base year;

- Break problems into component parts by analyzing factors that led to the results, such as DuPont analysis of return on equity.

For the variables under examination, analysts typically obtain descriptive statistics for them, such as the mean (average), median, and standard deviation. They may also analyze the distribution of the key variables to see how the individual values cluster around the mean.

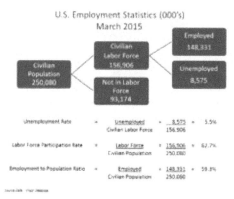

An illustration of the MECE principle used for data analysis.

The consultants at McKinsey and Company named a technique for breaking a quantitative problem down into its component parts called the MECE principle. Each layer can be broken down into its components; each of the sub-components must be mutually exclusive of each other and collectively add up to the layer above them. The relationship is referred to as "Mutually Exclusive and Collectively Exhaustive" or MECE. For example, profit by definition can be broken down into total revenue and total cost. In turn, total revenue can be analyzed by its components, such as revenue of divisions A, B, and C (which are mutually exclusive of each other) and should add to the total revenue (collectively exhaustive).

Analysts may use robust statistical measurements to solve certain analytical problems. Hypothesis testing is used when a particular hypothesis about the true state of affairs is made by the analyst and data is gathered to determine whether that state of affairs is true or false. For example, the hypothesis might be that "Unemployment has no effect on inflation", which relates to an economics concept called the Phillips Curve. Hypothesis testing involves considering the likelihood of Type I and type II errors, which relate to whether the data supports accepting or rejecting the hypothesis.

Regression analysis may be used when the analyst is trying to determine the extent to which independent variable X affects dependent variable Y (e.g., "To what extent do changes in the unemployment rate (X) affect the inflation rate (Y)?"). This is an attempt to model or fit an equation line or curve to the data, such that Y is a function of X.

Necessary condition analysis (NCA) may be used when the analyst is trying to determine the extent to which independent variable X allows variable Y (e.g., "To what extent is a certain unemployment rate (X) necessary for a certain inflation rate (Y)?"). Whereas (multiple) regression analysis uses additive logic where each X-variable can produce the outcome and the X's can compensate for each other (they are sufficient but not necessary), necessary condition analysis (NCA) uses necessity logic, where one or more X-variables allow the outcome to exist, but may not produce it (they are necessary but not sufficient). Each single necessary condition must be present and compensation is not possible.

Analytical Activities of Data Users

Users may have particular data points of interest within a data set, as opposed to general messaging outlined above. Such low-level user analytic activities are presented in the following table. The taxonomy can also be organized by three poles of activities: retrieving values, finding data points, and arranging data points.

#	Task	General Description	Pro Forma Abstract	Examples
1	Retrieve Value	Given a set of specific cases, find attributes of those cases.	What are the values of attributes {X, Y, Z, ...} in the data cases {A, B, C, ...}?	- What is the mileage per gallon of the Audi TT? - How long is the movie Gone with the Wind?
2	Filter	Given some concrete conditions on attribute values, find data cases satisfying those conditions.	Which data cases satisfy conditions {A, B, C...}?	- What Kellogg's cereals have high fiber? - What comedies have won awards? - Which funds underperformed the SP-500?
3	Compute Derived Value	Given a set of data cases, compute an aggregate numeric representation of those data cases.	What is the value of aggregation function F over a given set S of data cases?	- What is the average calorie content of Post cereals? - What is the gross income of all stores combined? - How many manufacturers of cars are there?
4	Find Extremum	Find data cases possessing an extreme value of an attribute over its range within the data set.	What are the top/bottom N data cases with respect to attribute A?	- What is the car with the highest MPG? - What director/film has won the most awards? - What Robin Williams film has the most recent release date?
5	Sort	Given a set of data cases, rank them according to some ordinal metric.	What is the sorted order of a set S of data cases according to their value of attribute A?	- Order the cars by weight. - Rank the cereals by calories.

6	Determine Range	Given a set of data cases and an attribute of interest, find the span of values within the set.	What is the range of values of attribute A in a set S of data cases?	- What is the range of film lengths? - What is the range of car horsepowers? - What actresses are in the data set?
7	Characterize Distribution	Given a set of data cases and a quantitative attribute of interest, characterize the distribution of that attribute's values over the set.	What is the distribution of values of attribute A in a set S of data cases?	- What is the distribution of carbohydrates in cereals? - What is the age distribution of shoppers?
8	Find Anomalies	Identify any anomalies within a given set of data cases with respect to a given relationship or expectation, e.g. statistical outliers.	Which data cases in a set S of data cases have unexpected/exceptional values?	- Are there exceptions to the relationship between horsepower and acceleration? - Are there any outliers in protein?
9	Cluster	Given a set of data cases, find clusters of similar attribute values.	Which data cases in a set S of data cases are similar in value for attributes {X, Y, Z, ...}?	- Are there groups of cereals w/ similar fat/calories/sugar? - Is there a cluster of typical film lengths?
10	Correlate	Given a set of data cases and two attributes, determine useful relationships between the values of those attributes.	What is the correlation between attributes X and Y over a given set S of data cases?	- Is there a correlation between carbohydrates and fat? - Is there a correlation between country of origin and MPG? - Do different genders have a preferred payment method? - Is there a trend of increasing film length over the years?

Barriers to Effective Analysis

Barriers to effective analysis may exist among the analysts performing the data analysis or among the audience. Distinguishing fact from opinion, cognitive biases, and innumeracy are all challenges to sound data analysis.

Confusing Fact and Opinion

Effective analysis requires obtaining relevant facts to answer questions, support a conclusion or formal opinion, or test hypotheses. Facts by definition are irrefutable, meaning that any person involved in the analysis should be able to agree upon them. For example, in August 2010, the Congressional Budget Office (CBO) estimated that extending the Bush tax cuts of 2001 and 2003 for the 2011-2020 time period would add approximately $3.3 trillion to the national debt. Everyone should be able to agree that indeed this is what CBO reported; they can all examine the report. This makes it a fact. Whether persons agree or disagree with the CBO is their own opinion.

As another example, the auditor of a public company must arrive at a formal opinion on whether financial statements of publicly traded corporations are "fairly stated, in all material respects." This requires extensive analysis of factual data and evidence to support their opinion. When making the leap from facts to opinions, there is always the possibility that the opinion is erroneous.

Cognitive Biases

There are a variety of cognitive biases that can adversely effect analysis. For example, confirmation bias is the tendency to search for or interpret information in a way that confirms one's preconceptions. In addition, individuals may discredit information that does not support their views.

Analysts may be trained specifically to be aware of these biases and how to overcome them. In his book *Psychology of Intelligence Analysis*, retired CIA analyst Richards Heuer wrote that analysts should clearly delineate their assumptions and chains of inference and specify the degree and source of the uncertainty involved in the conclusions. He emphasized procedures to help surface and debate alternative points of view.

Innumeracy

Effective analysts are generally adept with a variety of numerical techniques. However, audiences may not have such literacy with numbers or numeracy; they are said to be innumerate. Persons communicating the data may also be attempting to mislead or misinform, deliberately using bad numerical techniques.

For example, whether a number is rising or falling may not be the key factor. More important may be the number relative to another number, such as the size of government revenue or spending relative to the size of the economy (GDP) or the amount of cost relative to revenue in corporate financial statements. This numerical technique is referred to as normalization or common-sizing. There are many such techniques employed by analysts, whether adjusting for inflation (i.e., comparing real vs. nominal data) or considering population increases, demographics, etc. Analysts apply a variety of techniques to address the various quantitative messages described in the section above.

Analysts may also analyze data under different assumptions or scenarios. For example, when analysts perform financial statement analysis, they will often recast the financial statements under different assumptions to help arrive at an estimate of future cash flow, which they then discount to present value based on some interest rate, to determine the valuation of the company or its stock. Similarly, the CBO analyzes the effects of various policy options on the government's revenue, outlays and deficits, creating alternative future scenarios for key measures.

Other Topics

Analytics and Business Intelligence

Analytics is the "extensive use of data, statistical and quantitative analysis, explanatory and predictive models, and fact-based management to drive decisions and actions." It is a subset of business intelligence, which is a set of technologies and processes that use data to understand and analyze business performance.

Education

Analytic activities of data visualization users

In education, most educators have access to a data system for the purpose of analyzing student data. These data systems present data to educators in an over-the-counter data format (embedding labels, supplemental documentation, and a help system and making key package/display and content decisions) to improve the accuracy of educators' data analyses.

Initial Data Analysis

The most important distinction between the initial data analysis phase and the main analysis phase, is that during initial data analysis one refrains from any analysis that is aimed at answering the original research question. The initial data analysis phase is guided by the following four questions:

Quality of Data

The quality of the data should be checked as early as possible. Data quality can be assessed in several ways, using different types of analysis: frequency counts, descriptive statistics (mean, standard deviation, median), normality (skewness, kurtosis, frequency histograms, n: variables are compared with coding schemes of variables external to the data set, and possibly corrected if coding schemes are not comparable.

- Test for common-method variance.

The choice of analyses to assess the data quality during the initial data analysis phase depends on the analyses that will be conducted in the main analysis phase.

Quality of Measurements

The quality of the measurement instruments should only be checked during the initial data analysis phase when this is not the focus or research question of the study. One should check whether structure of measurement instruments corresponds to structure reported in the literature. There are two ways to assess measurement

- Analysis of homogeneity (internal consistency), which gives an indication of the reliability of a measurement instrument. During this analysis, one inspects the variances of the items and the scales, the Cronbach's α of the scales, and the change in the Cronbach's alpha when an item would be deleted from a scale.

Initial Transformations

After assessing the quality of the data and of the measurements, one might decide to impute missing data, or to perform initial transformations of one or more variables, although this can also be done during the main analysis phase.

Possible transformations of variables are:

- Square root transformation (if the distribution differs moderately from normal)

- Log-transformation (if the distribution differs substantially from normal)

- Inverse transformation (if the distribution differs severely from normal)

- Make categorical (ordinal / dichotomous) (if the distribution differs severely from normal, and no transformations help)

Did the Implementation of the Study Fulfill the Intentions of the Research Design?

One should check the success of the randomization procedure, for instance by checking whether background and substantive variables are equally distributed within and across groups. If the study did not need or use a randomization procedure, one should check the success of the non-random sampling, for instance by checking whether all subgroups of the population of interest are represented in sample.

Other possible data distortions that should be checked are:

- dropout (this should be identified during the initial data analysis phase)

- Item nonresponse (whether this is random or not should be assessed during the initial data analysis phase)

- Treatment quality (using manipulation checks).

Characteristics of Data Sample

In any report or article, the structure of the sample must be accurately described. It is especially important to exactly determine the structure of the sample (and specifically the size of the sub-groups) when subgroup analyses will be performed during the main analysis phase.

The characteristics of the data sample can be assessed by looking at:

- Basic statistics of important variables
- Scatter plots
- Correlations and associations
- Cross-tabulations

Final Stage of the Initial Data Analysis

During the final stage, the findings of the initial data analysis are documented, and necessary, preferable, and possible corrective actions are taken.
Also, the original plan for the main data analyses can and should be specified in more detail or rewritten.
In order to do this, several decisions about the main data analyses can and should be made:

- In the case of non-normals: should one transform variables; make variables categorical (ordinal/dichotomous); adapt the analysis method?

- In the case of missing data: should one neglect or impute the missing data; which imputation technique should be used?

- In the case of outliers: should one use robust analysis techniques?

- In case items do not fit the scale: should one adapt the measurement instrument by omitting items, or rather ensure comparability with other (uses of the) measurement instrument(s)?

- In the case of (too) small subgroups: should one drop the hypothesis about inter-group differences, or use small sample techniques, like exact tests or bootstrapping?

- In case the randomization procedure seems to be defective: can and should one calculate propensity scores and include them as covariates in the main analyses?

Analysis

Several analyses can be used during the initial data analysis phase:

- Univariate statistics (single variable)
- Bivariate associations (correlations)
- Graphical techniques (scatter plots)

It is important to take the measurement levels of the variables into account for the analyses, as special statistical techniques are available for each level:

- Nominal and ordinal variables
    - Frequency counts (numbers and percentages)
    - Associations
- circumambulations (crosstabulations)
- hierarchical loglinear analysis (restricted to a maximum of 8 variables)
- loglinear analysis (to identify relevant/important variables and possible confounders)
    - Exact tests or bootstrapping (in case subgroups are small)
    - Computation of new variables
- Continuous variables
    - Distribution
- Statistics (M, SD, variance, skewness, kurtosis)
- Stem-and-leaf displays
- Box plots

Nonlinear Analysis

Nonlinear analysis will be necessary when the data is recorded from a nonlinear system. Nonlinear systems can exhibit complex dynamic effects including bifurcations, chaos, harmonics and subharmonics that cannot be analyzed using simple linear methods. Nonlinear data analysis is closely related to nonlinear system identification.

Main Data Analysis

In the main analysis phase analyses aimed at answering the research question are performed as well as any other relevant analysis needed to write the first draft of the research report.

Exploratory and Confirmatory Approaches

In the main analysis phase either an exploratory or confirmatory approach can be adopted. Usually the approach is decided before data is collected. In an exploratory analysis no clear hypothesis is stated before analysing the data, and the data is searched for models that describe the data well. In a confirmatory analysis clear hypotheses about the data are tested.

Exploratory data analysis should be interpreted carefully. When testing multiple models at once there is a high chance on finding at least one of them to be significant, but this can be due to a type 1 error. It is important to always adjust the significance level when testing multiple models with, for example, a Bonferroni correction. Also, one should not follow up an exploratory analysis with a confirmatory analysis in the same dataset. An exploratory analysis is used to find ideas for a theory, but not to test that theory as well. When a model is found exploratory in a dataset, then following up that analysis with a confirmatory analysis in the same dataset could simply mean that the results of the confirmatory analysis are due to the same type 1 error that resulted in the exploratory model in the first place. The confirmatory analysis therefore will not be more informative than the original exploratory analysis.

Stability of Results

It is important to obtain some indication about how generalizable the results are. While this is hard to check, one can look at the stability of the results. Are the results reliable and reproducible? There are two main ways of doing this:

- Cross-validation: By splitting the data in multiple parts we can check if an analysis (like a fitted model) based on one part of the data generalizes to another part of the data as well.

- Sensitivity analysis: A procedure to study the behavior of a system or model when global parameters are (systematically) varied. One way to do this is with bootstrapping.

Statistical Methods

Many statistical methods have been used for statistical analyses. A very brief list of four of the more popular methods is:

- General linear model: A widely used model on which various methods are based (e.g. t test, ANOVA, ANCOVA, MANOVA). Usable for assessing the effect of several predictors on one or more continuous dependent variables.

- Generalized linear model: An extension of the general linear model for discrete dependent variables.

- Structural equation modelling: Usable for assessing latent structures from measured manifest variables.

- Item response theory: Models for (mostly) assessing one latent variable from several binary measured variables (e.g. an exam).

Free Software for Data Analysis

- DevInfo - a database system endorsed by the United Nations Development Group for monitoring and analyzing human development.

- ELKI - data mining framework in Java with data mining oriented visualization functions.

- KNIME - the Konstanz Information Miner, a user friendly and comprehensive data analytics framework.

- PAW - FORTRAN/C data analysis framework developed at CERN

- Orange - A visual programming tool featuring interactive data visualization and methods for statistical data analysis, data mining, and machine learning.

- R - a programming language and software environment for statistical computing and graphics.

- ROOT - C++ data analysis framework developed at CERN

- SciPy and Pandas - Python libraries for data analysis

Regression Analysis

In statistical modeling, regression analysis is a statistical process for estimating the relationships among variables. It includes many techniques for modeling and analyzing several variables, when the focus is on the relationship between a dependent variable and one or more independent variables (or 'predictors'). More specifically, regression analysis helps one understand how the typical value of the dependent variable (or 'criterion variable') changes when any one of the independent variables is varied, while the other independent variables are held fixed. Most commonly, regression analysis estimates the conditional expectation of the dependent variable given the independent variables – that is, the average value of the dependent variable when the independent variables are fixed. Less commonly, the focus is on a quantile, or other location parameter of the conditional distribution of the dependent variable given the independent variables. In all cases, the estimation target is a function of the independent variables called the regression function. In regression analysis, it is also of interest to characterize the variation of the dependent variable around the regression function which can be described by a probability distribution. A related but distinct approach is necessary condition analysis (NCA), which estimates the maximum (rather than average) value of the dependent variable for a given value of the independent variable (ceiling line rather than central line) in order to identify what value of the independent variable is necessary but not sufficient for a given value of the dependent variable.

Regression analysis is widely used for prediction and forecasting, where its use has substantial overlap with the field of machine learning. Regression analysis is also used to understand which among the independent variables are related to the dependent variable, and to explore the forms of these relationships. In restricted circumstances, regression analysis can be used to infer causal relationships between the independent and dependent variables. However this can lead to illusions or false relationships, so caution is advisable; for example, correlation does not imply causation.

Many techniques for carrying out regression analysis have been developed. Familiar methods such as linear regression and ordinary least squares regression are parametric, in that the regression function is defined in terms of a finite number of unknown parameters that are estimated from the data. Nonparametric regression refers to techniques that allow the regression function to lie in a specified set of functions, which may be infinite-dimensional.

The performance of regression analysis methods in practice depends on the form of the data generating process, and how it relates to the regression approach being used. Since the true form of the data-generating process is generally not known, regression analysis often depends to some extent on making assumptions about this process. These assumptions are sometimes testable if a sufficient quantity of data is available. Regression models for prediction are often useful even when the assumptions are moderately violated, although they may not perform optimally. However, in many applications, especially with small effects or questions of causality based on observational data, regression methods can give misleading results.

In a narrower sense, regression may refer specifically to the estimation of continuous response variables, as opposed to the discrete response variables used in classification. The case of a continuous output variable may be more specifically referred to as metric regression to distinguish it from related problems.

History

The earliest form of regression was the method of least squares, which was published by Legendre in 1805, and by Gauss in 1809. Legendre and Gauss both applied the method to the problem of determining, from astronomical observations, the orbits of bodies about the Sun (mostly comets, but also later the then newly discovered minor planets). Gauss published a further development of the theory of least squares in 1821, including a version of the Gauss–Markov theorem.

The term "regression" was coined by Francis Galton in the nineteenth century to describe a biological phenomenon. The phenomenon was that the heights of descendants of tall ancestors tend to regress down towards a normal average (a phenomenon also known as regression toward the mean). For Galton, regression had only this biological meaning, but his work was later extended by Udny Yule and Karl Pearson to a more general statistical context. In the work of Yule and Pearson, the joint distribution of the response and explanatory variables is assumed to be Gaussian. This assumption was weakened by R.A. Fisher in his works of 1922 and 1925. Fisher assumed that the conditional distribution of the response variable is Gaussian, but the joint distribution need not be. In this respect, Fisher's assumption is closer to Gauss's formulation of 1821.

In the 1950s and 1960s, economists used electromechanical desk calculators to calculate regressions. Before 1970, it sometimes took up to 24 hours to receive the result from one regression.

Regression methods continue to be an area of active research. In recent decades, new methods have been developed for robust regression, regression involving correlated responses such as time series and growth curves, regression in which the predictor (independent variable) or response variables are curves, images, graphs, or other complex data objects, regression methods accommodating various types of missing data, nonparametric regression, Bayesian methods for regression, regression in which the predictor variables are measured with error, regression with more predictor variables than observations, and causal inference with regression.

Regression Models

Regression models involve the following variables:

- The unknown parameters, denoted as β, which may represent a scalar or a vector.
- The independent variables, X.
- The dependent variable, Y.

In various fields of application, different terminologies are used in place of dependent and independent variables.

A regression model relates Y to a function of X and β.

$$Y \approx f(X, \beta)$$

The approximation is usually formalized as $E(Y \mid X) = f(X, \beta)$. To carry out regression analysis, the form of the function f must be specified. Sometimes the form of this function is based on knowledge about the relationship between Y and X that does not rely on the data. If no such knowledge is available, a flexible or convenient form for f is chosen.

Assume now that the vector of unknown parameters β is of length k. In order to perform a regression analysis the user must provide information about the dependent variable Y:

- If N data points of the form (Y, X) are observed, where $N < k$, most classical approaches to regression analysis cannot be performed: since the system of equations defining the regression model is underdetermined, there are not enough data to recover β.

- If exactly $N = k$ data points are observed, and the function f is linear, the equations $Y = f(X, \beta)$ can be solved exactly rather than approximately. This reduces to solving a set of N equations with N unknowns (the elements of β), which has a unique solution as long as the X are linearly independent. If f is nonlinear, a solution may not exist, or many solutions may exist.

- The most common situation is where $N > k$ data points are observed. In this case, there is enough information in the data to estimate a unique value for β that best fits the data in some sense, and the regression model when applied to the data can be viewed as an overdetermined system in β.

In the last case, the regression analysis provides the tools for:

1. Finding a solution for unknown parameters β that will, for example, minimize the distance between the measured and predicted values of the dependent variable Y (also known as method of least squares).

2. Under certain statistical assumptions, the regression analysis uses the surplus of information to provide statistical information about the unknown parameters β and predicted values of the dependent variable Y.

Necessary Number of Independent Measurements

Consider a regression model which has three unknown parameters, β_0, β_1, and β_2. Suppose an experimenter performs 10 measurements all at exactly the same value of independent variable vector X (which contains the independent variables X_1, X_2, and X_3). In this case, regression analysis fails to give a unique set of estimated values for the three unknown parameters; the experimenter did not provide enough information. The best one can do is to estimate the average value and the standard deviation of the dependent variable Y. Similarly, measuring at two different values of X would give enough data for a regression with two unknowns, but not for three or more unknowns.

If the experimenter had performed measurements at three different values of the independent variable vector X, then regression analysis would provide a unique set of estimates for the three unknown parameters in β.

In the case of general linear regression, the above statement is equivalent to the requirement that the matrix X^TX is invertible.

Statistical Assumptions

When the number of measurements, N, is larger than the number of unknown parameters, k, and the measurement errors ε_i are normally distributed then *the excess of information* contained in $(N - k)$ measurements is used to make statistical predictions about the unknown parameters. This excess of information is referred to as the degrees of freedom of the regression.

Underlying Assumptions

Classical assumptions for regression analysis include:

- The sample is representative of the population for the inference prediction.

- The error is a random variable with a mean of zero conditional on the explanatory variables.

- The independent variables are measured with no error. (Note: If this is not so, modeling may be done instead using errors-in-variables model techniques).

- The independent variables (predictors) are linearly independent, i.e. it is not possible to express any predictor as a linear combination of the others.

- The errors are uncorrelated, that is, the variance–covariance matrix of the errors is diagonal and each non-zero element is the variance of the error.

- The variance of the error is constant across observations (homoscedasticity). If not, weighted least squares or other methods might instead be used.

These are sufficient conditions for the least-squares estimator to possess desirable properties; in particular, these assumptions imply that the parameter estimates will be unbiased, consistent, and efficient in the class of linear unbiased estimators. It is important to note that actual data rarely satisfies the assumptions. That is, the method is used even though the assumptions are not true. Variation from the assumptions can sometimes be used as a measure of how far the model is from being useful. Many of these assumptions may be relaxed in more advanced treatments. Reports of statistical analyses usually include analyses of tests on the sample data and methodology for the fit and usefulness of the model.

Assumptions include the geometrical support of the variables. Independent and dependent variables often refer to values measured at point locations. There may be spatial trends and spatial autocorrelation in the variables that violate statistical assumptions of regression. Geographic weighted regression is one technique to deal with such data. Also, variables may include values aggregated by areas. With aggregated data the modifiable areal unit problem can cause extreme variation in regression parameters. When analyzing data aggregated by political boundaries, postal codes or census areas results may be very distinct with a different choice of units.

Linear Regression

In linear regression, the model specification is that the dependent variable, y_i s a linear combination of the *parameters* (but need not be linear in the *independent variables*). For example, in simple linear regression for modeling n data points there is one independent variable: x_i, and two parameters, β_0 and β_1:

straight line: $y_i = \beta_0 + \beta_1 x_i + \varepsilon_i, \quad i = 1, \ldots, n.$

In multiple linear regression, there are several independent variables or functions of independent variables.

Adding a term in x_i^2 to the preceding regression gives:

parabola: $y_i = \beta_0 + \beta_1 x_i + \beta_2 x_i^2 + \varepsilon_i, \; i = 1, \ldots, n.$

This is still linear regression; although the expression on the right hand side is quadratic in the independent variable x_i, it is linear in the parameters β_0, β_1 and β_2.

In both cases, ε_i is an error term and the subscript i indexes a particular observation.

Returning our attention to the straight line case: Given a random sample from the population, we estimate the population parameters and obtain the sample linear regression model:

$$\widehat{y}_i = \hat{\beta}_0 + \hat{\beta}_1 x_i.$$

The residual, $e_i = y_i - \hat{y}_i$, , is the difference between the value of the dependent variable predicted by the model, $\hat{y}_i$, and the true value of the dependent variable, y_i. One method of estimation is ordinary least squares. This method obtains parameter estimates that minimize the sum of squared residuals, SSE, also sometimes denoted RSS:

$$SSE = \sum_{i=1}^{n} e_i^2.$$

Minimization of this function results in a set of normal equations, a set of simultaneous linear equations in the parameters, which are solved to yield the parameter estimators, $\hat{\beta}_0, \hat{\beta}_1$.

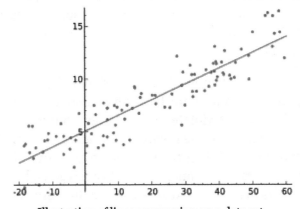

Illustration of linear regression on a data set.

In the case of simple regression, the formulas for the least squares estimates are

$$\widehat{\beta_1} = \frac{\sum (x_i - \bar{x})(y_i - \bar{y})}{\sum (x_i - \bar{x})^2} \text{ and } \widehat{\beta_0} = \bar{y} - \widehat{\beta_1}\bar{x}$$

where $\bar{x}$ is the mean (average) of the x values and $\bar{y}$ is the mean of the y values.

Under the assumption that the population error term has a constant variance, the estimate of that variance is given by:

$$\hat{\sigma}_\varepsilon^2 = \frac{SSE}{n-2}.$$

This is called the mean square error (MSE) of the regression. The denominator is the sample size reduced by the number of model parameters estimated from the same data, $(n-p)$ for p regressors or $(n-p-1)$ if an intercept is used. In this case, $p=1$ so the denominator is $n-2$.

The standard errors of the parameter estimates are given by

$$\hat{\sigma}_{\beta_0} = \hat{\sigma}_\varepsilon \sqrt{\frac{1}{n} + \frac{\bar{x}^2}{\sum (x_i - \bar{x})^2}}$$

$$\hat{\sigma}_{\beta_1} = \hat{\sigma}_\varepsilon \sqrt{\frac{1}{\sum (x_i - \bar{x})^2}}.$$

Under the further assumption that the population error term is normally distributed, the researcher can use these estimated standard errors to create confidence intervals and conduct hypothesis tests about the population parameters.

General Linear Model

In the more general multiple regression model, there are p independent variables:

$$y_i = \beta_1 x_{i1} + \beta_2 x_{i2} + \cdots + \beta_p x_{ip} + \varepsilon_i,$$

where x_{ij} is the ith observation on the jth independent variable. If the first independent variable takes the value 1 for all i, $x_{i1} = 1$, then β_1 is called the regression intercept.

The least squares parameter estimates are obtained from p normal equations. The residual can be written as

$$\varepsilon_i = y_i - \widehat{\beta_1} x_{i1} - \cdots - \widehat{\beta_p} x_{ip}.$$

The normal equations are

$$\sum_{i=1}^{n} \sum_{k=1}^{p} X_{ij} X_{ik} \widehat{\beta_k} = \sum_{i=1}^{n} X_{ij} y_i, \quad j = 1, \ldots, p.$$

In matrix notation, the normal equations are written as

$$(\mathbf{X}^{\top}\mathbf{X})\,\hat{\beta} = \mathbf{X}^{\top}\mathbf{Y},$$

where the ij element of X is x_{ij}, the i element of the column vector Y is y_i, and the j element of $\hat{\beta}$ is $\hat{\beta}_j$. Thus X is $n{\times}p$, Y is $n{\times}1$, and $\hat{\beta}$ is $p{\times}1$. The solution is

$$\hat{\beta} = (\mathbf{X}^{\top}\mathbf{X})^{-1}\mathbf{X}^{\top}\mathbf{Y}.$$

Diagnostics

Once a regression model has been constructed, it may be important to confirm the goodness of fit of the model and the statistical significance of the estimated parameters. Commonly used checks of goodness of fit include the R-squared, analyses of the pattern of residuals and hypothesis testing. Statistical significance can be checked by an F-test of the overall fit, followed by t-tests of individual parameters.

Interpretations of these diagnostic tests rest heavily on the model assumptions. Although examination of the residuals can be used to invalidate a model, the results of a t-test or F-test are sometimes more difficult to interpret if the model's assumptions are violated. For example, if the error term does not have a normal distribution, in small samples the estimated parameters will not follow normal distributions and complicate inference. With relatively large samples, however, a central limit theorem can be invoked such that hypothesis testing may proceed using asymptotic approximations.

"Limited Dependent" Variables

The phrase "limited dependent" is used in econometric statistics for categorical and constrained variables.

The response variable may be non-continuous ("limited" to lie on some subset of the real line). For binary (zero or one) variables, if analysis proceeds with least-squares linear regression, the model is called the linear probability model. Nonlinear models for binary dependent variables include the probit and logit model. The multivariate probit model is a standard method of estimating a joint relationship between several binary dependent variables and some independent variables. For categorical variables with more than two values there is the multinomial logit. For ordinal variables with more than two values, there are the ordered logit and ordered probit models. Censored regression models may be used when the dependent variable is only sometimes observed, and Heckman correction type models may be used when the sample is not randomly selected from the population of interest. An alternative to such procedures is linear regression based on polychoric correlation (or polyserial correlations) between the categorical variables. Such procedures differ in the assumptions made about the distribution of the variables in the population. If the variable is positive with low values and represents the repetition of the occurrence of an event, then count models like the Poisson regression or the negative binomial model may be used instead.

Interpolation and Extrapolation

Regression models predict a value of the Y variable given known values of the X variables. Prediction *within* the range of values in the dataset used for model-fitting is known informally as inter-polation. Prediction *outside* this range of the data is known as extrapolation. Performing extrapolation relies strongly on the regression assumptions. The further the extrapolation goes outside the data, the more room there is for the model to fail due to differences between the assumptions and the sample data or the true values.

It is generally advised that when performing extrapolation, one should accompany the estimated value of the dependent variable with a prediction interval that represents the uncertainty. Such intervals tend to expand rapidly as the values of the independent variable(s) moved outside the range covered by the observed data.

For such reasons and others, some tend to say that it might be unwise to undertake extrapolation.

However, this does not cover the full set of modelling errors that may be being made: in particular, the assumption of a particular form for the relation between Y and X. A properly conducted regression analysis will include an assessment of how well the assumed form is matched by the observed data, but it can only do so within the range of values of the independent variables actually available. This means that any extrapolation is particularly reliant on the assumptions being made about the structural form of the regression relationship. Best-practice advice here is that a linear-in-variables and linear-in-parameters relationship should not be chosen simply for computational convenience, but that all available knowledge should be deployed in constructing a regression model. If this knowledge includes the fact that the dependent variable cannot go outside a certain range of values, this can be made use of in selecting the model – even if the observed dataset has no values particularly near such bounds. The implications of this step of choosing an appropriate functional form for the regression can be great when extrapolation is considered. At a minimum, it can ensure that any extrapolation arising from a fitted model is "realistic" (or in accord with what is known).

Nonlinear Regression

When the model function is not linear in the parameters, the sum of squares must be minimized by an iterative procedure. This introduces many complications which are summarized in Differences between linear and non-linear least squares

Power and Sample Size Calculations

There are no generally agreed methods for relating the number of observations versus the number of independent variables in the model. One rule of thumb suggested by Good and Hardin is $N = m^n$, where N is the sample size, n is the number of independent variables and m is the number of observations needed to reach the desired precision if the model had only one independent variable. For example, a researcher is building a linear regression model using a dataset that contains 1000 patients (N). If the researcher decides that five observations are needed to precisely define a straight line (m), then the maximum number of independent variables the model can support is 4, because

$$\frac{\log 1000}{\log 5} = 4.29.$$

Other Methods

Although the parameters of a regression model are usually estimated using the method of least squares, other methods which have been used include:

- Bayesian methods, e.g. Bayesian linear regression

- Percentage regression, for situations where reducing *percentage* errors is deemed more appropriate.

- Least absolute deviations, which is more robust in the presence of outliers, leading to quantile regression

- Nonparametric regression, requires a large number of observations and is computationally intensive

- Distance metric learning, which is learned by the search of a meaningful distance metric in a given input space.

Software

All major statistical software packages perform least squares regression analysis and inference. Simple linear regression and multiple regression using least squares can be done in some spreadsheet applications and on some calculators. While many statistical software packages can perform various types of nonparametric and robust regression, these methods are less standardized; different software packages implement different methods, and a method with a given name may be implemented differently in different packages. Specialized regression software has been developed for use in fields such as survey analysis and neuroimaging.

Data Cleansing

Data cleansing, data cleaning, or data scrubbing is the process of detecting and correcting (or removing) corrupt or inaccurate records from a record set, table, or database and refers to identifying incomplete, incorrect, inaccurate or irrelevant parts of the data and then replacing, modifying, or deleting the dirty or coarse data. Data cleansing may be performed interactively with data wrangling tools, or as batch processing through scripting.

After cleansing, a data set should be consistent with other similar data sets in the system. The inconsistencies detected or removed may have been originally caused by user entry errors, by corruption in transmission or storage, or by different data dictionary definitions of similar entities in different stores. Data cleansing differs from data validation in that validation almost invariably means data is rejected from the system at entry and is performed at the time of entry, rather than on batches of data.

The actual process of data cleansing may involve removing typographical errors or validating and correcting values against a known list of entities. The validation may be strict (such as rejecting any address that does not have a valid postal code) or fuzzy (such as correcting records that partially match existing, known records). Some data cleansing solutions will clean data by cross checking with a validated data set. A common data cleansing practice is data enhancement, where data is made more complete by adding related information. For example, appending addresses with any phone numbers related to that address. Data cleansing may also involve activities like, harmonization of data, and standardization of data. For example, harmonization of short codes (st, rd, etc.) to actual words (street, road, etcetera). Standardization of data is a means of changing a reference data set to a new standard, ex, use of standard codes.

Motivation

Administratively, incorrect or inconsistent data can lead to false conclusions and misdirected investments on both public and private scales. For instance, the government may want to analyze population census figures to decide which regions require further spending and investment on infrastructure and services. In this case, it will be important to have access to reliable data to avoid erroneous fiscal decisions.

In the business world, incorrect data can be costly. Many companies use customer information databases that record data like contact information, addresses, and preferences. For instance, if the addresses are inconsistent, the company will suffer the cost of resending mail or even losing customers.

The profession of forensic accounting and fraud investigating uses data cleansing in preparing its data and is typically done before data is sent to a data warehouse for further investigation.

There are packages available so you can cleanse/wash address data while you enter it into your system. This is normally done via an API and will prompt staff as they type the address.

Data Quality

High-quality data needs to pass a set of quality criteria. Those include:

- Validity: The degree to which the measures conform to defined business rules or constraints. When modern database technology is used to design data-capture systems, validity is fairly easy to ensure: invalid data arises mainly in legacy contexts (where constraints were not implemented in software) or where inappropriate data-capture technology was used (e.g., spreadsheets, where it is very hard to limit what a user chooses to enter into a cell). Data constraints fall into the following categories:

    - *Data-Type Constraints* – e.g., values in a particular column must be of a particular datatype, e.g., Boolean, numeric (integer or real), date, etc.

    - *Range Constraints:* typically, numbers or dates should fall within a certain range. That is, they have minimum and/or maximum permissible values.

    - *Mandatory Constraints:* Certain columns cannot be empty.

    - *Unique Constraints:* A field, or a combination of fields, must be unique across a dataset. For example, no two persons can have the same social security number.

    - *Set-Membership constraints*: The values for a column come from a set of discrete values or codes. For example, a person's gender may be Female, Male or Unknown (not recorded).

- *Foreign-key constraints*: This is the more general case of set membership. The set of values in a column is defined in a column of another table that contains unique values. For example, in a US taxpayer database, the "state" column is required to belong to one of the US's defined states or territories: the set of permissible states/territories is recorded in a separate States table. The term foreign key is borrowed from relational database terminology.

- Regular expression patterns: Occasionally, text fields will have to be validated this way. For example, phone numbers may be required to have the pattern (999) 999-9999.

- Cross-field validation: Certain conditions that utilize multiple fields must hold. For example, in laboratory medicine, the sum of the components of the differential white blood cell count must be equal to 100 (since they are all percentages). In a hospital database, a patient's date of discharge from hospital cannot be earlier than the date of admission.

- Decleansing is detecting errors and syntactically removing them for better programming.

- Accuracy: The degree of conformity of a measure to a standard or a true value. Accuracy is very hard to achieve through data-cleansing in the general case, because it requires accessing an external source of data that contains the true value: such "gold standard" data is often unavailable. Accuracy has been achieved in some cleansing contexts, notably customer contact data, by using external databases that match up zip codes to geographical locations (city and state), and also help verify that street addresses within these zip codes actually exist.

- Completeness: The degree to which all required measures are known. Incompleteness is almost impossible to fix with data cleansing methodology: one cannot infer facts that were not captured when the data in question was initially recorded. (In some contexts, e.g., interview data, it may be possible to fix incompleteness by going back to the original source of data, i,e., re-interviewing the subject, but even this does not guarantee success because of problems of recall - e.g., in an interview to gather data on food consumption, no one is likely to remember exactly what one ate six months ago. In the case of systems that insist certain columns should not be empty, one may work around the problem by designating a value that indicates "unknown" or "missing", but supplying of default values does not imply that the data has been made complete.

- Consistency: The degree to which a set of measures are equivalent in across systems. Inconsistency occurs when two data items in the data set contradict each other: e.g., a customer is recorded in two different systems as having two different current addresses, and only one of them can be correct. Fixing inconsistency is not always possible: it requires a variety of strategies - e.g., deciding which data were recorded more recently, which data source is likely to be most reliable (the latter knowledge may be specific to a given organization), or simply trying to find the truth by testing both data items (e.g., calling up the customer).

- Uniformity: The degree to which a set data measures are specified using the same units of measure in all systems. In datasets pooled from different locales, weight may be recorded either in pounds or kilos, and must be converted to a single measure using an arithmetic transformation.

The term Integrity encompasses accuracy, consistency and some aspects of validation but is rarely used by itself in data-cleansing contexts because it is insufficiently specific. (For example, "referential integrity" is a term used to refer to the enforcement of foreign-key constraints above.)

The Process of Data Cleansing

- Data auditing: The data is audited with the use of statistical and database methods to detect anomalies and contradictions: this eventually gives an indication of the characteristics of the anomalies and their locations. Several commercial software packages will let you specify constraints of various kinds (using a grammar that conforms to that of a standard programming language, e.g., JavaScript or Visual Basic) and then generate code that checks the data for violation of these constraints. This process is referred to below in the bullets "workflow specification" and "workflow execution." For users who lack access to high-end cleansing software, Microcomputer database packages such as Microsoft Access or File Maker Pro will also let you perform such checks, on a constraint-by-constraint basis, interactively with little or no programming required in many cases.

- Workflow specification: The detection and removal of anomalies is performed by a sequence of operations on the data known as the workflow. It is specified after the process of auditing the data and is crucial in achieving the end product of high-quality data. In order to achieve a proper workflow, the causes of the anomalies and errors in the data have to be closely considered.

- Workflow execution: In this stage, the workflow is executed after its specification is complete and its correctness is verified. The implementation of the workflow should be efficient, even on large sets of data, which inevitably poses a trade-off because the execution of a data-cleansing operation can be computationally expensive.

- Post-processing and controlling: After executing the cleansing workflow, the results are inspected to verify correctness. Data that could not be corrected during execution of the workflow is manually corrected, if possible. The result is a new cycle in the data-cleansing process where the data is audited again to allow the specification of an additional workflow to further cleanse the data by automatic processing.

Good quality source data has to do with "Data Quality Culture" and must be initiated at the top of the organization. It is not just a matter of implementing strong validation checks on input screens, because almost no matter how strong these checks are, they can often still be circumvented by the users. There is a nine-step guide for organizations that wish to improve data quality:

- Declare a high level commitment to a data quality culture

- Drive process reengineering at the executive level

- Spend money to improve the data entry environment

- Spend money to improve application integration

- Spend money to change how processes work

- Promote end-to-end team awareness

- Promote interdepartmental cooperation

- Publicly celebrate data quality excellence

- Continuously measure and improve data quality

Decleanse

- Parsing: for the detection of syntax errors. A parser decides whether a string of data is acceptable within the allowed data specification. This is similar to the way a parser works with grammars and languages.

- Data transformation: Data transformation allows the mapping of the data from its given format into the format expected by the appropriate application. This includes value conversions or translation functions, as well as normalizing numeric values to conform to minimum and maximum values.

- Duplicate elimination: Duplicate detection requires an algorithm for determining whether data contains duplicate representations of the same entity. Usually, data is sorted by a key that would bring duplicate entries closer together for faster identification.

- Statistical methods: By analyzing the data using the values of mean, standard deviation, range, or clustering algorithms, it is possible for an expert to find values that are unexpected and thus erroneous. Although the correction of such data is difficult since the true value is not known, it can be resolved by setting the values to an average or other statistical value. Statistical methods can also be used to handle missing values which can be replaced by one or more plausible values, which are usually obtained by extensive data augmentation algorithms.

Data Cleansing System

The essential job of this system is to find a suitable balance between fixing dirty data and maintaining the data as close as possible to the original data from the source production system. This is a challenge for the Extract, transform, load architect.

The system should offer an architecture that can cleanse data, record quality events and measure/control quality of data in the data warehouse.

A good start is to perform a thorough data profiling analysis that will help define to the required complexity of the data cleansing system and also give an idea of the current data quality in the source system(s).

Quality Screens

Part of the data cleansing system is a set of diagnostic filters known as quality screens. They each implement a test in the data flow that, if it fails records an error in the Error Event Schema. Quality screens are divided into three categories:

- Column screens. Testing the individual column, e.g. for unexpected values like NULL values; non-numeric values that should be numeric; out of range values; etc.

- Structure screens. These are used to test for the integrity of different relationships between columns (typically foreign/primary keys) in the same or different tables. They are also used for testing that a group of columns is valid according to some structural definition it should adhere.

- Business rule screens. The most complex of the three tests. They test to see if data, maybe across multiple tables, follow specific business rules. An example could be, that if a customer is marked as a certain type of customer, the business rules that define this kind of customer should be adhered.

When a quality screen records an error, it can either stop the dataflow process, send the faulty data somewhere else than the target system or tag the data. The latter option is considered the best solution because the first option requires, that someone has to manually deal with the issue each time it occurs and the second implies that data are missing from the target system (integrity) and it is often unclear, what should happen to these data.

Criticism of Existing Tools and Processes

The main reasons cited are:

- Project costs: costs typically in the hundreds of thousands of dollars

- Time: lack of enough time to deal with large-scale data-cleansing software

- Security: concerns over sharing information, giving an application access across systems, and effects on legacy systems

Error Event Schema

This schema is the place, where all error events thrown by quality screens, are recorded. It consists of an Error Event Fact table with foreign keys to three dimension tables that represent date (when), batch job (where) and screen (who produced error). It also holds information about exactly when the error occurred and the severity of the error. In addition there is an Error Event Detail Fact table with a foreign key to the main table that contains detailed information about in which table, record and field the error occurred and the error condition.

Challenges and Problems

- Error correction and loss of information: The most challenging problem within data cleansing remains the correction of values to remove duplicates and invalid entries. In many cases, the available information on such anomalies is limited and insufficient to determine the necessary transformations or corrections, leaving the deletion of such entries as a primary solution. The deletion of data, though, leads to loss of information; this loss can be particularly costly if there is a large amount of deleted data.

- Maintenance of cleansed data: Data cleansing is an expensive and time-consuming process. So after having performed data cleansing and achieving a data collection free of errors, one would want to avoid the re-cleansing of data in its entirety after some values in data collection change. The process should only be repeated on values that have changed; this means that a cleansing lineage would need to be kept, which would require efficient data collection and management techniques.

- Data cleansing in virtually integrated environments: In virtually integrated sources like IBM's DiscoveryLink, the cleansing of data has to be performed every time the data is accessed, which considerably increases the response time and lowers efficiency.

- Data-cleansing framework: In many cases, it will not be possible to derive a complete data-cleansing graph to guide the process in advance. This makes data cleansing an iterative process involving significant exploration and interaction, which may require a framework in the form of a collection of methods for error detection and elimination in addition to data auditing. This can be integrated with other data-processing stages like integration and maintenance.

Data Transformation

In computing, a data transformation converts a set of data values from the data format of a source data system into the data format of a destination data system. It is often used in a data warehouse system.

Data transformation can be divided into two steps:

1. data mapping maps data elements from the source data system to the destination data system and captures any transformation that must occur

2. code generation that creates the actual transformation program

Data element to data element mapping is frequently complicated by complex transformations that require one-to-many and many-to-one transformation rules.

The code generation step takes the data element mapping specification and creates an executable program that can be run on a computer system. Code generation can also create transformation in easy-to-maintain computer languages such as Java or XSLT.

A master data recast is another form of data transformation where the entire database of data values is transformed or recast without extracting the data from the database. All data in a well designed database is directly or indirectly related to a limited set of master database tables by a network of foreign key constraints. Each foreign key constraint is dependent upon a unique database index from the parent database table. Therefore, when the proper master database table is recast with a different unique index, the directly and indirectly related data are also recast or restated. The directly and indirectly related data may also still be viewed in the original form since the original unique index still exists with the master data. Also, the database recast must be done in such a way as to not impact the applications architecture software.

When the data mapping is indirect via a mediating data model, the process is also called data mediation.

Transformational Languages

There are numerous languages available for performing data transformation. Many transformation languages require a grammar to be provided. In many cases the grammar is structured using something closely resembling Backus–Naur Form (BNF). There are numerous languages available for such purposes varying in their accessibility (cost) and general usefulness. Examples of such languages include:

- AWK - one of the oldest and popular textual data transformation language;

- Perl - a high-level language with both procedural and object-oriented syntax capable of powerful operations on binary or text data.

- Template languages - specialized for transform data into documents;

- TXL - prototyping language-based descriptions, used for source code or data transformation.

- XSLT - the standard XML data transformation language (suitable by XQuery in many applications);

Although transformational languages are typically best suited for transformation, something as simple as regular expressions can be used to achieve useful transformation. A text editor like emacs or Textpad supports the use of regular expressions with arguments. This would allow all instances of a particular pattern to be replaced with another pattern using parts of the original pattern. For example:

```
foo ("some string", 42, gCommon);

bar (someObj, anotherObj);

foo ("another string", 24, gCommon);

bar (myObj, myOtherObj);
```

could both be transformed into a more compact form like:

```
foobar("some string", 42, someObj, anotherObj);

foobar("another string", 24, myObj, myOtherObj);
```

In other words, all instances of a function invocation of foo with three arguments, followed by a function invocation with two invocations would be replaced with a single function invocation using some or all of the original set of arguments.

Another advantage to using regular expressions is that they will not fail the null transform test. That is, using your transformational language of choice, run a sample program through a transformation that doesn't perform any transformations. Many transformational languages will fail this test.

Data Fusion

Data fusion is the process of integration of multiple data and knowledge representing the same real-world object into a consistent, accurate, and useful representation. The goal of data fusion is to combine relevant information from two or more data sources into a single one that provides a more accurate description than any of the individual data sources.

Data fusion processes are often categorized as low, intermediate or high, depending on the processing stage at which fusion takes place. Low level data fusion combines several sources of raw data to produce new raw data. The expectation is that fused data is more informative and synthetic than the original inputs.

For example, sensor fusion is also known as (multi-sensor) data fusion and is a subset of information fusion.

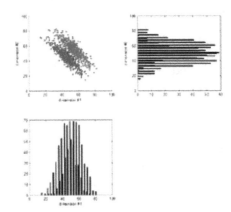

fusion of the data from 2 sources (dimension #1 & #2) can yield a classifier superior to any classifiers based on dimension #1 or dimension #2 alone

Geospatial Applications

In the geospatial (GIS) domain, data fusion is often synonymous with data integration. In these applications, there is often a need to combine diverse data sets into a unified (fused) data set which includes all of the data points and time steps from the input data sets. The fused data set is different from a simple combined superset in that the points in the fused data set contain attributes and metadata which might not have been included for these points in the original data set.

A simplified example of this process is shown below where data set "α" is fused with data set β to form the fused data set δ. Data points in set "α" have spatial coordinates X and Y and attributes A1 and A2. Data points in set β have spatial coordinates X and Y and attributes B1 and B2. The fused data set contains all points and attributes

Input Data Set α

Point	X	Y	A1	A2
α1	10	10	M	N
α2	10	30	M	N
α3	30	10	M	N
α4	30	30	M	N

Input Data Set β

Point	X	Y	B1	B2
β1	20	20	Q	R
β2	20	40	Q	R
β3	40	20	Q	R
β4	40	40	Q	R

Fused Data Set δ

Point	X	Y	A1	A2	B1	B2
δ1	10	10	M	N	Q	R
δ2	10	30	M	N	Q	R
δ3	30	10	M	N	Q	R
δ4	30	30	M	N	Q	R
δ5	20	20	M	N	Q	R
δ6	20	40	M	N	Q	R
δ7	40	20	M	N	Q	R
δ8	40	40	M	N	Q	R

In this simple case all attributes are uniform across the entire analysis domain, so attributes may be simply assigned. In more realistic applications, attributes are rarely uniform and some type of interpolation is usually required to properly assign attributes to the data points in the fused set.

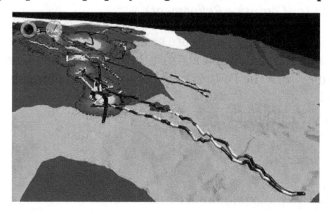

In a much more complicated application, marine animal researchers use data fusion to combine animal tracking data with bathymetric, meteorological, sea surface temperature (SST) and animal habitat data to examine and understand habitat utilization and animal behavior in reaction to external forces such as weather or water temperature. Each of these data sets exhibit a different spatial grid and sampling rate so a simple combination would likely create erroneous assumptions and taint the results of the analysis. But through the use of data fusion, all data and attributes are brought together into a single view in which a more complete picture of the environment is created. This enables scientists to identify key locations and times and form new insights into the interactions between the environment and animal behaviors.

In the figure at right, rock lobsters are studied off the coast of Tasmania. Dr. Hugh Pederson of the University of Tasmania used data fusion software to fuse southern rock lobster tracking data (color-coded for in yellow and black for day and night, respectively) with bathymetry and habitat data to create a unique 4D picture of rock lobster behavior.

Data Integration

In applications outside of the geospatial domain, differences in the usage of the terms Data integration and Data fusion apply. In areas such as business intelligence, for example, data integration is used to describe the combining of data, whereas data fusion is integration followed by reduction or replacement. Data integration might be viewed as set combination wherein the larger set is retained, whereas fusion is a set reduction technique with improved confidence.

The JDL/DFIG Model

In the mid-1980s, the Joint Directors of Laboratories formed the Data Fusion Subpanel (which later became known as the Data Fusion Group). With the advent of the World Wide Web, data fusion thus included data, sensor, and information fusion. The JDL/DFIG introduced a model of data fusion that divided the various processes. Currently, the six levels with the Data Fusion Information Group (DFIG) model are:

Level 0: *Source Preprocessing/subject Assessment*

Level 1: *Object Assessment*

Level 2: *Situation Assessment*

Level 3: *Impact Assessment* (or *Threat Refinement*)

Level 4: *Process Refinement*

Level 5: *User Refinement* (or *Cognitive Refinement*)

Although the JDL Model (Level 1-4) is still in use today, it is often criticized for its implication that the levels necessarily happen in order and also for its lack of adequate representation of the potential for a human-in-the-loop. The DFIG model (Level 0 - 5) explored the implications of situation awareness, user refinement, and mission management. Despite these shortcomings, the JDL/DFIG models are useful for visualizing the data fusion process, facilitating discussion and common understanding, and important for systems-level information fusion design.

Application Areas

- Geospatial Information Systems
- Soil Mapping
- Business intelligence
- Oceanography
- Discovery science
- Business performance management
- Intelligent transport systems
- Loyalty card

- Cheminformatics

- Quantitative structure-activity relationship

- Bioinformatics

- Intelligence services

- Wireless sensor networks

- Biometrics

Position Data Fusion

The distance or position of an object can be measured with different sensors. By taking sensors based on different physical principles (magnetic, optical, mechanical) as well the resolution can be lowered as the bandwidth of measurement can be increased. Optimal filtering (in sense of minimizing some norm over a frequency) is a very effective tool used for combining sensor data in real-time. Applied methods with Matlab(TM) code and explanation can be found in the Master Thesis 'Sensor Fusion for Nanopositioning'.

Data Fusion from Multiple Traffic Sensing Modalities

The data from the different sensing technologies can be combined in intelligent ways to determine the traffic state accurately. A Data fusion based approach that utilizes the road side collected acoustic, image and sensor data has been shown to combine the advantages of the different individual methods.

Decision Fusion

In many cases, geographically-dispersed sensors are severely energy- and bandwidth-limited. Therefore, the raw data concerning a certain phenomenon are often summarized in a few bits from each sensor. When inferring on a binary event (i.e., or), in the extreme case only binary decisions are sent from sensors to a Decision Fusion Center (DFC) and combined in order to obtain improved classification performance.

Data Fusion for Enhanced Contextual Awareness

With a multitude of built-in sensors including motion sensor, environmental sensor, position sensor, a modern mobile device typically gives mobile applications access to a number of sensory data which could be leveraged to enhance the contextual awareness. Using signal processing and data fusion techniques such as feature generation, feasibility study and Principal Component Analysis (PCA) to analyze such sensory data will greatly improve the positive rate of classifying the motion and contextual relevant status of the device.

Data Visualization

Data visualization or data visualisation is viewed by many disciplines as a modern equivalent of visual communication. It involves the creation and study of the visual representation of data, meaning "information that has been abstracted in some schematic form, including attributes or variables for the units of information".

A primary goal of data visualization is to communicate information clearly and efficiently via statistical graphics, plots and information graphics. Numerical data may be encoded using dots, lines, or bars, to visually communicate a quantitative message. Effective visualization helps users analyze and reason about data and evidence. It makes complex data more accessible, understandable and usable. Users may have particular analytical tasks, such as making comparisons or understanding causality, and the design principle of the graphic (i.e., showing comparisons or showing causality) follows the task. Tables are generally used where users will look up a specific measurement, while charts of various types are used to show patterns or relationships in the data for one or more variables.

Data visualization is both an art and a science. It is viewed as a branch of descriptive statistics by some, but also as a grounded theory development tool by others. The rate at which data is generated has increased. Data created by internet activity and an expanding number of sensors in the environment, such as satellites, are referred to as "Big Data". Processing, analyzing and communicating this data present a variety of ethical and analytical challenges for data visualization. The field of data science and practitioners called data scientists have emerged to help address this challenge.

Overview

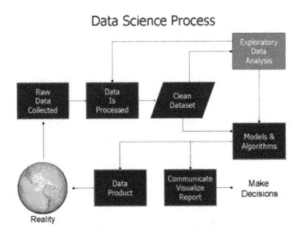

Data visualization is one of the steps in analyzing data and presenting it to users.

Data visualization refers to the techniques used to communicate data or information by encoding it as visual objects (e.g., points, lines or bars) contained in graphics. The goal is to communicate information clearly and efficiently to users. It is one of the steps in data analysis or data science. According to Friedman (2008) the "main goal of data visualization is to communicate information clearly and effectively through graphical means. It doesn't mean that data visualization needs to look boring to be functional or extremely sophisticated to look beautiful. To convey ideas effectively, both aesthetic form and functionality need to go hand in hand, providing insights into a rather sparse and complex data set by communicating its key-aspects in a more intuitive way. Yet designers often fail to achieve a balance between form and function, creating gorgeous data visualizations which fail to serve their main purpose — to communicate information".

Indeed, Fernanda Viegas and Martin M. Wattenberg have suggested that an ideal visualization should not only communicate clearly, but stimulate viewer engagement and attention.

Data visualization is closely related to information graphics, information visualization, scientific visualization, exploratory data analysis and statistical graphics. In the new millennium, data visualization has become an active area of research, teaching and development. According to Post et al. (2002), it has united scientific and information visualization.

Characteristics of Effective Graphical Displays

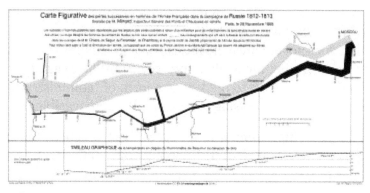

Charles Joseph Minard's 1869 diagram of Napoleon's March - an early example of an information graphic.

Professor Edward Tufte explained that users of information displays are executing particular *analytical tasks* such as making comparisons or determining causality. The *design principle* of the information graphic should support the analytical task, showing the comparison or causality.

In his 1983 book *The Visual Display of Quantitative Information*, Edward Tufte defines 'graphical displays' and principles for effective graphical display in the following passage: "Excellence in statistical graphics consists of complex ideas communicated with clarity, precision and efficiency. Graphical displays should:

- show the data
- induce the viewer to think about the substance rather than about methodology, graphic design, the technology of graphic production or something else
- avoid distorting what the data has to say
- present many numbers in a small space
- make large data sets coherent
- encourage the eye to compare different pieces of data
- reveal the data at several levels of detail, from a broad overview to the fine structure
- serve a reasonably clear purpose: description, exploration, tabulation or decoration

- be closely integrated with the statistical and verbal descriptions of a data set.

Graphics *reveal* data. Indeed graphics can be more precise and revealing than conventional statistical computations."

For example, the Minard diagram shows the losses suffered by Napoleon's army in the 1812–1813 period. Six variables are plotted: the size of the army, its location on a two-dimensional surface (x and y), time, direction of movement, and temperature. The line width illustrates a comparison (size of the army at points in time) while the temperature axis suggests a cause of the change in army size. This multivariate display on a two dimensional surface tells a story that can be grasped immediately while identifying the source data to build credibility. Tufte wrote in 1983 that: "It may well be the best statistical graphic ever drawn."

Not applying these principles may result in misleading graphs, which distort the message or support an erroneous conclusion. According to Tufte, chartjunk refers to extraneous interior decoration of the graphic that does not enhance the message, or gratuitous three dimensional or perspective effects. Needlessly separating the explanatory key from the image itself, requiring the eye to travel back and forth from the image to the key, is a form of "administrative debris." The ratio of "data to ink" should be maximized, erasing non-data ink where feasible.

The Congressional Budget Office summarized several best practices for graphical displays in a June 2014 presentation. These included: a) Knowing your audience; b) Designing graphics that can stand alone outside the context of the report; and c) Designing graphics that communicate the key messages in the report.

Quantitative Messages

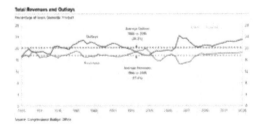

A time series illustrated with a line chart demonstrating trends in U.S. federal spending and revenue over time.

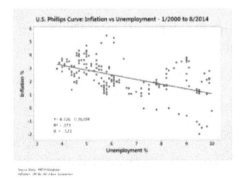

A scatterplot illustrating negative correlation between two variables (inflation and unemployment) measured at points in time.

Author Stephen Few described eight types of quantitative messages that users may attempt to understand or communicate from a set of data and the associated graphs used to help communicate the message:

1. Time-series: A single variable is captured over a period of time, such as the unemployment rate over a 10-year period. A line chart may be used to demonstrate the trend.

2. Ranking: Categorical subdivisions are ranked in ascending or descending order, such as a ranking of sales performance (the *measure*) by sales persons (the *category*, with each sales person a *categorical subdivision*) during a single period. A bar chart may be used to show the comparison across the sales persons.

3. Part-to-whole: Categorical subdivisions are measured as a ratio to the whole (i.e., a percentage out of 100%). A pie chart or bar chart can show the comparison of ratios, such as the market share represented by competitors in a market.

4. Deviation: Categorical subdivisions are compared against a reference, such as a comparison of actual vs. budget expenses for several departments of a business for a given time period. A bar chart can show comparison of the actual versus the reference amount.

5. Frequency distribution: Shows the number of observations of a particular variable for given interval, such as the number of years in which the stock market return is between intervals such as 0-10%, 11-20%, etc. A histogram, a type of bar chart, may be used for this analysis. A boxplot helps visualize key statistics about the distribution, such as median, quartiles, outliers, etc.

6. Correlation: Comparison between observations represented by two variables (X,Y) to determine if they tend to move in the same or opposite directions. For example, plotting unemployment (X) and inflation (Y) for a sample of months. A scatter plot is typically used for this message.

7. Nominal comparison: Comparing categorical subdivisions in no particular order, such as the sales volume by product code. A bar chart may be used for this comparison.

8. Geographic or geospatial: Comparison of a variable across a map or layout, such as the unemployment rate by state or the number of persons on the various floors of a building. A cartogram is a typical graphic used.

Analysts reviewing a set of data may consider whether some or all of the messages and graphic types above are applicable to their task and audience. The process of trial and error to identify meaningful relationships and messages in the data is part of exploratory data analysis.

Visual Perception and Data Visualization

A human can distinguish differences in line length, shape orientation, and color (hue) readily without significant processing effort; these are referred to as "pre-attentive attributes." For example, it may require significant time and effort ("attentive processing") to identify the number of times the digit "5" appears in a series of numbers; but if that digit is different in size, orientation, or color, instances of the digit can be noted quickly through pre-attentive processing.

Effective graphics take advantage of pre-attentive processing and attributes and the relative strength of these attributes. For example, since humans can more easily process differences in line length than surface area, it may be more effective to use a bar chart (which takes advantage of line length to show comparison) rather than pie charts (which use surface area to show comparison).

Human Perception/Cognition and Data Visualization

There is a human side to data visualization. With the "studying [of] human perception and cognition …" we are better able to understand the target of the data which we display. Cognition refers to processes in human beings like perception, attention, learning, memory, thought, concept formation, reading, and problem solving. The basis of data visualization evolved because as a picture is worth a thousand words, data displayed graphically allows for an easier comprehension of the information. Proper visualization provides a different approach to show potential connections, relationships, etc. which are not as obvious in non-visualized quantitative data. Visualization becomes a means of data exploration. Human brain neurons involve multiple functions but 2/3 of the brain's neurons are dedicated to vision. With a well-developed sense of sight, analysis of data can be made on data, whether that data is quantitative or qualitative. Effective visualization follows from understanding the processes of human perception and being able to apply this to intuitive visualizations is important. Understanding how humans see and organize the world is critical to effectively communicating data to the reader. This leads to more intuitive designs.

History of Data Visualization

There is a history of data visualization: beginning in the 2nd century C.E. with data arrangement into columns and rows and evolving to the initial quantitative representations in the 17th century. According to the Interaction Design Foundation, French philosopher and mathematician René Descartes laid the ground work for Scotsman William Playfair. Descartes developed a two-dimensional coordinate system for displaying values, which in the late 18th century Playfair saw potential for graphical communication of quantitative data. In the second half of the 20th century, Jacques Bertin used quantitative graphs to represent information "intuitively, clearly, accurately, and efficiently". John Tukey and more notably Edward Tufte pushed the bounds of data visualization. Tukey with his new statistical approach: exploratory data analysis and Tufte with his book "The Visual Display of Quantitative Information", the path was paved for refining data visualization techniques for more than statisticians. With the progression of technology came the progression of data visualization; starting with hand drawn visualizations and evolving into more technical applications – including interactive designs leading to software visualization. Programs like SAS, SOFA, R, Minitab, and more allow for data visualization in the field of statistics. Other data visualization applications, more focused and unique to individuals, programming languages such as D3, Python and JavaScript help to make the visualization of quantitative data a possibility.

Terminology

Data visualization involves specific terminology, some of which is derived from statistics. For example, author Stephen Few defines two types of data, which are used in combination to support a meaningful analysis or visualization:

- Categorical: Text labels describing the nature of the data, such as "Name" or "Age". This term also covers qualitative (non-numerical) data.

- Quantitative: Numerical measures, such as "25" to represent the age in years.

- Two primary types of information displays are tables and graphs.

- A *table* contains quantitative data organized into rows and columns with categorical labels. It is primarily used to look up specific values. In the example above, the table might have categorical column labels representing the name (a *qualitative variable*) and age (a *quantitative variable*), with each row of data representing one person (the sampled *experimental unit* or *category subdivision*).

- A *graph* is primarily used to show relationships among data and portrays values encoded as *visual objects* (e.g., lines, bars, or points). Numerical values are displayed within an area delineated by one or more *axes*. These axes provide *scales* (quantitative and categorical) used to label and assign values to the visual objects. Many graphs are also referred to as *charts*.

KPI Library has developed the "Periodic Table of Visualization Methods," an interactive chart displaying various data visualization methods. It includes six types of data visualization methods: data, information, concept, strategy, metaphor and compound.

Examples of Diagrams used for Data Visualization

	Name	Visual Dimensions	Example Usages
Bar chart of tips by day of week	Bar chart	- length/count - category - (color)	- Comparison of values, such as sales performance for several persons or businesses in a single time period. For a single variable measured over time (trend) a line chart is preferable.
Histogram of housing prices	Histogram	- bin limits - count/length - (color)	- Determining frequency of annual stock market percentage returns within particular ranges (bins) such as 0-10%, 11-20%, etc. The height of the bar represents the number of observations (years) with a return % in the range represented by the bin.

		• x position	• Determining the relationship (e.g., correlation) between unemployment (x) and inflation (y) for multiple time periods.
Basic scatterplot of two variables	Scatter plot	• y position • (symbol/glyph) • (color) • (size)	
Scatter Plot	Scatter plot (3D)	• position x • position y • position z • color	
Network Analysis	Network	• nodes size • nodes color • ties thickness • ties color • spatialization	• Finding clusters in the network (e.g. grouping Facebook friends into different clusters). • Determining the most influential nodes in the network (e.g. A company wants to target a small group of people on Twitter for a marketing campaign).
Streamgraph	Streamgraph	• width • color • time (flow)	

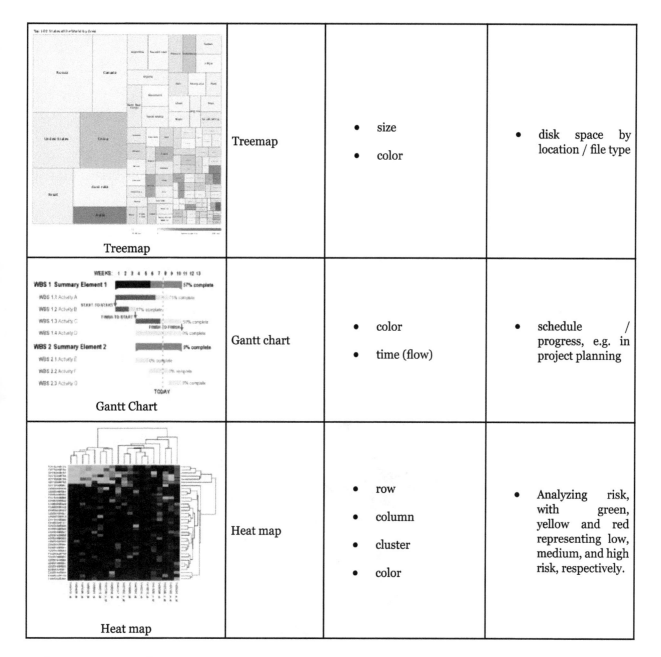

Treemap	Treemap	• size • color	• disk space by location / file type
Gantt Chart	Gantt chart	• color • time (flow)	• schedule / progress, e.g. in project planning
Heat map	Heat map	• row • column • cluster • color	• Analyzing risk, with green, yellow and red representing low, medium, and high risk, respectively.

Other Perspectives

There are different approaches on the scope of data visualization. One common focus is on information presentation, such as Friedman (2008) presented it. In this way Friendly (2008) presumes two main parts of data visualization: statistical graphics, and thematic cartography. In this line the "Data Visualization: Modern Approaches" (2007) article gives an overview of seven subjects of data visualization:

- Articles & resources

- Displaying connections

- Displaying data

- Displaying news
- Displaying websites
- Mind maps
- Tools and services

All these subjects are closely related to graphic design and information representation.

On the other hand, from a computer science perspective, Frits H. Post (2002) categorized the field into a number of sub-fields:

- Information visualization
- Interaction techniques and architectures
- Modelling techniques
- Multiresolution methods
- Visualization algorithms and techniques
- Volume visualization

Data Presentation Architecture

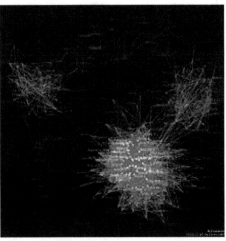

A data visualization from social media

Data presentation architecture (DPA) is a skill-set that seeks to identify, locate, manipulate, format and present data in such a way as to optimally communicate meaning and proper knowledge.

Historically, the term *data presentation architecture* is attributed to Kelly Lautt: "Data Presentation Architecture (DPA) is a rarely applied skill set critical for the success and value of Business Intelligence. Data presentation architecture weds the science of numbers, data and statistics in discovering valuable information from data and making it usable, relevant and actionable with the arts of data visualization, communications, organizational psychology and change management in order to provide business intelligence solutions with the data scope, delivery timing, format and visualizations that will most effectively support and drive operational, tactical and strategic behaviour toward understood business (or organizational) goals. DPA is neither an IT nor a business skill set but exists as a separate field of expertise. Often confused with data visualization, data presentation architecture is a much broader skill set that includes determining what data on what schedule and in what exact format is to be presented, not just the best way to present data that has already been chosen (which is data visualization). Data visualization skills are one element of DPA."

Objectives

DPA has two main objectives:

- To use data to provide knowledge in the most efficient manner possible (minimize noise, complexity, and unnecessary data or detail given each audience's needs and roles)

- To use data to provide knowledge in the most effective manner possible (provide relevant, timely and complete data to each audience member in a clear and understandable manner that conveys important meaning, is actionable and can affect understanding, behavior and decisions)

Scope

With the above objectives in mind, the actual work of data presentation architecture consists of:

- Creating effective delivery mechanisms for each audience member depending on their role, tasks, locations and access to technology

- Defining important meaning (relevant knowledge) that is needed by each audience member in each context

- Determining the required periodicity of data updates (the currency of the data)

- Determining the right timing for data presentation (when and how often the user needs to see the data)

- Finding the right data (subject area, historical reach, breadth, level of detail, etc.)

- Utilizing appropriate analysis, grouping, visualization, and other presentation formats

Related Fields

DPA work shares commonalities with several other fields, including:

- Business analysis in determining business goals, collecting requirements, mapping processes.

- Business process improvement in that its goal is to improve and streamline actions and decisions in furtherance of business goals

- Data visualization in that it uses well-established theories of visualization to add or highlight meaning or importance in data presentation.

- Graphic or user design: As the term DPA is used, it falls just short of design in that it does not consider such detail as colour palates, styling, branding and other aesthetic concerns, unless these design elements are specifically required or beneficial for communication of meaning, impact, severity or other information of business value. For example:

- choosing locations for various data presentation elements on a presentation page (such as in a company portal, in a report or on a web page) in order to convey hierarchy, priority, importance or a rational progression for the user is part of the DPA skill-set.

- choosing to provide a specific colour in graphical elements that represent data of specific meaning or concern is part of the DPA skill-set

- Information architecture, but information architecture's focus is on unstructured data and therefore excludes both analysis (in the statistical/data sense) and direct transformation of the actual content (data, for DPA) into new entities and combinations.

- Solution architecture in determining the optimal detailed solution, including the scope of data to include, given the business goals

- Statistical analysis or data analysis in that it creates information and knowledge out of data

Data Science

Data science is an interdisciplinary field about processes and systems to extract knowledge or insights from data in various forms, either structured or unstructured, which is a continuation of some of the data analysis fields such as statistics, machine learning, data mining, and predictive analytics, similar to Knowledge Discovery in Databases (KDD).

Overview

Data science employs techniques and theories drawn from many fields within the broad areas of mathematics, statistics, operations research, information science, and computer science, including signal processing, probability models, machine learning, statistical learning, data mining, database, data engineering, pattern recognition and learning, visualization, predictive analytics, uncertainty modeling, data warehousing, data compression, computer programming, artificial intelligence, and high performance computing. Methods that scale to big data are of particular interest in data science, although the discipline is not generally considered to be restricted to such big data, and big data technologies are often focused on organizing and preprocessing the data instead of analysis. The development of machine learning has enhanced the growth and importance of data science.

Data science affects academic and applied research in many domains, including machine translation, speech recognition, robotics, search engines, digital economy, but also the biological sciences, medical informatics, health care, social sciences and the humanities. It heavily influences economics, business and finance. From the business perspective, data science is an integral part of competitive intelligence, a newly emerging field that encompasses a number of activities, such as data mining and data analysis.

Data Scientist

Data scientists use their data and analytical ability to find and interpret rich data sources; manage large amounts of data despite hardware, software, and bandwidth constraints; merge data sources; ensure consistency of datasets; create visualizations to aid in understanding data; build mathematical models using the data; and present and communicate the data insights/findings. They are often expected to produce answers in days rather than months, work by exploratory analysis and rapid iteration, and to produce and present results with dashboards (displays of current values) rather than papers/reports, as statisticians normally do.

"Data Scientist" has become a popular occupation with Harvard Business Review dubbing it "The Sexiest Job of the 21st Century" and McKinsey & Company projecting a global excess demand of 1.5 million new data scientists. Universities are offering masters courses in data science. Shorter private bootcamps are also offering data science certificates including student-paid programs like General Assembly to employer-paid programs like The Data Incubator.

History

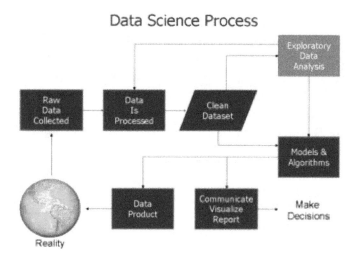

Data science process flowchart

The term "data science" (originally used interchangeably with "datalogy") has existed for over thirty years and was used initially as a substitute for computer science by Peter Naur in 1960. In 1974, Naur published *Concise Survey of Computer Methods*, which freely used the term data science in its survey of the contemporary data processing methods that are used in a wide range of applications. In 1996, members of the International Federation of Classification Societies (IFCS) met in Kobe for their biennial conference. Here, for the first time, the term data science is included in the title of the conference ("Data Science, classification, and related methods").

In November 1997, C.F. Jeff Wu gave the inaugural lecture entitled "Statistics = Data Science?" for his appointment to the H. C. Carver Professorship at the University of Michigan. In this lecture, he characterized statistical work as a trilogy of data collection, data modeling and analysis, and decision making. In his conclusion, he initiated the modern, non-computer science, usage of the term "data science" and advocated that statistics be renamed data science and statisticians data scientists. Later, he presented his lecture entitled "Statistics = Data Science?" as the first of his 1998 P.C. Mahalanobis Memorial Lectures. These lectures honor Prasanta Chandra Mahalanobis, an Indian scientist and statistician and founder of the Indian Statistical Institute.

In 2001, William S. Cleveland introduced data science as an independent discipline, extending the field of statistics to incorporate "advances in computing with data" in his article "Data Science: An Action Plan for Expanding the Technical Areas of the Field of Statistics," which was published in Volume 69, No. 1, of the April 2001 edition of the International Statistical Review / Revue Internationale de Statistique. In his report, Cleveland establishes six technical areas which he believed to encompass the field of data science: multidisciplinary investigations, models and methods for data, computing with data, pedagogy, tool evaluation, and theory.

In April 2002, the International Council for Science: Committee on Data for Science and Technology (CODATA) started the *Data Science Journal*, a publication focused on issues such as the description of data systems, their publication on the internet, applications and legal issues. Shortly thereafter, in January 2003, Columbia University began publishing *The Journal of Data Science*, which provided a platform for all data workers to present their views and exchange ideas. The journal was largely devoted to the application of statistical methods and quantitative research. In 2005, The National Science Board published "Long-lived Digital Data Collections: Enabling Research and Education in the 21st Century" defining data scientists as "the information and computer scientists, database and software and programmers, disciplinary experts, curators and expert annotators, librarians, archivists, and others, who are crucial to the successful management of a digital data collection" whose primary activity is to "conduct creative inquiry and analysis." In 2013, the IEEE Task Force on Data Science and Advanced Analytics was launched, and the first international conference: IEEE International Conference on Data Science and Advanced Analytics was launched in 2014. In 2015, the International Journal on Data Science and Analytics was launched by Springer to publish original work on data science and big data analytics.

In 2008, DJ Patil and Jeff Hammerbacher used the term "data scientist" to define their jobs at LinkedIn and Facebook, respectively.

Criticism

Although use of the term "data science" has exploded in business environments, many academics and journalists see no distinction between data science and statistics. Writing in Forbes, Gil Press argues that data science is a buzzword without a clear definition and has simply replaced "business analytics" in contexts such as graduate degree programs. In the question-and-answer section of his keynote address at the Joint Statistical Meetings of American Statistical Association, noted applied statistician Nate Silver said, "I think data-scientist is a sexed up term for a statistician....Statistics is a branch of science. Data scientist is slightly redundant in some way and people shouldn't berate the term statistician."

Software

In the 2010-2011 time frame, data science software reached an inflection point where open source software started supplanting proprietary software. The use of open source software enables modifying and extending the software, and it allows sharing of the resulting algorithms.

Data Reduction

Data reduction is the transformation of numerical or alphabetical digital information derived empirically or experimentally into a corrected, ordered, and simplified form. The basic concept is the reduction of multitudinous amounts of data down to the meaningful parts.

When information is derived from instrument readings there may also be a transformation from analog to digital form. When the data are already in digital form the 'reduction' of the data typically involves some editing, scaling, coding, sorting, collating, and producing tabular summaries. When the observations are discrete but the underlying phenomenon is continuous then smoothing and interpolation are often needed. Often the data reduction is undertaken in the presence of reading or measurement errors. Some idea of the nature of these errors is needed before the most likely value may be determined.

An example in astronomy is the data reduction in the *Kepler* satellite. This satellite records 95-megapixel images once every six seconds, generating tens of megabytes of data per second, which is orders of magnitudes more than the downlink bandwidth of 550 KBps. The on-board data reduction encompasses co-adding the raw frames for thirty minutes, reducing the bandwidth by a factor of 300. Furthermore, interesting targets are pre-selected and only the relevant pixels are processed, which is 6% of the total. This reduced data is then sent to Earth where it is processed further.

Best Practices

These are common techniques used in data reduction.

- Order by some aspect of size.
- Table diagonalization, whereby rows and columns of tables are re-arranged to make patterns easier to see (refer to the diagram).
- Round drastically to one, or at most two, effective digits (effective digits are ones that vary in that part of the data).
- Use averages to provide a visual focus as well as a summary.
- Use layout and labeling to guide the eye.
- Remove Chartjunk, such as pictures and lines.
- Give a brief verbal summary.

Automatic Summarization

Automatic summarization is the process of reducing a text document with a computer program in order to create a summary that retains the most important points of the original document. Technologies that can make a coherent summary take into account variables such as length, writing style and syntax. Automatic data summarization is part of machine learning and data mining. The main idea of summarization is to find a representative subset of the data, which contains the *information* of the entire set. Summarization technologies are used in a large number of sectors in industry today. An example of the use of summarization technology is search engines such as Google. Other examples include document summarization, image collection summarization and video summarization. Document summarization, tries to automatically create a *representative summary* or *abstract* of the entire document, by finding the most *informative* sentences. Similarly, in image summarization the system finds the most representative and important (or salient) images. Similarly, in consumer videos one would want to remove the boring or repetitive scenes, and extract out a much shorter and concise version of the video. This is also important, say for surveillance videos, where one might want to extract only important events in the recorded video, since most part of the video may be uninteresting with nothing going on. As the problem of information overload grows, and as the amount of data increases, the interest in automatic summarization is also increasing.

Generally, there are two approaches to automatic summarization: *extraction* and *abstraction*. Extractive methods work by selecting a subset of existing words, phrases, or sentences in the original text to form the summary. In contrast, abstractive methods build an internal semantic representation and then use natural language generation techniques to create a summary that is closer to what a human might generate. Such a summary might contain words not explicitly present in the original. Research into abstractive methods is an increasingly important and active research area, however due to complexity constraints, research to date has focused primarily on extractive methods. In some application domains, extractive summarization makes more sense. Examples of these include image collection summarization and video summarization.

Extraction-based Summarization

In this summarization task, the automatic system extracts objects from the entire collection, without modifying the objects themselves. Examples of this include keyphrase extraction, where the goal is to select individual words or phrases to "tag" a document, and document summarization, where the goal is to select whole sentences (without modifying them) to create a short paragraph summary. Similarly, in image collection summarization, the system extracts images from the collection without modifying the images themselves.

Abstraction-based Summarization

Extraction techniques merely copy the information deemed most important by the system to the summary (for example, key clauses, sentences or paragraphs), while abstraction involves paraphrasing sections of the source document. In general, abstraction can condense a text more strongly than extraction, but the programs that can do this are harder to develop as they require use of natural language generation technology, which itself is a growing field.

While some work has been done in abstractive summarization (creating an abstract synopsis like that of a human), the majority of summarization systems are extractive (selecting a subset of sentences to place in a summary).

Aided Summarization

Machine learning techniques from closely related fields such as information retrieval or text mining have been successfully adapted to help automatic summarization.

Apart from Fully Automated Summarizers (FAS), there are systems that aid users with the task of summarization (MAHS = Machine Aided Human Summarization), for example by highlighting candidate passages to be included in the summary, and there are systems that depend on post-processing by a human (HAMS = Human Aided Machine Summarization).

Applications and Systems for Summarization

There are broadly two types of extractive summarization tasks depending on what the summarization program focuses on. The first is *generic summarization*, which focuses on obtaining a generic summary or abstract of the collection (whether documents, or sets of images, or videos, news stories etc.). The second is *query relevant summarization*, sometimes called *query-based summarization*, which summarizes objects specific to a query. Summarization systems are able to create both query relevant text summaries and generic machine-generated summaries depending on what the user needs.

An example of a summarization problem is document summarization, which attempts to automatically produce an abstract from a given document. Sometimes one might be interested in generating a summary from a single source document, while others can use multiple source documents. This problem is called multi-document summarization. A related application is summarizing news articles. Imagine a system, which automatically pulls together news articles on a given topic (from the web), and concisely represents the latest news as a summary.

Image collection summarization is another application example of automatic summarization. It consists in selecting a representative set of images from a larger set of images. A summary in this context is useful to show the most representative images of results in an image collection exploration system. Video summarization is a related domain, where the system automatically creates a trailer of a long video. This also has applications in consumer or personal videos, where one might want to skip the boring or repetitive actions. Similarly, in surveillance videos, one would want to extract important and suspicious activity, while ignoring all the boring and redundant frames captured.

At a very high level, summarization algorithms try to find subsets of objects (like set of sentences, or a set of images), which cover information of the entire set. This is also called the *core-set*. These algorithms model notions like diversity, coverage, information and representativeness of the summary. Query based summarization techniques, additionally model for relevance of the summary with the query. Some techniques and algorithms which naturally model summarization problems are TextRank and PageRank, Submodular set function, Determinantal point process, maximal marginal relevance (MMR) etc.

Keyphrase Extraction

The task is the following. You are given a piece of text, such as a journal article, and you must produce a list of keywords or key[phrase]s that capture the primary topics discussed in the text. In the case of research articles, many authors provide manually assigned keywords, but most text lacks pre-existing keyphrases. For example, news articles rarely have keyphrases attached, but it would be useful to be able to automatically do so for a number of applications discussed below. Consider the example text from a news article:

"The Army Corps of Engineers, rushing to meet President Bush's promise to protect New Orleans by the start of the 2006 hurricane season, installed defective flood-control pumps last year despite warnings from its own expert that the equipment would fail during a storm, according to documents obtained by The Associated Press".

A keyphrase extractor might select "Army Corps of Engineers", "President Bush", "New Orleans", and "defective flood-control pumps" as keyphrases. These are pulled directly from the text. In contrast, an abstractive keyphrase system would somehow internalize the content and generate keyphrases that do not appear in the text, but more closely resemble what a human might produce, such as "political negligence" or "inadequate protection from floods". Abstraction requires a deep understanding of the text, which makes it difficult for a computer system. Keyphrases have many applications. They can enable document browsing by providing a short summary, improve information retrieval (if documents have keyphrases assigned, a user could search by keyphrase to produce more reliable hits than a full-text search), and be employed in generating index entries for a large text corpus.

Depending on the different literature and the definition of key terms, words or phrases, highly related theme is certainly the Keyword extraction.

Supervised Learning Approaches

Beginning with the work of Turney, many researchers have approached keyphrase extraction as a supervised machine learning problem. Given a document, we construct an example for each unigram, bigram, and trigram found in the text (though other text units are also possible, as discussed below). We then compute various features describing each example (e.g., does the phrase begin with an upper-case letter?). We assume there are known keyphrases available for a set of training documents. Using the known keyphrases, we can assign positive or negative labels to the examples. Then we learn a classifier that can discriminate between positive and negative examples as a function of the features. Some classifiers make a binary classification for a test example, while others assign a probability of being a keyphrase. For instance, in the above text, we might learn a rule that says phrases with initial capital letters are likely to be keyphrases. After training a learner, we can select keyphrases for test documents in the following manner. We apply the same example-generation strategy to the test documents, then run each example through the learner. We can determine the keyphrases by looking at binary classification decisions or probabilities returned from our learned model. If probabilities are given, a threshold is used to select the keyphrases. Keyphrase extractors are generally evaluated using precision and recall. Precision measures how many of the proposed keyphrases are actually correct. Recall measures how many of the true keyphrases your system proposed. The two measures can be combined in an F-score, which is the harmonic mean of the two ($F = 2PR/(P + R)$). Matches between the proposed keyphrases and the known keyphrases can be checked after stemming or applying some other text normalization.

Designing a supervised keyphrase extraction system involves deciding on several choices (some of these apply to unsupervised, too). The first choice is exactly how to generate examples. Turney and others have used all possible unigrams, bigrams, and trigrams without intervening punctuation and after removing stopwords. Hulth showed that you can get some improvement by selecting examples to be sequences of tokens that match certain patterns of part-of-speech tags. Ideally, the mechanism for generating examples produces all the known labeled keyphrases as candidates, though this is often not the case. For example, if we use only unigrams, bigrams, and trigrams, then we will never be able to extract a known keyphrase containing four words. Thus, recall may suffer. However, generating too many examples can also lead to low precision.

We also need to create features that describe the examples and are informative enough to allow a learning algorithm to discriminate keyphrases from non- keyphrases. Typically features involve various term frequencies (how many times a phrase appears in the current text or in a larger corpus), the length of the example, relative position of the first occurrence, various boolean syntactic features (e.g., contains all caps), etc. The Turney paper used about 12 such features. Hulth uses a reduced set of features, which were found most successful in the KEA (Keyphrase Extraction Algorithm) work derived from Turney's seminal paper.

In the end, the system will need to return a list of keyphrases for a test document, so we need to have a way to limit the number. Ensemble methods (i.e., using votes from several classifiers) have been used to produce numeric scores that can be thresholded to provide a user-provided number of keyphrases. This is the technique used by Turney with C4.5 decision trees. Hulth used a single binary classifier so the learning algorithm implicitly determines the appropriate number.

Once examples and features are created, we need a way to learn to predict keyphrases. Virtually any supervised learning algorithm could be used, such as decision trees, Naive Bayes, and rule induction. In the case of Turney's GenEx algorithm, a genetic algorithm is used to learn parameters for a domain-specific keyphrase extraction algorithm. The extractor follows a series of heuristics to identify keyphrases. The genetic algorithm optimizes parameters for these heuristics with respect to performance on training documents with known key phrases.

Unsupervised Approach: Textrank

Another keyphrase extraction algorithm is TextRank. While supervised methods have some nice properties, like being able to produce interpretable rules for what features characterize a keyphrase, they also require a large amount of training data. Many documents with known keyphrases are needed. Furthermore, training on a specific domain tends to customize the extraction process to that domain, so the resulting classifier is not necessarily portable, as some of Turney's results demonstrate. Unsupervised keyphrase extraction removes the need for training data. It approaches the problem from a different angle. Instead of trying to learn explicit features that characterize keyphrases, the TextRank algorithm exploits the structure of the text itself to determine keyphrases that appear "central" to the text in the same way that PageRank selects important Web pages. Recall this is based on the notion of "prestige" or "recommendation" from social networks. In this way, TextRank does not rely on any previous training data at all, but rather can be run on any arbitrary piece of text, and it can produce output simply based on the text's intrinsic properties. Thus the algorithm is easily portable to new domains and languages.

TextRank is a general purpose graph-based ranking algorithm for NLP. Essentially, it runs PageRank on a graph specially designed for a particular NLP task. For keyphrase extraction, it builds a graph using some set of text units as vertices. Edges are based on some measure of semantic or lexical similarity between the text unit vertices. Unlike PageRank, the edges are typically undirected and can be weighted to reflect a degree of similarity. Once the graph is constructed, it is used to form a stochastic matrix, combined with a damping factor (as in the "random surfer model"), and the ranking over vertices is obtained by finding the eigenvector corresponding to eigenvalue 1 (i.e., the stationary distribution of the random walk on the graph).

The vertices should correspond to what we want to rank. Potentially, we could do something similar to the supervised methods and create a vertex for each unigram, bigram, trigram, etc. However, to keep the graph small, the authors decide to rank individual unigrams in a first step, and then include a second step that merges highly ranked adjacent unigrams to form multi-word phrases. This has a nice side effect of allowing us to produce keyphrases of arbitrary length. For example, if we rank unigrams and find that "advanced", "natural", "language", and "processing" all get high ranks, then we would look at the original text and see that these words appear consecutively and create a final keyphrase using all four together. Note that the unigrams placed in the graph can be filtered by part of speech. The authors found that adjectives and nouns were the best to include. Thus, some linguistic knowledge comes into play in this step.

Edges are created based on word co-occurrence in this application of TextRank. Two vertices are connected by an edge if the unigrams appear within a window of size N in the original text. N is typically around 2–10. Thus, "natural" and "language" might be linked in a text about NLP. "Natural" and "processing" would also be linked because they would both appear in the same string of N words. These edges build on the notion of "text cohesion" and the idea that words that appear near each other are likely related in a meaningful way and "recommend" each other to the reader.

Since this method simply ranks the individual vertices, we need a way to threshold or produce a limited number of keyphrases. The technique chosen is to set a count T to be a user-specified fraction of the total number of vertices in the graph. Then the top T vertices/unigrams are selected based on their stationary probabilities. A post-processing step is then applied to merge adjacent instances of these T unigrams. As a result, potentially more or less than T final keyphrases will be produced, but the number should be roughly proportional to the length of the original text.

It is not initially clear why applying PageRank to a co-occurrence graph would produce useful keyphrases. One way to think about it is the following. A word that appears multiple times throughout a text may have many different co-occurring neighbors. For example, in a text about machine learning, the unigram "learning" might co-occur with "machine", "supervised", "un-supervised", and "semi-supervised" in four different sentences. Thus, the "learning" vertex would be a central "hub" that connects to these other modifying words. Running PageRank/TextRank on the graph is likely to rank "learning" highly. Similarly, if the text contains the phrase "supervised classification", then there would be an edge between "supervised" and "classification". If "classification" appears several other places and thus has many neighbors, its importance would contribute to the importance of "supervised". If it ends up with a high rank, it will be selected as one of the top T unigrams, along with "learning" and probably "classification". In the final post-processing step, we would then end up with keyphrases "supervised learning" and "supervised classification".

In short, the co-occurrence graph will contain densely connected regions for terms that appear often and in different contexts. A random walk on this graph will have a stationary distribution that assigns large probabilities to the terms in the centers of the clusters. This is similar to densely connected Web pages getting ranked highly by PageRank. This approach has also been used in document summarization, considered below.

Document Summarization

Like keyphrase extraction, document summarization aims to identify the essence of a text. The only real difference is that now we are dealing with larger text units—whole sentences instead of words and phrases.

Before getting into the details of some summarization methods, we will mention how summarization systems are typically evaluated. The most common way is using the so-called ROUGE (Recall-Oriented Understudy for Gisting Evaluation) measure. This is a recall-based measure that determines how well a system-generated summary covers the content present in one or more human-generated model summaries known as references. It is recall-based to encourage systems to include all the important topics in the text. Recall can be computed with respect to unigram, bigram, trigram, or 4-gram matching. For example, ROUGE-1 is computed as division of count of unigrams in reference that appear in system and count of unigrams in reference summary.

If there are multiple references, the ROUGE-1 scores are averaged. Because ROUGE is based only on content overlap, it can determine if the same general concepts are discussed between an automatic summary and a reference summary, but it cannot determine if the result is coherent or the sentences flow together in a sensible manner. High-order n-gram ROUGE measures try to judge fluency to some degree. Note that ROUGE is similar to the BLEU measure for machine translation, but BLEU is precision- based, because translation systems favor accuracy.

A promising line in document summarization is adaptive document/text summarization. The idea of adaptive summarization involves preliminary recognition of document/text genre and subsequent application of summarization algorithms optimized for this genre. First summarizes that perform adaptive summarization have been created.

Supervised Learning Approaches

Supervised text summarization is very much like supervised keyphrase extraction. Basically, if you have a collection of documents and human-generated summaries for them, you can learn features of sentences that make them good candidates for inclusion in the summary. Features might include the position in the document (i.e., the first few sentences are probably important), the number of words in the sentence, etc. The main difficulty in supervised extractive summarization is that the known summaries must be manually created by extracting sentences so the sentences in an original training document can be labeled as "in summary" or "not in summary". This is not typically how people create summaries, so simply using journal abstracts or existing summaries is usually not sufficient. The sentences in these summaries do not necessarily match up with sentences in the original text, so it would be difficult to assign labels to examples for training. Note, however, that these natural summaries can still be used for evaluation purposes, since ROUGE-1 only cares about unigrams.

Maximum Entropy-based Summarization

During the DUC 2001 and 2002 evaluation workshops, TNO developed a sentence extraction system for multi-document summarization in the news domain. The system was based on a hybrid system using a naive Bayes classifier and statistical language models for modeling salience. Although the system exhibited good results, the researchers wanted to explore the effectiveness of a maximum entropy (ME) classifier for the meeting summarization task, as ME is known to be robust against feature dependencies. Maximum entropy has also been applied successfully for summarization in the broadcast news domain.

TextRank and LexRank

The unsupervised approach to summarization is also quite similar in spirit to unsupervised keyphrase extraction and gets around the issue of costly training data. Some unsupervised summarization approaches are based on finding a "centroid" sentence, which is the mean word vector of all the sentences in the document. Then the sentences can be ranked with regard to their similarity to this centroid sentence.

A more principled way to estimate sentence importance is using random walks and eigenvector centrality. LexRank is an algorithm essentially identical to TextRank, and both use this approach for document summarization. The two methods were developed by different groups at the same time, and LexRank simply focused on summarization, but could just as easily be used for keyphrase extraction or any other NLP ranking task.

In both LexRank and TextRank, a graph is constructed by creating a vertex for each sentence in the document.

The edges between sentences are based on some form of semantic similarity or content overlap. While LexRank uses cosine similarity of TF-IDF vectors, TextRank uses a very similar measure based on the number of words two sentences have in common (normalized by the sentences' lengths). The LexRank paper explored using unweighted edges after applying a threshold to the cosine values, but also experimented with using edges with weights equal to the similarity score. TextRank uses continuous similarity scores as weights.

In both algorithms, the sentences are ranked by applying PageRank to the resulting graph. A summary is formed by combining the top ranking sentences, using a threshold or length cutoff to limit the size of the summary.

It is worth noting that TextRank was applied to summarization exactly as described here, while LexRank was used as part of a larger summarization system (MEAD) that combines the LexRank score (stationary probability) with other features like sentence position and length using a linear combination with either user-specified or automatically tuned weights. In this case, some training documents might be needed, though the TextRank results show the additional features are not absolutely necessary.

Another important distinction is that TextRank was used for single document summarization, while LexRank has been applied to multi-document summarization. The task remains the same in both cases—only the number of sentences to choose from has grown. However, when summarizing multiple documents, there is a greater risk of selecting duplicate or highly redundant sentences to place in the same summary. Imagine you have a cluster of news articles on a particular event, and you want to produce one summary. Each article is likely to have many similar sentences, and you would only want to include distinct ideas in the summary. To address this issue, LexRank applies a heuristic post-processing step that builds up a summary by adding sentences in rank order, but discards any sentences that are too similar to ones already placed in the summary. The method used is called Cross-Sentence Information Subsumption (CSIS).

These methods work based on the idea that sentences "recommend" other similar sentences to the reader. Thus, if one sentence is very similar to many others, it will likely be a sentence of great importance. The importance of this sentence also stems from the importance of the sentences "recommending" it. Thus, to get ranked highly and placed in a summary, a sentence must be similar to many sentences that are in turn also similar to many other sentences. This makes intuitive sense and allows the algorithms to be applied to any arbitrary new text. The methods are domain-independent and easily portable. One could imagine the features indicating important sentences in the news domain might vary considerably from the biomedical domain. However, the unsupervised "recommendation"-based approach applies to any domain.

Multi-document Summarization

Multi-document summarization is an automatic procedure aimed at extraction of information from multiple texts written about the same topic. Resulting summary report allows individual users, such as professional information consumers, to quickly familiarize themselves with information contained in a large cluster of documents. In such a way, multi-document summarization systems are complementing the news aggregators performing the next step down the road of coping with information overload. Multi-document summarization may also be done in response to a question.

Multi-document summarization creates information reports that are both concise and comprehensive. With different opinions being put together and outlined, every topic is described from multiple perspectives within a single document. While the goal of a brief summary is to simplify information search and cut the time by pointing to the most relevant source documents, comprehensive multi-document summary should itself contain the required information, hence limiting the need for accessing original files to cases when refinement is required. Automatic summaries present information extracted from multiple sources algorithmically, without any editorial touch or subjective human intervention, thus making it completely unbiased.

Incorporating Diversity

Multi-document extractive summarization faces a problem of potential redundancy. Ideally, we would like to extract sentences that are both "central" (i.e., contain the main ideas) and "diverse" (i.e., they differ from one another). LexRank deals with diversity as a heuristic final stage using CSIS, and other systems have used similar methods, such as Maximal Marginal Relevance (MMR), in trying to eliminate redundancy in information retrieval results. There is a general purpose graph-based ranking algorithm like Page/Lex/TextRank that handles both "centrality" and "diversity" in a unified mathematical framework based on absorbing Markov chain random walks. (An absorbing random walk is like a standard random walk, except some states are now absorbing states that act as "black holes" that cause the walk to end abruptly at that state.) The algorithm is called GRASSHOPPER. In addition to explicitly promoting diversity during the ranking process, GRASSHOPPER incorporates a prior ranking (based on sentence position in the case of summarization).

The state of the art results for multi-document summarization, however, are obtained using mixtures of submodular functions. These methods have achieved the state of the art results for Document Summarization Corpora, DUC 04 - 07. Similar results were also achieved with the use of determinantal point processes (which are a special case of submodular functions) for DUC-04.

Submodular Functions as Generic Tools for Summarization

The idea of a Submodular set function has recently emerged as a powerful modeling tool for various summarization problems. Submodular functions naturally model notions of *coverage, information, representation* and *diversity*. Moreover, several important combinatorial optimization problems occur as special instances of submodular optimization. For example, the set cover problem is a special case of submodular optimization, since the set cover function is submodular. The set cover function attempts to find a subset of objects which *cover* a given set of concepts. For example, in document summarization, one would like the summary to cover all important and relevant concepts in the document. This is an instance of set cover. Similarly, the facility location problem is a special case of submodular functions. The Facility Location function also naturally models coverage and diversity. Another example of a submodular optimization problem is using a Determinantal point process to model diversity. Similarly, the Maximum-Marginal-Relevance procedure can also be seen as an instance of submodular optimization. All these important models encouraging coverage, diversity and information are all submodular. Moreover, submodular functions can be efficiently combined together, and the resulting function is still submodular. Hence, one could combine one submodular function which models diversity, another one which models coverage and use human supervision to learn a right model of a submodular function for the problem.

While submodular functions are fitting problems for summarization, they also admit very efficient algorithms for optimization. For example, a simple greedy algorithm admits a constant factor guarantee. Moreover, the greedy algorithm is extremely simple to implement and can scale to large datasets, which is very important for summarization problems.

Submodular functions have achieved state-of-the-art for almost all summarization problems. For example, work by Lin and Bilmes, 2012 shows that submodular functions achieve the best results to date on DUC-04, DUC-05, DUC-06 and DUC-07 systems for document summarization. Similarly, work by Lin and Bilmes, 2011, shows that many existing systems for automatic summarization are instances of submodular functions. This was a break through result establishing submodular functions as the right models for summarization problems.

Submodular Functions have also been used for other summarization tasks. Tschiatschek et al., 2014 show that mixtures of submodular functions achieve state-of-the-art results for image collection summarization. Similarly, Bairi et al., 2015 show the utility of submodular functions for summarizing multi-document topic hierarchies. Submodular Functions have also successfully been used for summarizing machine learning datasets.

Evaluation Techniques

The most common way to evaluate the informativeness of automatic summaries is to compare them with human-made model summaries.

Evaluation techniques fall into intrinsic and extrinsic, inter-textual and intra-textual.

Intrinsic and Extrinsic Evaluation

An intrinsic evaluation tests the summarization system in and of itself while an extrinsic evaluation tests the summarization based on how it affects the completion of some other task. Intrinsic evaluations have assessed mainly the coherence and informativeness of summaries. Extrinsic evaluations, on the other hand, have tested the impact of summarization on tasks like relevance assessment, reading comprehension, etc.

Inter-textual and Intra-textual

Intra-textual methods assess the output of a specific summarization system, and the inter-textual ones focus on contrastive analysis of outputs of several summarization systems.

Human judgement often has wide variance on what is considered a "good" summary, which means that making the evaluation process automatic is particularly difficult. Manual evaluation can be used, but this is both time and labor-intensive as it requires humans to read not only the summaries but also the source documents. Other issues are those concerning coherence and coverage.

One of the metrics used in NIST's annual Document Understanding Conferences, in which research groups submit their systems for both summarization and translation tasks, is the ROUGE metric (Recall-Oriented Understudy for Gisting Evaluation). It essentially calculates n-gram overlaps between automatically generated summaries and previously-written human summaries. A high level of overlap should indicate a high level of shared concepts between the two summaries. Note that overlap metrics like this are unable to provide any feedback on a summary's coherence. Anaphor resolution remains another problem yet to be fully solved. Similarly, for image summarization, Tschiatschek et al., developed a Visual-ROUGE score which judges the performance of algorithms for image summarization.

Current Challenges in Evaluating Summaries Automatically

Evaluating summaries, either manually or automatically, is a hard task. The main difficulty in evaluation comes from the impossibility of building a fair gold-standard against which the results of the systems can be compared. Furthermore, it is also very hard to determine what a correct summary is, because there is always the possibility of a system to generate a good summary that is quite different from any human summary used as an approximation to the correct output.

Content selection is not a deterministic problem. People are subjective, and different authors would choose different sentences. And individuals may not be consistent. A particular person may chose different sentences at different times. Two distinct sentences expressed in different words can express the same meaning. This phenomenon is known as paraphrasing. We can find an approach to automatically evaluating summaries using paraphrases (ParaEval).

Most summarization systems perform an extractive approach, selecting and copying important sentences from the source documents. Although humans can also cut and paste relevant information of a text, most of the times they rephrase sentences when necessary, or they join different related information into one sentence.

Domain Specific Versus Domain Independent Summarization Techniques

Domain independent summarization techniques generally apply sets of general features which can be used to identify information-rich text segments. Recent research focus has drifted to domain-specific summarization techniques that utilize the available knowledge specific to the domain of text. For example, automatic summarization research on medical text generally attempts to utilize the various sources of codified medical knowledge and ontologies.

Evaluating Summaries Qualitatively

The main drawback of the evaluation systems existing so far is that we need at least one reference summary, and for some methods more than one, to be able to compare automatic summaries with models. This is a hard and expensive task. Much effort has to be done in order to have corpus of texts and their corresponding summaries. Furthermore, for some methods, not only do we need to have human-made summaries available for comparison, but also manual annotation has to be performed in some of them (e.g. SCU in the Pyramid Method). In any case, what the evaluation methods need as an input, is a set of summaries to serve as gold standards and a set of automatic summaries. Moreover, they all perform a quantitative evaluation with regard to different similarity metrics. To overcome these problems, we think that the quantitative evaluation might not be the only way to evaluate summaries, and a qualitative automatic evaluation would be also important. A new method which works by simplifying and generating ideograms that represent the meaning of each sentence in a document and then evaluates similarity "qualitatively" by comparing the shape and position of said ideograms has recently been developed. The Simplish Simplifying & Summarizing tool - performs automatic multi-lingual multi-document summarization. This tool does not need training of any kind and works by generating ideograms that represent the meaning of each sentence and then summarizes using two user-supplied parameters: equivalence (when are two sentences to be considered equivalent) and relevance (how long is the desired summary).

Data Pre-processing

Data pre-processing is an important step in the data mining process. The phrase "garbage in, garbage out" is particularly applicable to data mining and machine learning projects. Data-gathering methods are often loosely controlled, resulting in out-of-range values (e.g., Income: −100), impossible data combinations (e.g., Sex: Male, Pregnant: Yes), missing values, etc. Analyzing data that has not been carefully screened for such problems can produce misleading results. Thus, the representation and quality of data is first and foremost before running an analysis.

If there is much irrelevant and redundant information present or noisy and unreliable data, then knowledge discovery during the training phase is more difficult. Data preparation and filtering steps can take considerable amount of processing time. Data pre-processing includes cleaning, normalization, transformation, feature extraction and selection, etc. The product of data pre-processing is the final training set. Kotsiantis et al. (2006) present a well-known algorithm for each step of data pre-processing.

Data Editing

Data editing is defined as the process involving the review and adjustment of collected survey data. The purpose is to control the quality of the collected data. Data editing can be performed manually, with the assistance of a computer or a combination of both.

Editing Methods

Interactive Editing

The term interactive editing is commonly used for modern computer-assisted manual editing. Most interactive data editing tools applied at National Statistical Institutes (NSIs) allow one to check the specified edits during or after data entry, and if necessary to correct erroneous data immediately. Several approaches can be followed to correct erroneous data:

- Recontact the respondent
- Compare the respondent's data to his data from previous year
- Compare the respondent's data to data from similar respondents
- Use the subject matter knowledge of the human editor

Interactive editing is a standard way to edit data. It can be used to edit both categorical and continuous data. Interactive editing reduces the time frame needed to complete the cyclical process of review and adjustment.

Selective Editing

Selective editing is an umbrella term for several methods to identify the influential errors, and outliers. Selective editing techniques aim to apply interactive editing to a well-chosen subset of the records, such that the limited time and resources available for interactive editing are allocated to those records where it has the most effect on the quality of the final estimates of publication figures. In selective editing, data is split into two streams:

- The critical stream
- The non-critical stream

The critical stream consists of records that are more likely to contain influential errors. These critical records are edited in a traditional interactive manner. The records in the non-critical stream which are unlikely to contain influential errors are not edited in a computer assisted manner.

Macro Editing

There are two methods of macro editing:

Aggregation Method

This method is followed in almost every statistical agency before publication: verifying whether figures to be published seem plausible. This is accomplished by comparing quantities in publication tables with same quantities in previous publications. If an unusual value is observed, a micro-editing procedure is applied to the individual records and fields contributing to the suspicious quantity.

Distribution Method

Data available is used to characterize the distribution of the variables. Then all individual values are compared with the distribution. Records containing values that could be considered uncommon (given the distribution) are candidates for further inspection and possibly for editing.

Automatic Editing

In automatic editing records are edited by a computer without human intervention. Prior knowledge on the values of a single variable or a combination of variables can be formulated as a set of edit rules which specify or constrain the admissible values.

References

- Mogull, Robert G. (2004). Second-Semester Applied Statistics. Kendall/Hunt Publishing Company. p. 59. ISBN 0-7575-1181-3.

- Ronald A. Fisher (1954). Statistical Methods for Research Workers (Twelfth ed.). Edinburgh: Oliver and Boyd. ISBN 0-05-002170-2.

- Fotheringham, A. Stewart; Brunsdon, Chris; Charlton, Martin (2002). Geographically weighted regression: the analysis of spatially varying relationships (Reprint ed.). Chichester, England: John Wiley. ISBN 978-0-471-49616-8.

- Chiang, C.L, (2003) Statistical methods of analysis, World Scientific. ISBN 981-238-310-7 - page 274 section 9.7.4 "interpolation vs extrapolation"

- Good, P. I.; Hardin, J. W. (2009). Common Errors in Statistics (And How to Avoid Them) (3rd ed.). Hoboken, New Jersey: Wiley. p. 211. ISBN 978-0-470-45798-6.

- Kimball, R., Ross, M., Thornthwaite, W., Mundy, J., Becker, B. The Data Warehouse Lifecycle Toolkit, Wiley Publishing, Inc., 2008. ISBN 978-0-470-14977-5

- Klein, Lawrence A. (2004). Sensor and data fusion: A tool for information assessment and decision making. SPIE Press. p. 51. ISBN 0-8194-5435-4.

- Blasch, Erik P.; Bossé, Éloi; Lambert, Dale A. (2012). High-Level Information Fusion Management and System Design. Norwood, MA: Artech House Publishers. ISBN 978-1-6080-7151-7.

- Liggins, Martin E.; Hall, David L.; Llinas, James (2008). Multisensor Data Fusion, Second Edition: Theory and Practice (Multisensor Data Fusion). CRC. ISBN 978-1-4200-5308-1.

- Foreman, John (2013). Data Smart: Using Data Science to Transform Information into Insight. John Wiley & Sons. p. xiv. ISBN 9781118839867.

- M. Haghighat, M. Abdel-Mottaleb, & W. Alhalabi (2016). Discriminant Correlation Analysis: Real-Time Feature Level Fusion for Multimodal Biometric Recognition. IEEE Transactions on Information Forensics and Security, 11(9), 1984-1996.

- Chalef, Daniel (2016-03-20). "Data Science Tools – Are Proprietary Vendors Still Relevant?". kdnuggets.com. Retrieved 2016-11-07.

- Friendly, Michael (2006). "A Brief History of Data Visualization" (PDF). York University. Springer-Verlag. Retrieved 2015-11-22.

- Kai Wei, Rishabh Iyer, and Jeff Bilmes, Submodularity in Data Subset Selection and Active Learning, To Appear In Proc. International Conference on Machine Learning (ICML), Lille, France, June - 2015

- Ciuonzo, D.; Salvo Rossi, P. (2014-02-01). "Decision Fusion With Unknown Sensor Detection Probability". IEEE Signal Processing Letters. 21 (2): 208–212. doi:10.1109/LSP.2013.2295054. ISSN 1070-9908.

- Billings S.A. "Nonlinear System Identification: NARMAX Methods in the Time, Frequency, and Spatio-Temporal Domains". Wiley, 2013

- Hellerstein, Joseph (27 February 2008). "Quantitative Data Cleaning for Large Databases" (PDF). EECS Computer Science Division: 3. Retrieved 26 October 2013.

- Ciuonzo, D.; Papa, G.; Romano, G.; Salvo Rossi, P.; Willett, P. (2013-09-01). "One-Bit Decentralized Detection With a Rao Test for Multisensor Fusion". IEEE Signal Processing Letters. 20 (9): 861–864. doi:10.1109/LSP.2013.2271847. ISSN 1070-9908.

- Lengler, Ralph; Eppler, Martin. J. "Periodic Table of Visualization Methods". www.visual-literacy.org. Retrieved 15 March 2013.

4

Various Data Mining Techniques

The various data mining techniques are sequential pattern mining, process mining, text mining, data stream mining, bibliomining etc. Sequential pattern mining is concerned with searching for relevant patterns between data examples. The section serves as a source to understand the various data mining techniques.

Sequential Pattern Mining

Sequential pattern mining is a topic of data mining concerned with finding statistically relevant patterns between data examples where the values are delivered in a sequence. It is usually presumed that the values are discrete, and thus time series mining is closely related, but usually considered a different activity. Sequential pattern mining is a special case of structured data mining.

There are several key traditional computational problems addressed within this field. These include building efficient databases and indexes for sequence information, extracting the frequently occurring patterns, comparing sequences for similarity, and recovering missing sequence members. In general, sequence mining problems can be classified as *string mining* which is typically based on string processing algorithms and *itemset mining* which is typically based on association rule learning.

String Mining

String mining typically deals with a limited alphabet for items that appear in a sequence, but the sequence itself may be typically very long. Examples of an alphabet can be those in the ASCII character set used in natural language text, nucleotide bases 'A', 'G', 'C' and 'T' in DNA sequences, or amino acids for protein sequences. In biology applications analysis of the arrangement of the alphabet in strings can be used to examine gene and protein sequences to determine their properties. Knowing the sequence of letters of a DNA or a protein is not an ultimate goal in itself. Rather, the major task is to understand the sequence, in terms of its structure and biological function. This is typically achieved first by identifying individual regions or structural units within each sequence and then assigning a function to each structural unit. In many cases this requires comparing a given sequence with previously studied ones. The comparison between the strings becomes complicated when insertions, deletions and mutations occur in a string.

A survey and taxonomy of the key algorithms for sequence comparison for bioinformatics is presented by Abouelhoda & Ghanem (2010), which include:

- Repeat-related problems: that deal with operations on single sequences and can be based on exact string matching or approximate string matching methods for finding dispersed fixed length and maximal length repeats, finding tandem repeats, and finding unique subsequences and missing (un-spelled) subsequences.

- Alignment problems: that deal with comparison between strings by first aligning one or more sequences; examples of popular methods include BLAST for comparing a single sequence with multiple sequences in a database, and ClustalW for multiple alignments. Alignment algorithms can be based on either exact or approximate methods, and can also be classified as global alignments, semi-global alignments and local alignment.

Itemset Mining

Some problems in sequence mining lend themselves discovering frequent itemsets and the order they appear, for example, one is seeking rules of the form "if a {customer buys a car}, he or she is likely to {buy insurance} within 1 week", or in the context of stock prices, "if {Nokia up and Ericsson up}, it is likely that {Motorola up and Samsung up} within 2 days". Traditionally, itemset mining is used in marketing applications for discovering regularities between frequently co-occurring items in large transactions. For example, by analysing transactions of customer shopping baskets in a supermarket, one can produce a rule which reads "if a customer buys onions and potatoes together, he or she is likely to also buy hamburger meat in the same transaction".

A survey and taxonomy of the key algorithms for item set mining is presented by Han et al. (2007).

The two common techniques that are applied to sequence databases for frequent itemset mining are the influential apriori algorithm and the more-recent FP-growth technique.

Applications

With a great variation of products and user buying behaviors, shelf on which products are being displayed is one of the most important resources in retail environment. Retailers can not only increase their profit but, also decrease cost by proper management of shelf space allocation and products display. To solve this problem, George and Binu (2013) have proposed an approach to mine user buying patterns using PrefixSpan algorithm and place the products on shelves based on the order of mined purchasing patterns.

Algorithms

Commonly used algorithms include:

- GSP algorithm
- Sequential PAttern Discovery using Equivalence classes (SPADE)
- FreeSpan
- PrefixSpan
- MAPres

Process Mining

Process mining is a process management technique that allows for the analysis of business processes based on event logs. During process mining, specialized data-mining algorithms are applied to event log datasets in order to identify trends, patterns and details contained in event logs recorded by an information system. Process mining aims to improve process efficiency and understanding of processes. Process mining is also known as *Automated Business Process Discovery* (ABPD).

Overview

Process mining techniques are often used when no formal description of the process can be obtained by other approaches, or when the quality of existing documentation is questionable. For example, application of process mining methodology to the audit trails of a workflow management system, the transaction logs of an enterprise resource planning system, or the electronic patient records in a hospital can result in models describing processes, organizations, and products. Event log analysis can also be used to compare event logs with *prior* model(s) to understand whether the observations conform to a prescriptive or descriptive model.

Contemporary management trends such as BAM (Business Activity Monitoring), BOM (Business Operations Management), and BPI (business process intelligence) illustrate the interest in supporting diagnosis functionality in the context of Business Process Management technology (e.g., Workflow Management Systems and other *process-aware* information systems).

Application

Process mining follows the options established in business process engineering, then goes beyond those options by providing feedback for business process modeling:

- process analysis filters, orders and compresses logfiles for further insight into the connex of process operations.

- process design may be supported by feedback from process monitoring (action or event recording or logging)

- process enactment uses results from process mining based on logging for triggering further process operations

Classification

There are three classes of process mining techniques. This classification is based on whether there is a prior model and, if so, how the prior model is used during process mining.

- *Discovery*: Previous (*a priori*) models do not exist. Based on an event log, a new model is constructed or discovered based on low-level events. For example, using the alpha algorithm (a didactically driven approach). Many established techniques exist for automatically constructing process models (for example, Petri net, pi-calculus expression) based on an event log. Recently, process mining research has started targeting the other perspectives (e.g., data, resources, time, etc.). One example is the technique described in (Aalst, Reijers, & Song, 2005), which can be used to construct a social network.

- *Conformance checking*: Used when there is an *a priori* model. The existing model is compared with the process event log; discrepancies between the log and the model are analyzed. For example, there may be a process model indicating that purchase orders of more than 1 million Euro require two checks. Another example is the checking of the so-called "four-eyes" principle. Conformance checking may be used to detect deviations to enrich the model. An example is the extension of a process model with performance data, i.e., some *a priori* process model is used to project the potential bottlenecks. Another example is the *decision miner* described in (Rozinat & Aalst, 2006b) which takes an *a priori* process model and analyzes every choice in the process model. For each choice the event log is consulted to see which information is typically available the moment the choice is made. Then classical data mining techniques are used to see which data elements influence the choice. As a result, a decision tree is generated for each choice in the process.

- *Extension*: Used when there is an *a priori* model. The model is extended with a new aspect or perspective, so that the goal is *not* to check conformance, but rather to improve the existing model. An example is the extension of a process model with performance data, i.e., some prior process model dynamically annotated with performance data.

Software for Process Mining

A software framework for the evaluation of process mining algorithms has been developed at the Eindhoven University of Technology by Wil van der Aalst and others, and is available as an open source toolkit.

- Process Mining

- ProM Framework

- ProM Import Framework

Process Mining functionality is also offered by the following commercial vendors:

- Interstage Automated Process Discovery, a Process Mining service offered by Fujitsu, Ltd. as part of the Interstage Integration Middleware Suite.

- Disco is a complete Process Mining software by Fluxicon.

- ARIS Process Performance Manager, a Process Mining and Process Intelligence Tool offered by Software AG as part of the Process Intelligence Solution.

- QPR ProcessAnalyzer, Process Mining software for Automated Business Process Discovery (ABPD).

- Perceptive Process Mining, the Process Mining solution by Perceptive Software (formerly Futura Reflect / Pallas Athena Reflect).

- Celonis Process Mining, the Process Mining solution offered by Celonis

- SNP Business Process Analysis, the SAP-focused Process Mining solution by SNP Schneider-Neureither & Partner AG

- minit is a Process Mining software offered by Gradient ECM

- myInvenio cloud and on-premises solution by Cognitive Technology Ltd.

- LANA is a process mining tool featuring discovery and conformance checking.

- ProcessGold Enterprise Platform, an integration of Process Mining & Business Intelligence.

Text Mining

Text mining, also referred to as *text data mining*, roughly equivalent to text analytics, is the process of deriving high-quality information from text. High-quality information is typically derived through the devising of patterns and trends through means such as statistical pattern learning. Text mining usually involves the process of structuring the input text (usually parsing, along with the addition of some derived linguistic features and the removal of others, and subsequent insertion into a database), deriving patterns within the structured data, and finally evaluation and interpretation of the output. 'High quality' in text mining usually refers to some combination of relevance, novelty, and interestingness. Typical text mining tasks include text categorization, text clustering, concept/entity extraction, production of granular taxonomies, sentiment analysis, document summarization, and entity relation modeling (*i.e.*, learning relations between named entities).

Text analysis involves information retrieval, lexical analysis to study word frequency distributions, pattern recognition, tagging/annotation, information extraction, data mining techniques including link and association analysis, visualization, and predictive analytics. The overarching goal is, essentially, to turn text into data for analysis, via application of natural language processing (NLP) and analytical methods.

A typical application is to scan a set of documents written in a natural language and either model the document set for predictive classification purposes or populate a database or search index with the information extracted.

Text Analytics

The term text analytics describes a set of linguistic, statistical, and machine learning techniques that model and structure the information content of textual sources for business intelligence, exploratory data analysis, research, or investigation. The term is roughly synonymous with text mining; indeed, Ronen Feldman modified a 2000 description of "text mining" in 2004 to describe "text analytics." The latter term is now used more frequently in business settings while "text mining" is used in some of the earliest application areas, dating to the 1980s, notably life-sciences research and government intelligence.

The term text analytics also describes that application of text analytics to respond to business problems, whether independently or in conjunction with query and analysis of fielded, numerical data. It is a truism that 80 percent of business-relevant information originates in unstructured form, primarily text. These techniques and processes discover and present knowledge – facts, business rules, and relationships – that is otherwise locked in textual form, impenetrable to automated processing.

History

Labor-intensive manual text mining approaches first surfaced in the mid-1980s, but technological advances have enabled the field to advance during the past decade. Text mining is an interdisciplinary field that draws on information retrieval, data mining, machine learning, statistics, and computational linguistics. As most information (common estimates say over 80%) is currently stored as text, text mining is believed to have a high commercial potential value. Increasing interest is being paid to multilingual data mining: the ability to gain information across languages and cluster similar items from different linguistic sources according to their meaning.

The challenge of exploiting the large proportion of enterprise information that originates in "unstructured" form has been recognized for decades. It is recognized in the earliest definition of business intelligence (BI), in an October 1958 IBM Journal article by H.P. Luhn, A Business Intelligence System, which describes a system that will:

"...utilize data-processing machines for auto-abstracting and auto-encoding of documents and for creating interest profiles for each of the 'action points' in an organization. Both incoming and internally generated documents are automatically abstracted, characterized by a word pattern, and sent automatically to appropriate action points."

Yet as management information systems developed starting in the 1960s, and as BI emerged in the '80s and '90s as a software category and field of practice, the emphasis was on numerical data stored in relational databases. This is not surprising: text in "unstructured" documents is hard to process. The emergence of text analytics in its current form stems from a refocusing of research in the late 1990s from algorithm development to application, as described by Prof. Marti A. Hearst in the paper Untangling Text Data Mining:

For almost a decade the computational linguistics community has viewed large text collections as a resource to be tapped in order to produce better text analysis algorithms. In this paper, I have attempted to suggest a new emphasis: the use of large online text collections to discover new facts and trends about the world itself. I suggest that to make progress we do not need fully artificial intelligent text analysis; rather, a mixture of computationally-driven and user-guided analysis may open the door to exciting new results.

Hearst's 1999 statement of need fairly well describes the state of text analytics technology and practice a decade later.

Text Analysis Processes

Subtasks—components of a larger text-analytics effort—typically include:

- Information retrieval or identification of a corpus is a preparatory step: collecting or identifying a set of textual materials, on the Web or held in a file system, database, or content corpus manager, for analysis.

- Although some text analytics systems apply exclusively advanced statistical methods, many others apply more extensive natural language processing, such as part of speech tagging, syntactic parsing, and other types of linguistic analysis.

- Named entity recognition is the use of gazetteers or statistical techniques to identify named text features: people, organizations, place names, stock ticker symbols, certain abbreviations, and so on. Disambiguation—the use of contextual clues—may be required to decide where, for instance, "Ford" can refer to a former U.S. president, a vehicle manufacturer, a movie star, a river crossing, or some other entity.

- Recognition of Pattern Identified Entities: Features such as telephone numbers, e-mail addresses, quantities (with units) can be discerned via regular expression or other pattern matches.

- Coreference: identification of noun phrases and other terms that refer to the same object.

- Relationship, fact, and event Extraction: identification of associations among entities and other information in text

- Sentiment analysis involves discerning subjective (as opposed to factual) material and extracting various forms of attitudinal information: sentiment, opinion, mood, and emotion. Text analytics techniques are helpful in analyzing, sentiment at the entity, concept, or topic level and in distinguishing opinion holder and opinion object.

- Quantitative text analysis is a set of techniques stemming from the social sciences where either a human judge or a computer extracts semantic or grammatical relationships between words in order to find out the meaning or stylistic patterns of, usually, a casual personal text for the purpose of psychological profiling etc.

Applications

The technology is now broadly applied for a wide variety of government, research, and business needs. Applications can be sorted into a number of categories by analysis type or by business function. Using this approach to classifying solutions, application categories include:

- Enterprise Business Intelligence/Data Mining, Competitive Intelligence

- E-Discovery, Records Management

- National Security/Intelligence

- Scientific discovery, especially Life Sciences

- Sentiment Analysis Tools, Listening Platforms

- Natural Language/Semantic Toolkit or Service

- Publishing

- Automated ad placement

- Search/Information Access

- Social media monitoring

Security Applications

Many text mining software packages are marketed for security applications, especially monitoring and analysis of online plain text sources such as Internet news, blogs, etc. for national security purposes. It is also involved in the study of text encryption/decryption.

Biomedical Applications

A range of text mining applications in the biomedical literature has been described.

One online text mining application in the biomedical literature is PubGene that combines biomedical text mining with network visualization as an Internet service.

GoPubMed is a knowledge-based search engine for biomedical texts.

Software Applications

Text mining methods and software is also being researched and developed by major firms, including IBM and Microsoft, to further automate the mining and analysis processes, and by different firms working in the area of search and indexing in general as a way to improve their results. Within public sector much effort has been concentrated on creating software for tracking and monitoring terrorist activities.

Online Media Applications

Text mining is being used by large media companies, such as the Tribune Company, to clarify information and to provide readers with greater search experiences, which in turn increases site "stickiness" and revenue. Additionally, on the back end, editors are benefiting by being able to share, associate and package news across properties, significantly increasing opportunities to monetize content.

Marketing Applications

Text mining is starting to be used in marketing as well, more specifically in analytical customer relationship management. Coussement and Van den Poel (2008) apply it to improve predictive analytics models for customer churn (customer attrition).

Sentiment Analysis

Sentiment analysis may involve analysis of movie reviews for estimating how favorable a review is for a movie. Such an analysis may need a labeled data set or labeling of the affectivity of words. Resources for affectivity of words and concepts have been made for WordNet and ConceptNet, respectively.

Text has been used to detect emotions in the related area of affective computing. Text based approaches to affective computing have been used on multiple corpora such as students evaluations, children stories and news stories.

Academic Applications

The issue of text mining is of importance to publishers who hold large databases of information needing indexing for retrieval. This is especially true in scientific disciplines, in which highly specific information is often contained within written text. Therefore, initiatives have been taken such as Nature's proposal for an Open Text Mining Interface (OTMI) and the National Institutes of Health's common Journal Publishing Document Type Definition (DTD) that would provide semantic cues to machines to answer specific queries contained within text without removing publisher barriers to public access.

Academic institutions have also become involved in the text mining initiative:

- The National Centre for Text Mining (NaCTeM), is the first publicly funded text mining centre in the world. NaCTeM is operated by the University of Manchester in close collaboration with the Tsujii Lab, University of Tokyo. NaCTeM provides customised tools, research facilities and offers advice to the academic community. They are funded by the Joint Information Systems Committee (JISC) and two of the UK Research Councils (EPSRC & BBSRC). With an initial focus on text mining in the biological and biomedical sciences, research has since expanded into the areas of social sciences.

- In the United States, the School of Information at University of California, Berkeley is developing a program called BioText to assist biology researchers in text mining and analysis.

Digital Humanities and Computational Sociology

The automatic analysis of vast textual corpora has created the possibility for scholars to analyse millions of documents in multiple languages with very limited manual intervention. Key enabling technologies have been parsing, machine translation, topic categorization, and machine learning.

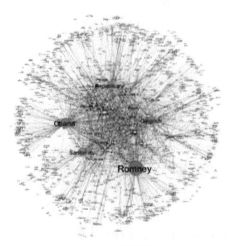

Narrative network of US Elections 2012

The automatic parsing of textual corpora has enabled the extraction of actors and their relational networks on a vast scale, turning textual data into network data. The resulting networks, which can contain thousands of nodes, are then analysed by using tools from network theory to identify the key actors, the key communities or parties, and general properties such as robustness or structural stability of the overall network, or centrality of certain nodes. This automates the approach introduced by quantitative narrative analysis, whereby subject-verb-object triplets are identified with pairs of actors linked by an action, or pairs formed by actor-object.

Content analysis has been a traditional part of social sciences and media studies for a long time. The automation of content analysis has allowed a "big data" revolution to take place in that field, with studies in social media and newspaper content that include millions of news items. Gender bias, readability, content similarity, reader preferences, and even mood have been analyzed based on text mining methods over millions of documents. The analysis of readability, gender bias and topic bias was demonstrated in Flaounas et al. showing how different topics have different gender biases and levels of readability; the possibility to detect mood shifts in a vast population by analysing Twitter content was demonstrated as well.

Software

Text mining computer programs are available from many commercial and open source companies and sources.

Intellectual Property Law

Situation in Europe

Due to a lack of flexibilities in European copyright and database law, the mining of in-copyright works such as web mining without the permission of the copyright owner is not legal. In the UK in 2014, on the recommendation of the Hargreaves review the government amended copyright law to allow text mining as a limitation and exception. Only the second country in the world to do so after Japan, which introduced a mining specific exception in 2009. However, due to the restriction of the Copyright Directive, the UK exception only allows content mining for non-commercial purposes. UK copyright law does not allow this provision to be overridden by contractual terms and conditions.

The European Commission facilitated stakeholder discussion on text and data mining in 2013, under the title of Licences for Europe. The focus on the solution to this legal issue being licences and not limitations and exceptions to copyright law led to representatives of universities, researchers, libraries, civil society groups and open access publishers to leave the stakeholder dialogue in May 2013.

Situation in the United States

By contrast to Europe, the flexible nature of US copyright law, and in particular fair use means that text mining in America, as well as other fair use countries such as Israel, Taiwan and South Korea is viewed as being legal. As text mining is transformative, meaning that it does not supplant the original work, it is viewed as being lawful under fair use. For example, as part of the Google Book settlement the presiding judge on the case ruled that Google's digitisation project of in-copyright books was lawful, in part because of the transformative uses that the digitisation project displayed—one such use being text and data mining.

Implications

Until recently, websites most often used text-based searches, which only found documents containing specific user-defined words or phrases. Now, through use of a semantic web, text mining can find content based on meaning and context (rather than just by a specific word). Additionally, text mining software can be used to build large dossiers of information about specific people and events. For example, large datasets based on data extracted from news reports can be built to facilitate social networks analysis or counter-intelligence. In effect, the text mining software may act in a capacity similar to an intelligence analyst or research librarian, albeit with a more limited scope of analysis. Text mining is also used in some email spam filters as a way of determining the characteristics of messages that are likely to be advertisements or other unwanted material. Text mining plays an important role in determining financial market sentiment.

Data Stream Mining

Data Stream Mining is the process of extracting knowledge structures from continuous, rapid data records. A data stream is an ordered sequence of instances that in many applications of data stream mining can be read only once or a small number of times using limited computing and storage capabilities. Examples of data streams include computer network traffic, phone conversations, ATM transactions, web searches, and sensor data. Data stream mining can be considered a subfield of data mining, machine learning, and knowledge discovery.

In many data stream mining applications, the goal is to predict the class or value of new instances in the data stream given some knowledge about the class membership or values of previous instances in the data stream. Machine learning techniques can be used to learn this prediction task from labeled examples in an automated fashion. Often, concepts from the field of incremental learning, a generalization of Incremental heuristic search are applied to cope with structural changes, on-line learning and real-time demands. In many applications, especially operating within non-stationary environments, the distribution underlying the instances or the rules underlying their labeling may change over time, i.e. the goal of the prediction, the class to be predicted or the target value to be predicted, may change over time. This problem is referred to as concept drift.

Software for Data Stream Mining

- MOA (Massive Online Analysis): free open-source software specific for mining data streams with concept drift. It has several machine learning algorithms (classification, regression, clustering, outlier detection and recommender systems). Also it contains a prequential evaluation method, the EDDM concept drift methods, a reader of ARFF real datasets, and artificial stream generators as SEA concepts, STAGGER, rotating hyperplane, random tree, and random radius based functions. MOA supports bi-directional interaction with Weka (machine learning).

- RapidMiner: commercial software for knowledge discovery, data mining, and machine learning also featuring data stream mining, learning time-varying concepts, and tracking drifting concept (if used in combination with its data stream mining plugin (formerly: concept drift plugin))

Events

- International Workshop on Ubiquitous Data Mining held in conjunction with the International

Joint Conference on Artificial Intelligence (IJCAI) in Beijing, China, August 3–5, 2013.

- International Workshop on Knowledge Discovery from Ubiquitous Data Streams held in conjunction with the 18th European Conference on Machine Learning (ECML) and the 11th European Conference on Principles and Practice of Knowledge Discovery in Databases (PKDD) in Warsaw, Poland, in September 2007.

- ACM Symposium on Applied Computing Data Streams Track held in conjunction with the 2007 ACM Symposium on Applied Computing (SAC-2007) in Seoul, Korea, in March 2007.

- IEEE International Workshop on Mining Evolving and Streaming Data (IWMESD 2006) to be held in conjunction with the 2006 IEEE International Conference on Data Mining (ICDM-2006) in Hong Kong in December 2006.

- Fourth International Workshop on Knowledge Discovery from Data Streams (IWKDDS) to be held in conjunction with the 17th European Conference on Machine Learning (ECML) and the 10th European Conference on Principles and Practice of Knowledge Discovery in Databases (PKDD) (ECML/PKDD-2006) in Berlin, Germany, in September 2006.

Data Scraping

Data scraping is a technique in which a computer program extracts data from human-readable output coming from another program.

Description

Normally, data transfer between programs is accomplished using data structures suited for automated processing by computers, not people. Such interchange formats and protocols are typically rigidly structured, well-documented, easily parsed, and keep ambiguity to a minimum. Very often, these transmissions are not human-readable at all.

Thus, the key element that distinguishes data scraping from regular parsing is that the output being scraped was intended for display to an end-user, rather than as input to another program, and is therefore usually neither documented nor structured for convenient parsing. Data scraping often involves ignoring binary data (usually images or multimedia data), display formatting, redundant labels, superfluous commentary, and other information which is either irrelevant or hinders automated processing.

Data scraping is most often done either to interface to a legacy system which has no other mechanism which is compatible with current hardware, or to interface to a third-party system which does not provide a more convenient API. In the second case, the operator of the third-party system will often see screen scraping as unwanted, due to reasons such as increased system load, the loss of advertisement revenue, or the loss of control of the information content.

Data scraping is generally considered an *ad hoc*, inelegant technique, often used only as a "last resort" when no other mechanism for data interchange is available. Aside from the higher programming and processing overhead, output displays intended for human consumption often change structure frequently. Humans can cope with this easily, but a computer program may report non-sense, have been told to read data in a particular format or from a particular place, and with no knowledge of how to check its results for validity.

Technical Variants

Screen Scraping

Screen scraping is normally associated with the programmatic collection of visual data from a source, instead of parsing data as in Web scraping. Originally, screen scraping referred to the practice of reading text data from a computer display terminal's screen. This was generally done by reading the terminal's memory through its auxiliary port, or by connecting the terminal output port of one computer system to an input port on another. The term screen scraping is also commonly used to refer to the bidirectional exchange of data. This could be the simple cases where the controlling program navigates through the user interface, or more complex scenarios where the controlling program is entering data into an interface meant to be used by a human.

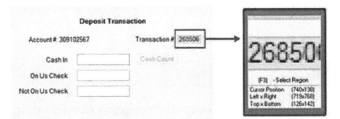

A screen fragment and a screen-scraping interface (blue box with red arrow) to customize data capture process.

As a concrete example of a classic screen scraper, consider a hypothetical legacy system dating from the 1960s — the dawn of computerized data processing. Computer to user interfaces from that era were often simply text-based dumb terminals which were not much more than virtual teleprinters (such systems are still in use today, for various reasons). The desire to interface such a system to more modern systems is common. A robust solution will often require things no longer available, such as source code, system documentation, APIs, or programmers with experience in a 50-year-old computer system. In such cases, the only feasible solution may be to write a screen scraper which "pretends" to be a user at a terminal. The screen scraper might connect to the legacy system via Telnet, emulate the keystrokes needed to navigate the old user interface, process the resulting display output, extract the desired data, and pass it on to the modern system. (A sophisticated and resilient implementation of this kind, built on a platform providing the governance and control required by a major enterprise — e.g. change control, security, user management, data protection, operational audit, load balancing and queue management, etc. — could be said to be an example of robotic process automation software.)

In the 1980s, financial data providers such as Reuters, Telerate, and Quotron displayed data in 24×80 format intended for a human reader. Users of this data, particularly investment banks, wrote applications to capture and convert this character data as numeric data for inclusion into calculations for trading decisions without re-keying the data. The common term for this practice, especially in the United Kingdom, was *page shredding*, since the results could be imagined to have passed through a paper shredder. Internally Reuters used the term 'logicized' for this conversion process, running a sophisticated computer system on VAX/VMS called the Logicizer.

More modern screen scraping techniques include capturing the bitmap data from the screen and running it through an OCR engine, or for some specialised automated testing systems, matching the screen's bitmap data against expected results. This can be combined in the case of GUI applications, with querying the graphical controls by programmatically obtaining references to their underlying programming objects. A sequence of screens is automatically captured and converted into a database.

Another modern adaptation to these techniques is to use, instead of a sequence of screens as input, a set of images or PDF files, so there are some overlaps with generic "document scraping" and report mining techniques.

Web Scraping

Web pages are built using text-based mark-up languages (HTML and XHTML), and frequently contain a wealth of useful data in text form. However, most web pages are designed for human end-users and not for ease of automated use. Because of this, tool kits that scrape web content were created. A web scraper is an API to extract data from a web site. Companies like Amazon AWS and Google provide web scraping tools, services and public data available free of cost to end users. Newer forms of web scraping involve listening to data feeds from web servers. For example, JSON is commonly used as a transport storage mechanism between the client and the web server.

Recently, companies have developed web scraping systems that rely on using techniques in DOM parsing, computer vision and natural language processing to simulate the human processing that occurs when viewing a webpage to automatically extract useful information.

Report Mining

Report mining is the extraction of data from human readable computer reports. Conventional data extraction requires a connection to a working source system, suitable connectivity standards or an API, and usually complex querying. By using the source system's standard reporting options, and directing the output to a spool file instead of to a printer, static reports can be generated suitable for offline analysis via report mining. This approach can avoid intensive CPU usage during business hours, can minimise end-user licence costs for ERP customers, and can offer very rapid prototyping and development of custom reports. Whereas data scraping and web scraping involve interacting with dynamic output, report mining involves extracting data from files in a human readable format, such as HTML, PDF, or text. These can be easily generated from almost any system by intercepting the data feed to a printer. This approach can provide a quick and simple route to obtaining data without needing to program an API to the source system.

Bibliomining

Bibliomining is the use of a combination of data mining, data warehousing, and bibliometrics for the purpose of analyzing library services. The term was created in 2003 by Scott Nicholson, Assistant Professor, Syracuse University School of Information Studies, in order to distinguish data mining in a library setting from other types of data mining.

How Bibliomining Works

First a data warehouse must be created. This is done by compiling information on the resources, such as titles and authors, subject headings, and descriptions of the collections. Then the demographic surrogate information is organized. Finally the library information (such as the librarian, whether or not the information came from the reference desk or circulation desk, and the location of the library) is obtained.

Once this is organized, the data can be processed and analyzed. This can be done via a few methods, such as online analytical processing (OLAP), using a data mining program, or through data visualization.

Uses of Bibliomining

Bibliomining is used to discover patterns in what people are reading and researching and allows librarians to target their community better. Bibliomining can also help library directors focus their budgets on resources that will be utilized. Another use is to determine when people use the library more often, so staffing needs can be adequately met. Combining bibliomining with other research techniques such as focus groups, surveys and cost-benefit analysis, will help librarians to get a better picture of their patrons and their needs.

Issues

There is some concern that data mining violates patron privacy. But by extracting the data, all personally identifiable information is deleted, and the data warehouse is clean. The original patron data can then be totally deleted and there will be no way to link the new data to a particular patron. This can be done in a few ways. One, used with information regarding database access, is to track the IP address, but then replace it with a similar code, that will allow identification without violating privacy. Another is to keep track of an item returned to the library and create a "demographic surrogate" of the patron. The demographic surrogate would not give any identifiable information such as names, library card numbers or addresses.

The other concern in bibliomining is that it only provides data in a very detached manner. Information is given as to how a patron uses library resources, but there is no way to track if the resources met the user's needs completely. Someone could take out a book on a topic, but not find the information they were seeking. Bibliomining only helps identify which books are used, not how useful they actually were. Bibliomining cannot provide information on how well a collection serves a patron. In order to counteract this, bibliomining must be used in accordance with other research techniques.

References

- Abouelhoda, M.; Ghanem, M. (2010). "String Mining in Bioinformatics". In Gaber, M. M. Scientific Data Mining and Knowledge Discovery. Springer. doi:10.1007/978-3-642-02788-8_9. ISBN 978-3-642-02787-1.

- Hearst, Marti A. (1999). "Proceedings of the 37th annual meeting of the Association for Computational Linguistics on Computational Linguistics": 3–10. doi:10.3115/1034678.1034679. ISBN 1-55860-609-2.

- Mehl, Matthias R. (2006). "Handbook of multimethod measurement in psychology": 141. doi:10.1037/11383-011. ISBN 1-59147-318-7.

- Zanasi, Alessandro (2009). "Proceedings of the International Workshop on Computational Intelligence in Security for Information Systems CISIS'08". Advances in Soft Computing. 53: 53. doi:10.1007/978-3-540-88181-0_7. ISBN 978-3-540-88180-3.

- Automated analysis of the US presidential elections using Big Data and network analysis; S Sudhahar, GA Veltri, N Cristianini; Big Data & Society 2 (1), 1-28, 2015

- "Text and Data Mining:Its importance and the need for change in Europe". Association of European Research Libraries. Retrieved 14 November 2014.

- "Judge grants summary judgment in favor of Google Books — a fair use victory". Lexology.com. Antonelli Law Ltd. Retrieved 14 November 2014.

5

Data Mining Algorithms

The data mining algorithms are alpha algorithm, apriori algorithm, GSP algorithm and Teiresias algorithm. Alpha algorithm is an algorithm that is aimed at reconstructing causality while Teiresias algorithm enables the discovery of rigidity in biological sequences. The topics discussed in the chapter are of great importance to broaden the existing knowledge on data mining algorithms.

Alpha Algorithm

The α-algorithm is an algorithm used in process mining, aimed at reconstructing causality from a set of sequences of events. It was first put forward by van der Aalst, Weijters and Mărușter. Several extensions or modifications of it have since been presented, which will be listed below.

It constructs P/T nets with special properties (workflow nets) from event logs (as might be collected by an ERP system). Each transition in the net corresponds to an observed task.

Short Description

The algorithm takes a workflow log $W \subseteq T^*$ as input and results in a workflow net being constructed.

It does so by examining causal relationships observed between tasks. For example, one specific task might always precede another specific task in every execution trace, which would be useful information.

Definitions Used

- A workflow trace or execution trace is a string over an alphabet T of *tasks*.
- A workflow log is a set of workflow traces.

Description

Declaratively, the algorithm can be presented as follows. Three sets of tasks are determined:

- T_W is the set of all tasks which occur in at least one trace
- T_I is the set of all tasks which occur trace-initially
- T_O is the set of all tasks which occur trace-terminally

Basic ordering relations are determined ($\succ_W$ first, the latter three can be constructed therefrom)

- $a \succ_W b$ iff a directly precedes b in some trace

- $a \rightarrow_W b$ iff $a \succ_W b \wedge b \nsucc_W a$
- $a \#_W b$ iff $a \nsucc_W b \wedge b \nsucc_W a$
- $a \setminus_W b$ iff $a \succ_W b \wedge b \succ_W a$

Places are discovered. Each place is identified with a pair of *sets of* tasks, in order to keep the number of places low.

- Y_W is the set of all pairs (A, B) of maximal sets of tasks such that
  - Neither $A \times A$ and $B \times B$ contain any members of $\succ_W$ and
  - $A \times B$ is a subset of $\rightarrow_W$
- P_W contains one place $p_{(A,B)}$ for every member of Y_W, plus the input place i_W and the output place o_W

The flow relation F_W is the union of the following:

- $\{(a, p_{(A,B)}) \mid (A, B) \in Y_W \wedge a \in A\}$
- $\{(p_{(A,B)}, b) \mid (A, B) \in Y_W \wedge b \in B\}$
- $\{(i_W, t) \mid t \in T_I\}$
- $\{(t, i_O) \mid t \in T_O\}$

The result is

- a petri net structure $\alpha(W) = (P_W, T_W, F_W)$
- with one input place i_W and one output place o_W
- because every transition of T_W is on a F_W – path from i_W to o_W, it is indeed a workflow net.

Properties

It can be shown that in the case of a complete workflow log generated by a sound SWF net, the net generating it can be reconstructed. Complete means that its $\succ_W$ relation is maximal. It is *not* required that all possible traces be present (which would be countably infinite for a net with a loop).

Limitations

General workflow nets may contain several types of constructs which the α-algorithm cannot re-discover.

Constructing Y_W takes exponential time in the number of tasks, since $\succ_W$ is not constrained and arbitrary subsets of T_W must be considered.

Apriori Algorithm

Apriori is an algorithm for frequent item set mining and association rule learning over transactional databases. It proceeds by identifying the frequent individual items in the database and extending them to larger and larger item sets as long as those item sets appear sufficiently often in the database. The frequent item sets determined by Apriori can be used to determine association rules which highlight general trends in the database: this has applications in domains such as market basket analysis.

Overview

The Apriori algorithm was proposed by Agrawal and Srikant in 1994. Apriori is designed to operate on databases containing transactions (for example, collections of items bought by customers, or details of a website frequentation). Other algorithms are designed for finding association rules in data having no transactions (Winepi and Minepi), or having no timestamps (DNA sequencing). Each transaction is seen as a set of items (an *itemset*). Given a threshold C, the Apriori algorithm identifies the item sets which are subsets of at least C transactions in the database.

Apriori uses a "bottom up" approach, where frequent subsets are extended one item at a time (a step known as *candidate generation*), and groups of candidates are tested against the data. The algorithm terminates when no further successful extensions are found.

Apriori uses breadth-first search and a Hash tree structure to count candidate item sets efficiently. It generates candidate item sets of length k from item sets of length $k-1$. Then it prunes the candidates which have an infrequent sub pattern. According to the downward closure lemma, the candidate set contains all frequent k-length item sets. After that, it scans the transaction database to determine frequent item sets among the candidates.

The pseudo code for the algorithm is given below for a transaction database T, and a support threshold of ϵ. Usual set theoretic notation is employed, though note that T is a multiset. C_k is the candidate set for level k. At each step, the algorithm is assumed to generate the candidate sets from the large item sets of the preceding level, heeding the downward closure lemma. $count[c]$ accesses a field of the data structure that represents candidate set c, which is initially assumed to be zero. Many details are omitted below, usually the most important part of the implementation is the data structure used for storing the candidate sets, and counting their frequencies.

```
Apriori(T, ε)
    L₁ ← {large 1-itemsets}
    k ← 2
    while L_{k-1} ≠ ∅
        C_k ← {a ∪ {b} | a ∈ L_{k-1} ∧ b ∉ a} − {c | {s | s ⊆ c ∧ |s| = k−1} ⊄ L_{k-1}}
        for transactions t ∈ T
            C_t ← {c | c ∈ C_k ∧ c ⊆ t}
            for candidates c ∈ C_t
                count[c] ← count[c]+1
        L_k ← {c | c ∈ C_k ∧ count[c] ≥ ε}
        k ← k+1
    return ∪_k L_k
```

Examples

Example 1

Consider the following database, where each row is a transaction and each cell is an individual item of the transaction:

alpha	beta	epsilon
alpha	beta	theta
alpha	beta	epsilon
alpha	beta	theta

The association rules that can be determined from this database are the following:

1. 100% of sets with alpha also contain beta
2. 50% of sets with alpha, beta also have epsilon
3. 50% of sets with alpha, beta also have theta

we can also illustrate this through a variety of examples

Example 2

Assume that a large supermarket tracks sales data by stock-keeping unit (SKU) for each item: each item, such as "butter" or "bread", is identified by a numerical SKU. The supermarket has a database of transactions where each transaction is a set of SKUs that were bought together.

Let the database of transactions consist of following itemsets:

Itemsets
{1,2,3,4}
{1,2,4}
{1,2}
{2,3,4}
{2,3}
{3,4}
{2,4}

We will use Apriori to determine the frequent item sets of this database. To do so, we will say that an item set is frequent if it appears in at least 3 transactions of the database: the value 3 is the *support threshold*.

The first step of Apriori is to count up the number of occurrences, called the support, of each member item separately, by scanning the database a first time. We obtain the following result

Item	Support
{1}	3
{2}	6
{3}	4
{4}	5

All the itemsets of size 1 have a support of at least 3, so they are all frequent.

The next step is to generate a list of all pairs of the frequent items.

For example, regarding the pair {1,2}: the first table of Example 2 shows items 1 and 2 appearing together in three of the itemsets; therefore, we say item {1,2} has support of three.

Item	Support
{1,2}	3
{1,3}	1
{1,4}	2
{2,3}	3
{2,4}	4
{3,4}	3

The pairs {1,2}, {2,3}, {2,4}, and {3,4} all meet or exceed the minimum support of 3, so they are frequent. The pairs {1,3} and {1,4} are not. Now, because {1,3} and {1,4} are not frequent, any larger set which contains {1,3} or {1,4} cannot be frequent. In this way, we can *prune* sets: we will now look for frequent triples in the database, but we can already exclude all the triples that contain one of these two pairs:

Item	Support
{2,3,4}	2

in the example, there are no frequent triplets -- {2,3,4} is below the minimal threshold, and the other triplets were excluded because they were super sets of pairs that were already below the threshold.

We have thus determined the frequent sets of items in the database, and illustrated how some items were not counted because one of their subsets was already known to be below the threshold.

Limitations

Apriori, while historically significant, suffers from a number of inefficiencies or trade-offs, which have spawned other algorithms. Candidate generation generates large numbers of subsets (the algorithm attempts to load up the candidate set with as many as possible before each scan). Bottom-up subset exploration (essentially a breadth-first traversal of the subset lattice) finds any maximal subset S only after all $2^{|S|} - 1$ of its proper subsets.

Later algorithms such as Max-Miner try to identify the maximal frequent item sets without enumerating their subsets, and perform "jumps" in the search space rather than a purely bottom-up approach.

GSP Algorithm

GSP algorithm (*Generalized Sequential Pattern* algorithm) is an algorithm used for sequence mining. The algorithms for solving sequence mining problems are mostly based on the *a priori* (level-wise) algorithm. One way to use the level-wise paradigm is to first discover all the frequent items in a level-wise fashion. It simply means counting the occurrences of all singleton elements in the database. Then, the transactions are filtered by removing the non-frequent items. At the end of this step, each transaction consists of only the frequent elements it originally contained. This modified database becomes an input to the GSP algorithm. This process requires one pass over the whole database.

GSP algorithm makes multiple database passes. In the first pass, all single items (1-sequences) are counted. From the frequent items, a set of candidate 2-sequences are formed, and another pass is made to identify their frequency. The frequent 2-sequences are used to generate the candidate 3-sequences, and this process is repeated until no more frequent sequences are found. There are two main steps in the algorithm.

- Candidate Generation. Given the set of frequent (k-1)-frequent sequences F(k-1), the candidates for the next pass are generated by joining F(k-1) with itself. A pruning phase eliminates any sequence, at least one of whose subsequences is not frequent.

- Support Counting. Normally, a hash tree–based search is employed for efficient support counting. Finally non-maximal frequent sequences are removed.

Algorithm

```
F1 = the set of frequent 1-sequence

k=2,

do while F(k-1)!= Null;

    Generate candidate sets Ck (set of candidate k-sequences);

        For all input sequences s in the database D

            do

        Increment count of all a in Ck if s supports a

        Fk = {a ∈ Ck such that its frequency exceeds the threshold}

            k = k+1;

        Result = Set of all frequent sequences is the union of all Fks

            End do

    End do
```

The above algorithm looks like the Apriori algorithm. One main difference is however the generation of candidate sets. Let us assume that:

A → B and A → C

are two frequent 2-sequences. The items involved in these sequences are (A, B) and (A,C) respectively. The candidate generation in a usual Apriori style would give (A, B, C) as a 3-itemset, but in the present context we get the following 3-sequences as a result of joining the above 2- sequences

$A \rightarrow B \rightarrow C, A \rightarrow C \rightarrow B$ and $A \rightarrow BC$

The candidate–generation phase takes this into account. The GSP algorithm discovers frequent sequences, allowing for time constraints such as maximum gap and minimum gap among the sequence elements. Moreover, it supports the notion of a sliding window, i.e., of a time interval within which items are observed as belonging to the same event, even if they originate from different events.

Teiresias Algorithm

The Teiresias algorithm is a combinatorial algorithm for the discovery of rigid patterns (motifs) in biological sequences. It is named after the Greek prophet Teiresias and was created in 1997 by Isidore Rigoutsos and Aris Floratos.

The problem of finding sequence similarities in the primary structure of related proteins or genes is one of the problems arising in the analysis of biological sequences. It can be shown that pattern discovery in its general form is NP-hard. The Teiresias algorithm, is based on the observation that if a pattern spans many positions and appears exactly k times in the input then all fragments (sub patterns) of the pattern have to appear at least k times in the input. The algorithm is able to produce all patterns that have a user-defined number of copies in the given input, and manages to be very efficient by avoiding the enumeration of the entire space. Finally, the algorithm reports motifs that are maximal in both length and composition.

A new implementation of the Teiresias algorithm was recently made available by the Computational Medicine Center at Thomas Jefferson University. Teiresias is also accessible through an interactive web-based user interface by the same center.

Pattern Description

The Teiresias algorithm uses regular expressions to define the patterns. This allows the patterns reported to consist not only from the characters that appear in each position (literals) but from a specific group of characters (bracketed literals) or even from any character (wild card). The patterns created by the algorithm are <L,W> patterns that have at least k instances in the input, where L ≤ W and L, W, k positive integers. A pattern is called an <L,W> pattern if and only if any L consecutive literals or bracketed literals span at most W positions (i.e. there can be no more than W-L wild cards).

The algorithm reports only maximal patterns. Given a set of sequences S, a pattern P that appears k times in S is called maximal if and only if there exists no pattern P' which is more specific than P and also appears exactly k times in S. If there exists such a pattern P' then we say that P cannot be maximal and P is considered to be subsumed by P'. A pattern P' is said to be more specific than a pattern P if and only if P' can be obtained from P by a) dereferencing a wild card or b) instantiating a bracketed literal to a literal, or c) by appending a string of literals, bracketed literals or/and wild cards to the right of P, or d) by prepending a string of literals, bracketed literals or/and wild cards to the left of P.

Algorithm Description

Teiresias consists of two phases. Scanning and Convolution. During the first phase the input is scanned for the patterns that satisfy the minimum requirements, the elementary patterns. The elementary patterns consist of exactly L literals and/or bracketed literals and includes at most W-L wild cards. During convolution, the elementary patterns are recursively combined and maximal patterns are created. The order in which the convolutions are performed is very important since it guarantees that all patterns will be generated and all maximal patterns are generated before all the patterns that are subsumed by them. The order is dictated by the following rules

- The priority of each pattern is defined by its contents from left to right.

- A literal has higher priority than a bracketed literal and both have higher priority than wild cards (the more specific first).

- Longer patterns have higher priority than shorter ones.

- Ties are resolved alphabetically.

Given the assurance that all maximal patterns will be created first, it is easy to check a newly created pattern against all maximal ones to ensure that it is subsumed in which case it is discarded. If the newly created pattern is not subsumed then it is added to the list of maximal patterns. When no more patterns can be combined to form new maximal patterns then the algorithm terminates. The length of any maximal pattern is bounded from above by the length of the longest input sequence.

Time Complexity

The algorithm is "output-sensitive." The time complexity of the TEIRESIAS algorithm is

$$O\left(W^L m \log m + (C^m + t_H) \sum_{P_{max}} rc(P) \right)$$

where L and W are user-specified parameters that define the "minimum density" of a pattern (any L literals or brackets cannot span more than W positions), m is the number of characters the input includes, $C \leq 1$ is the average number of patterns found in a hash entry, t_H is the time needed for locating the hash entry corresponding to any given hash value, and the summation Σ is the maximum number of patterns that will ever be placed in the stack that keeps the patterns for extension during convolution.

6

Cluster Analysis and its Algorithms

Cluster analysis is the task of grouping objects in a manner where the same group is more similar to other groups in some manner. Cluster analysis is used in many fields such as pattern recognition, image analysis, bioinformatics, information retrieval and computer graphics. The aspects explained in the following section are of vital importance and provide a better understanding of cluster analysis and examples of its algorithms.

Cluster Analysis

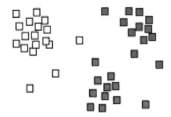

The result of a cluster analysis shown as the coloring of the squares into three clusters.

Cluster analysis or clustering is the task of grouping a set of objects in such a way that objects in the same group (called a cluster) are more similar (in some sense or another) to each other than to those in other groups (clusters). It is a main task of exploratory data mining, and a common technique for statistical data analysis, used in many fields, including machine learning, pattern recognition, image analysis, information retrieval, bioinformatics, data compression, and computer graphics.

Cluster analysis itself is not one specific algorithm, but the general task to be solved. It can be achieved by various algorithms that differ significantly in their notion of what constitutes a cluster and how to efficiently find them. Popular notions of clusters include groups with small distances among the cluster members, dense areas of the data space, intervals or particular statistical distributions. Clustering can therefore be formulated as a multi-objective optimization problem. The appropriate clustering algorithm and parameter settings (including values such as the distance function to use, a density threshold or the number of expected clusters) depend on the individual data set and intended use of the results. Cluster analysis as such is not an automatic task, but an iterative process of knowledge discovery or interactive multi-objective optimization that involves trial and failure. It is often necessary to modify data preprocessing and model parameters until the result achieves the desired properties.

Besides the term *clustering*, there are a number of terms with similar meanings, including *automatic classification, numerical taxonomy, botryology* and *typological analysis*. The subtle differences are often in the usage of the results: while in data mining, the resulting groups are the matter of interest, in automatic classification the resulting discriminative power is of interest.

Cluster analysis was originated in anthropology by Driver and Kroeber in 1932 and introduced to psychology by Zubin in 1938 and Robert Tryon in 1939 and famously used by Cattell beginning in 1943 for trait theory classification in personality psychology.

Definition

The notion of a "cluster" cannot be precisely defined, which is one of the reasons why there are so many clustering algorithms. There is a common denominator: a group of data objects. However, different researchers employ different cluster models, and for each of these cluster models again different algorithms can be given. The notion of a cluster, as found by different algorithms, varies significantly in its properties. Understanding these "cluster models" is key to understanding the differences between the various algorithms. Typical cluster models include:

- Connectivity models: for example, hierarchical clustering builds models based on distance connectivity.

- Centroid models: for example, the k-means algorithm represents each cluster by a single mean vector.

- Distribution models: clusters are modeled using statistical distributions, such as multivariate normal distributions used by the Expectation-maximization algorithm.

- Density models: for example, DBSCAN and OPTICS defines clusters as connected dense regions in the data space.

- Subspace models: in Biclustering (also known as Co-clustering or two-mode-clustering), clusters are modeled with both cluster members and relevant attributes.

- Group models: some algorithms do not provide a refined model for their results and just provide the grouping information.

- Graph-based models: a clique, that is, a subset of nodes in a graph such that every two nodes in the subset are connected by an edge can be considered as a prototypical form of cluster. Relaxations of the complete connectivity requirement (a fraction of the edges can be missing) are known as quasi-cliques, as in the HCS clustering algorithm.

A "clustering" is essentially a set of such clusters, usually containing all objects in the data set. Additionally, it may specify the relationship of the clusters to each other, for example, a hierarchy of clusters embedded in each other. Clusterings can be roughly distinguished as:

- hard clustering: each object belongs to a cluster or not

- soft clustering (also: fuzzy clustering): each object belongs to each cluster to a certain degree (for example, a likelihood of belonging to the cluster)

There are also finer distinctions possible, for example:

- strict partitioning clustering: here each object belongs to exactly one cluster

- strict partitioning clustering with outliers: objects can also belong to no cluster, and are considered outliers.

- overlapping clustering (also: alternative clustering, multi-view clustering): while usually a hard clustering, objects may belong to more than one cluster.

- hierarchical clustering: objects that belong to a child cluster also belong to the parent cluster

- subspace clustering: while an overlapping clustering, within a uniquely defined subspace, clusters are not expected to overlap.

Algorithms

Clustering algorithms can be categorized based on their cluster model, as listed above. The following overview will only list the most prominent examples of clustering algorithms, as there are possibly over 100 published clustering algorithms. Not all provide models for their clusters and can thus not easily be categorized.

There is no objectively "correct" clustering algorithm, but as it was noted, "clustering is in the eye of the beholder." The most appropriate clustering algorithm for a particular problem often needs to be chosen experimentally, unless there is a mathematical reason to prefer one cluster model over another. It should be noted that an algorithm that is designed for one kind of model has no chance on a data set that contains a radically different kind of model. For example, k-means cannot find non-convex clusters.

Connectivity-based Clustering (Hierarchical Clustering)

Connectivity based clustering, also known as *hierarchical clustering*, is based on the core idea of objects being more related to nearby objects than to objects farther away. These algorithms connect "objects" to form "clusters" based on their distance. A cluster can be described largely by the maximum distance needed to connect parts of the cluster. At different distances, different clusters will form, which can be represented using a dendrogram, which explains where the common name "hierarchical clustering" comes from: these algorithms do not provide a single partitioning of the data set, but instead provide an extensive hierarchy of clusters that merge with each other at certain distances. In a dendrogram, the y-axis marks the distance at which the clusters merge, while the objects are placed along the x-axis such that the clusters don't mix.

Connectivity based clustering is a whole family of methods that differ by the way distances are computed. Apart from the usual choice of distance functions, the user also needs to decide on the linkage criterion (since a cluster consists of multiple objects, there are multiple candidates to compute the distance to) to use. Popular choices are known as single-linkage clustering (the minimum of object distances), complete linkage clustering (the maximum of object distances) or UPGMA ("Unweighted Pair Group Method with Arithmetic Mean", also known as average linkage clustering). Furthermore, hierarchical clustering can be agglomerative (starting with single elements and aggregating them into clusters) or divisive (starting with the complete data set and dividing it into partitions).

These methods will not produce a unique partitioning of the data set, but a hierarchy from which the user still needs to choose appropriate clusters. They are not very robust towards outliers, which will either show up as additional clusters or even cause other clusters to merge (known as "chaining phenomenon", in particular with single-linkage clustering). In the general case, the complexity is $\mathcal{O}(n^3)$ for agglomerative clustering and $\mathcal{O}(2^{n-1})$ for divisive clustering, which makes them too slow for large data sets. For some special cases, optimal efficient methods (of complexity $\mathcal{O}(n^2)$) are known: SLINK for single-linkage and CLINK for complete-linkage clustering. In the data mining community these methods are recognized as a theoretical foundation of cluster analysis, but often considered obsolete. They did however provide inspiration for many later methods such as density based clustering.

- Linkage clustering examples

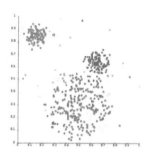

Single-linkage on Gaussian data. At 35 clusters, the biggest cluster starts fragmenting into smaller parts, while before it was still connected to the second largest due to the single-link effect.

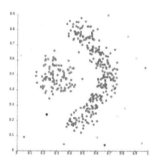

Single-linkage on density-based clusters. 20 clusters extracted, most of which contain single elements, since linkage clustering does not have a notion of "noise".

Centroid-based Clustering

In centroid-based clustering, clusters are represented by a central vector, which may not necessarily be a member of the data set. When the number of clusters is fixed to k, k-means clustering gives a formal definition as an optimization problem: find the k cluster centers and assign the objects to the nearest cluster center, such that the squared distances from the cluster are minimized.

The optimization problem itself is known to be NP-hard, and thus the common approach is to search only for approximate solutions. A particularly well known approximative method is Lloyd's algorithm, often actually referred to as *"k-means algorithm"*. It does however only find a local optimum, and is commonly run multiple times with different random initializations. Variations of k-means often include such optimizations as choosing the best of multiple runs, but also restricting the centroids to members of the data set (k-medoids), choosing medians (k-medians clustering), choosing the initial centers less randomly (K-means++) or allowing a fuzzy cluster assignment (Fuzzy c-means).

Most k-means-type algorithms require the number of clusters - k - to be specified in advance, which is considered to be one of the biggest drawbacks of these algorithms. Furthermore, the algorithms prefer clusters of approximately similar size, as they will always assign an object to the nearest centroid. This often leads to incorrectly cut borders in between of clusters (which is not surprising, as the algorithm optimized cluster centers, not cluster borders).

K-means has a number of interesting theoretical properties. First, it partitions the data space into a structure known as a Voronoi diagram. Second, it is conceptually close to nearest neighbor classification, and as such is popular in machine learning. Third, it can be seen as a variation of model based classification, and Lloyd's algorithm as a variation of the Expectation-maximization algorithm for this model discussed below.

- k-Means clustering examples

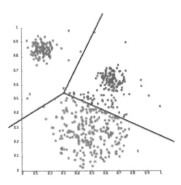

K-means separates data into Voronoi-cells, which assumes equal-sized clusters (not adequate here)

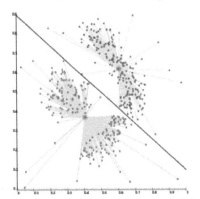

K-means cannot represent density-based clusters

Distribution-based Clustering

The clustering model most closely related to statistics is based on distribution models. Clusters can then easily be defined as objects belonging most likely to the same distribution. A convenient property of this approach is that this closely resembles the way artificial data sets are generated: by sampling random objects from a distribution.

While the theoretical foundation of these methods is excellent, they suffer from one key problem known as overfitting, unless constraints are put on the model complexity. A more complex model will usually be able to explain the data better, which makes choosing the appropriate model complexity inherently difficult.

One prominent method is known as Gaussian mixture models (using the expectation-maximization-tion algorithm). Here, the data set is usually modelled with a fixed (to avoid overfitting) number of Gaussian distributions that are initialized randomly and whose parameters are iteratively optimized to fit better to the data set. This will converge to a local optimum, so multiple runs may produce different results. In order to obtain a hard clustering, objects are often then assigned to the Gaussian distribution they most likely belong to; for soft clusterings, this is not necessary.

Distribution-based clustering produces complex models for clusters that can capture correlation and dependence between attributes. However, these algorithms put an extra burden on the user: for many real data sets, there may be no concisely defined mathematical model (e.g. assuming Gaussian distributions is a rather strong assumption on the data).

- Expectation-Maximization (EM) clustering examples

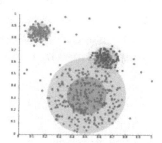

On Gaussian-distributed data, EM works well, since it uses Gaussians for modelling clusters

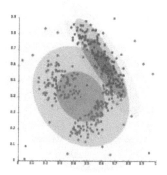

Density-based clusters cannot be modeled using Gaussian distributions

Density-based Clustering

In density-based clustering, clusters are defined as areas of higher density than the remainder of the data set. Objects in these sparse areas - that are required to separate clusters - are usually considered to be noise and border points.

The most popular density based clustering method is DBSCAN. In contrast to many newer methods, it features a well-defined cluster model called "density-reachability". Similar to linkage based clustering, it is based on connecting points within certain distance thresholds. However, it only connects points that satisfy a density criterion, in the original variant defined as a minimum number of other objects within this radius. A cluster consists of all density-connected objects (which can form a cluster of an arbitrary shape, in contrast to many other methods) plus all objects that are within these objects' range. Another interesting property of DBSCAN is that its complexity is fairly low - it requires a linear number of range queries on the database - and that it will discover essentially the same results (it is deterministic for core and noise points, but not for border points) in each run, therefore there is no need to run it multiple times. OPTICS is a generalization of DBSCAN that removes the need to choose an appropriate value for the range parameter , and produces a hierarchical result related to that of linkage clustering. DeLi-Clu, Density-Link-Clustering combines ideas from single-linkage clustering and OPTICS, eliminating the ε parameter entirely and offering performance improvements over OPTICS by using an R-tree index.

The key drawback of DBSCAN and OPTICS is that they expect some kind of density drop to detect cluster borders. Moreover, they cannot detect intrinsic cluster structures which are prevalent in the majority of real life data. A variation of DBSCAN, EnDBSCAN, efficiently detects such kinds of structures. On data sets with, for example, overlapping Gaussian distributions - a common use case in artificial data - the cluster borders produced by these algorithms will often look arbitrary, because the cluster density decreases continuously. On a data set consisting of mixtures of Gaussians, these algorithms are nearly always outperformed by methods such as EM clustering that are able to precisely model this kind of data.

Mean-shift is a clustering approach where each object is moved to the densest area in its vicinity, based on kernel density estimation. Eventually, objects converge to local maxima of density. Similar to k-means clustering, these "density attractors" can serve as representatives for the data set, but mean-shift can detect arbitrary-shaped clusters similar to DBSCAN. Due to the expensive iterative procedure and density estimation, mean-shift is usually slower than DBSCAN or k-Means.

- Density-based clustering examples

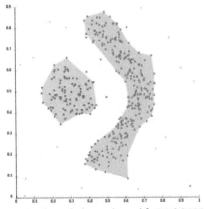

Density-based clustering with DBSCAN.

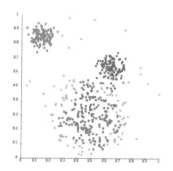

DBSCAN assumes clusters of similar density, and may have problems separating nearby clusters

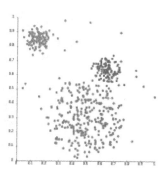

OPTICS is a DBSCAN variant that handles different densities much better

Recent Developments

In recent years considerable effort has been put into improving the performance of existing algorithms. Among them are *CLARANS* (Ng and Han, 1994), and *BIRCH* (Zhang et al., 1996). With the recent need to process larger and larger data sets (also known as big data), the willingness to trade semantic meaning of the generated clusters for performance has been increasing. This led to the development of pre-clustering methods such as canopy clustering, which can process huge data sets efficiently, but the resulting "clusters" are merely a rough pre-partitioning of the data set to then analyze the partitions with existing slower methods such as k-means clustering. Various other approaches to clustering have been tried such as seed based clustering.

For high-dimensional data, many of the existing methods fail due to the curse of dimensionality, which renders particular distance functions problematic in high-dimensional spaces. This led to new clustering algorithms for high-dimensional data that focus on subspace clustering (where only some attributes are used, and cluster models include the relevant attributes for the cluster) and correlation clustering that also looks for arbitrary rotated ("correlated") subspace clusters that can be modeled by giving a correlation of their attributes. Examples for such clustering algorithms are CLIQUE and SUBCLU.

Ideas from density-based clustering methods (in particular the DBSCAN/OPTICS family of algorithms) have been adopted to subspace clustering (HiSC, hierarchical subspace clustering and

DiSH) and correlation clustering (HiCO, hierarchical correlation clustering, 4C using "correlation connectivity" and ERiC exploring hierarchical density-based correlation clusters).

Several different clustering systems based on mutual information have been proposed. One is Marina Meilă's *variation of information* metric; another provides hierarchical clustering. Using genetic algorithms, a wide range of different fit-functions can be optimized, including mutual information. Also message passing algorithms, a recent development in Computer Science and Statistical Physics, has led to the creation of new types of clustering algorithms.

Other Methods

- Basic sequential algorithmic scheme (BSAS)

Evaluation and Assessment

Evaluation of clustering results sometimes is referred to as cluster validation.

There have been several suggestions for a measure of similarity between two clusterings. Such a measure can be used to compare how well different data clustering algorithms perform on a set of data. These measures are usually tied to the type of criterion being considered in assessing the quality of a clustering method.

Internal Evaluation

When a clustering result is evaluated based on the data that was clustered itself, this is called internal evaluation. These methods usually assign the best score to the algorithm that produces clusters with high similarity within a cluster and low similarity between clusters. One drawback of using internal criteria in cluster evaluation is that high scores on an internal measure do not necessarily result in effective information retrieval applications. Additionally, this evaluation is biased towards algorithms that use the same cluster model. For example, k-Means clustering naturally optimizes object distances, and a distance-based internal criterion will likely overrate the resulting clustering.

Therefore, the internal evaluation measures are best suited to get some insight into situations where one algorithm performs better than another, but this shall not imply that one algorithm produces more valid results than another. Validity as measured by such an index depends on the claim that this kind of structure exists in the data set. An algorithm designed for some kind of models has no chance if the data set contains a radically different set of models, or if the evaluation measures a radically different criterion. For example, k-means clustering can only find convex clusters, and many evaluation indexes assume convex clusters. On a data set with non-convex clusters neither the use of k-means, nor of an evaluation criterion that assumes convexity, is sound.

The following methods can be used to assess the quality of clustering algorithms based on internal criterion:

- Davies–Bouldin index

The Davies–Bouldin index can be calculated by the following formula:

$$DB = \frac{1}{n} \sum_{i=1}^{n} \max_{j \neq i} \left(\frac{\sigma_i + \sigma_j}{d(c_i, c_j)} \right)$$

where n is the number of clusters, c_x is the centroid of cluster x, σ_x is the average distance of all elements in cluster x to centroid c_x, and $d(c_i, c_j)$ is the distance between centroids c_i and c_j. Since algorithms that produce clusters with low intra-cluster distances (high intra-cluster similarity) and high inter-cluster distances (low inter-cluster similarity) will have a low Davies–Bouldin index, the clustering algorithm that produces a collection of clusters with the smallest Davies–Bouldin index is considered the best algorithm based on this criterion.

- Dunn index

The Dunn index aims to identify dense and well-separated clusters. It is defined as the ratio between the minimal inter-cluster distance to maximal intra-cluster distance. For each cluster partition, the Dunn index can be calculated by the following formula:

$$D = \frac{\min_{1 \leq i < j \leq n} d(i, j)}{\max_{1 \leq k \leq n} d'(k)},$$

where $d(i,j)$ represents the distance between clusters i and j, and $d'(k)$ measures the intra-cluster distance of cluster k. The inter-cluster distance $d(i,j)$ between two clusters may be any number of distance measures, such as the distance between the centroids of the clusters. Similarly, the intra-cluster distance $d'(k)$ may be measured in a variety ways, such as the maximal distance between any pair of elements in cluster k. Since internal criterion seek clusters with high intra-cluster similarity and low inter-cluster similarity, algorithms that produce clusters with high Dunn index are more desirable.

- Silhouette coefficient

The silhouette coefficient contrasts the average distance to elements in the same cluster with the average distance to elements in other clusters. Objects with a high silhouette value are considered well clustered, objects with a low value may be outliers. This index works well with k-means clustering, and is also used to determine the optimal number of clusters.

External Evaluation

In external evaluation, clustering results are evaluated based on data that was not used for clustering, such as known class labels and external benchmarks. Such benchmarks consist of a set of pre-classified items, and these sets are often created by (expert) humans. Thus, the benchmark sets can be thought of as a gold standard for evaluation. These types of evaluation methods measure how close the clustering is to the predetermined benchmark classes. However, it has recently been discussed whether this is adequate for real data, or only on synthetic data sets with a factual ground truth, since classes can contain internal structure, the attributes present may not allow separation of clusters or the classes may contain anomalies. Additionally, from a knowledge discovery point of view, the reproduction of known knowledge may not necessarily be the intended result. In the special scenario of constrained clustering, where meta information (such as class labels) is used already in the clustering process, the hold-out of information for evaluation purposes is non-trivial.

A number of measures are adapted from variants used to evaluate classification tasks. In place of counting the number of times a class was correctly assigned to a single data point (known as true positives), such *pair counting* metrics assess whether each pair of data points that is truly in the same cluster is predicted to be in the same cluster.

Some of the measures of quality of a cluster algorithm using external criterion include:

- Rand measure (William M. Rand 1971)

The Rand index computes how similar the clusters (returned by the clustering algorithm) are to the benchmark classifications. One can also view the Rand index as a measure of the percentage of correct decisions made by the algorithm. It can be computed using the following formula:

$$RI = \frac{TP + TN}{TP + FP + FN + TN}$$

where TP is the number of true positives, TN is the number of true negatives, FP is the number of false positives, and FN is the number of false negatives. One issue with the Rand index is that false positives and false negatives are equally weighted. This may be an undesirable characteristic for some clustering applications. The F-measure addresses this concern, as does the chance-corrected adjusted Rand index.

- F-measure

The F-measure can be used to balance the contribution of false negatives by weighting recall through a parameter $\beta \geq 0$. Let precision and recall be defined as follows:

$$P = \frac{TP}{TP + FP}$$

$$R = \frac{TP}{TP + FN}$$

where P is the precision rate and R is the recall rate. We can calculate the F-measure by using the following formula:

$$F_\beta = \frac{(\beta^2 + 1) \cdot P \cdot R}{\beta^2 \cdot P + R}$$

Notice that when $\beta = 0$, $F_0 = P$. In other words, recall has no impact on the F-measure when $\beta = 0$, and increasing $F_0 = P$ allocates an increasing amount of weight to recall in the final F-measure.

- Jaccard index

The Jaccard index is used to quantify the similarity between two datasets. The Jaccard index takes on a value between 0 and 1. An index of 1 means that the two dataset are identical, and an index of 0 indicates that the datasets have no common elements. The Jaccard index is defined by the following formula:

$$J(A, B) = \frac{|A \cap B|}{|A \cup B|} = \frac{TP}{TP + FP + FN}$$

This is simply the number of unique elements common to both sets divided by the total number of unique elements in both sets.

- Fowlkes–Mallows index (E. B. Fowlkes & C. L. Mallows 1983)

The Fowlkes-Mallows index computes the similarity between the clusters returned by the clustering algorithm and the benchmark classifications. The higher the value of the Fowlkes-Mallows index the more similar the clusters and the benchmark classifications are. It can be computed using the following formula:

$$FM = \sqrt{\frac{TP}{TP + FP} \cdot \frac{TP}{TP + FN}}$$

where TP is the number of true positives, FP is the number of false positives, and FN is the number of false negatives. The FM index is the geometric mean of the precision and recall P and R, while the F-measure is their harmonic mean. Moreover, precision and recall are also known as Wallace's indices B^{I} and B^{II}.

- The Mutual Information is an information theoretic measure of how much information is shared between a clustering and a ground-truth classification that can detect a non-linear similarity between two clusterings. Adjusted mutual information is the corrected-for-chance variant of this that has a reduced bias for varying cluster numbers.

- Confusion matrix

A confusion matrix can be used to quickly visualize the results of a classification (or clustering) algorithm. It shows how different a cluster is from the gold standard cluster.

Applications

Biology, computational biology and bioinformatics

Plant and animal ecology

cluster analysis is used to describe and to make spatial and temporal comparisons of communities (assemblages) of organisms in heterogeneous environments; it is also used in plant systematics to generate artificial phylogenies or clusters of organisms (individuals) at the species, genus or higher level that share a number of attributes

Transcriptomics

clustering is used to build groups of genes with related expression patterns (also known as coexpressed genes) as in HCS clustering algorithm . Often such groups contain functionally related proteins, such as enzymes for a specific pathway, or genes that are co-regulated. High throughput experiments using expressed sequence tags (ESTs) or DNA microarrays can be a powerful tool for genome annotation, a general aspect of genomics.

Sequence analysis

clustering is used to group homologous sequences into gene families. This is a very important concept in bioinformatics, and evolutionary biology in general.

High-throughput genotyping platforms

clustering algorithms are used to automatically assign genotypes.

Human genetic clustering

The similarity of genetic data is used in clustering to infer population structures.

Medicine

Medical imaging

On PET scans, cluster analysis can be used to differentiate between different types of tissue in a three-dimensional image for many different purposes.

Business and marketing

Market research

Cluster analysis is widely used in market research when working with multivariate data from surveys and test panels. Market researchers use cluster analysis to partition the general population of consumers into market segments and to better understand the relationships between different groups of consumers/potential customers, and for use in market segmentation, Product positioning, New product development and Selecting test markets.

Grouping of shopping items

Clustering can be used to group all the shopping items available on the web into a set of unique products. For example, all the items on eBay can be grouped into unique products. (eBay doesn't have the concept of a SKU)

World wide web

Social network analysis

In the study of social networks, clustering may be used to recognize communities within large groups of people.

Search result grouping

In the process of intelligent grouping of the files and websites, clustering may be used to create a more relevant set of search results compared to normal search engines like Google. There are currently a number of web based clustering tools such as Clusty.

Slippy map optimization

Flickr's map of photos and other map sites use clustering to reduce the number of markers on a map. This makes it both faster and reduces the amount of visual clutter.

Computer science

Software evolution

Clustering is useful in software evolution as it helps to reduce legacy properties in code by reforming functionality that has become dispersed. It is a form of restructuring and hence is a way of direct preventative maintenance.

Image segmentation

Clustering can be used to divide a digital image into distinct regions for border detection or object recognition.

Evolutionary algorithms

Clustering may be used to identify different niches within the population of an evolutionary algorithm so that reproductive opportunity can be distributed more evenly amongst the evolving species or subspecies.

Recommender systems

Recommender systems are designed to recommend new items based on a user's tastes. They sometimes use clustering algorithms to predict a user's preferences based on the preferences of other users in the user's cluster.

Markov chain Monte Carlo methods

Clustering is often utilized to locate and characterize extrema in the target distribution.

Anomaly detection

Anomalies/outliers are typically - be it explicitly or implicitly - defined with respect to clustering structure in data.

Social science

Crime analysis

Cluster analysis can be used to identify areas where there are greater incidences of particular types of crime. By identifying these distinct areas or "hot spots" where a similar crime has happened over a period of time, it is possible to manage law enforcement resources more effectively.

Educational data mining

Cluster analysis is for example used to identify groups of schools or students with similar properties.

Typologies

From poll data, projects such as those undertaken by the Pew Research Center use cluster analysis to discern typologies of opinions, habits, and demographics that may be useful in politics and marketing.

Others

Field robotics

Clustering algorithms are used for robotic situational awareness to track objects and detect outliers in sensor data.

Mathematical chemistry

To find structural similarity, etc., for example, 3000 chemical compounds were clustered in the space of 90 topological indices.

Climatology

To find weather regimes or preferred sea level pressure atmospheric patterns.

Petroleum geology

Cluster analysis is used to reconstruct missing bottom hole core data or missing log curves in order to evaluate reservoir properties.

Physical geography

The clustering of chemical properties in different sample locations.

Fuzzy Clustering

Fuzzy clustering (also referred to as soft clustering) is a form of clustering in which each data point can belong to more than one cluster.

Clustering or cluster analysis involves assigning data points to clusters (also called buckets, bins, or classes), or homogeneous classes, such that items in the same class or cluster are as similar as possible, while items belonging to different classes are as dissimilar as possible. Clusters are identified via similarity measures. These similarity measures include distance, connectivity, and intensity. Different similarity measures may be chosen based on the data or the application.

Comparison to Hard Clustering

In non-fuzzy clustering (also known as hard clustering), data is divided into distinct clusters, where each data point can only belong to exactly one cluster. In fuzzy clustering, data points can potentially belong to multiple clusters.

Membership

Membership grades are assigned to each of the data points. These membership grades indicate the degree to which data points belong to each cluster. Thus, points on the edge of a cluster, with lower membership grades, may be *in the cluster* to a lesser degree than points in the center of cluster.

Fuzzy C-means Clustering

One of the most widely used fuzzy clustering algorithms is the Fuzzy C-Means (FCM) Algorithm.

History

Fuzzy c-means (FCM) clustering was developed by J.C. Dunn in 1973, and improved by J.C. Bezdek in 1981.

General Description

The fuzzy c-means algorithm is very similar to the k-means algorithm:

- Choose a number of clusters.

- Assign randomly to each point coefficients for being in the clusters.

- Repeat until the algorithm has converged (that is, the coefficients' change between two iterations is no more than ε, the given sensitivity threshold) :

    - Compute the centroid for each cluster.

    - For each point, compute its coefficients of being in the clusters.

Centroid

Any point x has a set of coefficients giving the degree of being in the kth cluster $w_k(x)$. With fuzzy c-means, the centroid of a cluster is the mean of all points, weighted by their degree of belonging to the cluster:

$$c_k = \frac{\sum_x w_k(x)^m x}{\sum_x w_k(x)^m}.$$

Algorithm

The FCM algorithm attempts to partition a finite collection of n elements $X = \{\mathbf{x}_1,...,\mathbf{x}_n\}$ into a collection of c fuzzy clusters with respect to some given criterion.

Given a finite set of data, the algorithm returns a list of c cluster centres $C = \{\mathbf{c}_1,...,\mathbf{c}_c\}$ and a partition matrix

$W = w_{i,j} \in [0,1], i = 1,...,n, j = 1,...,c,$ where each element, w_{ij}, tells the degree to which element, $\mathbf{x}_i$, belongs to cluster $\mathbf{c}_j$.

The FCM aims to minimize an objective function:

$$\underset{C}{\arg\min} \sum_{i=1}^{n} \sum_{j=1}^{c} w_{ij}^{m} \left\| \mathbf{x}_i - \mathbf{c}_j \right\|^2 ,$$

where:

$$w_{ij} = \frac{1}{\sum_{k=1}^{c} \left(\dfrac{\left\| \mathbf{x}_i - \mathbf{c}_j \right\|}{\left\| \mathbf{x}_i - \mathbf{c}_k \right\|} \right)^{\frac{2}{m-1}}}.$$

Comparison to K-means Clustering

K-means clustering also attempts to minimize the objective function shown above. This method differs from the k-means objective function by the addition of the membership values w_{ij} and the fuzzifier, $m \in R$, with $m \geq 1$. The fuzzifier m determines the level of cluster fuzziness. A large m results in smaller membership values, w_{ij}, and hence, fuzzier clusters. In the limit $m = 1$, the memberships, w_{ij}, converge to 0 or 1, which implies a crisp partitioning. In the absence of experimentation or domain knowledge, m is commonly set to 2. The algorithm minimizes intra-cluster variance as well, but has the same problems as k-means; the minimum is a local minimum, and the results depend on the initial choice of weights.

Related Algorithms

Using a mixture of Gaussians along with the expectation-maximization algorithm is a more statistically formalized method which includes some of these ideas: partial membership in classes.

Another algorithm closely related to Fuzzy C-Means is Soft K-means.

Applications

Clustering problems have applications in biology, medicine, psychology, economics, and many other disciplines.

Bioinformatics

In the field of bioinformatics, clustering is used for a number of applications. One use is as a pattern recognition technique to analyze gene expression data from microarrays or other technology. In this case, genes with similar expression patterns are grouped into the same cluster, and different clusters display distinct, well-separated patterns of expression. Use of clustering can provide insight into gene function and regulation. Because fuzzy clustering allows genes to belong to more than one cluster, it allows for the identification of genes that are conditionally co-regulated or co-expressed. For example, one gene may be acted on by more than one Transcription factor, and one gene may encode a protein that has more than one function. Thus, fuzzy clustering is more appropriate than hard clustering.

Image Analysis

Fuzzy c-means has been a very important tool for image processing in clustering objects in an image. In the 70's, mathematicians introduced the spatial term into the FCM algorithm to improve the accuracy of clustering under noise. Alternatively, A fuzzy logic model can be described on fuzzy sets that are defined on three components of the HSL color space HSL and HSV; The membership functions aim to describe colors follow the human intuition of color identification.

Marketing

In marketing, customers can be grouped into fuzzy clusters based on their needs, brand choices, psycho-graphic profiles, or other marketing related partitions.

FLAME Clustering

Fuzzy clustering by Local Approximation of MEmberships (FLAME) is a data clustering algorithm that defines clusters in the dense parts of a dataset and performs cluster assignment solely based on the neighborhood relationships among objects. The key feature of this algorithm is that the neighborhood relationships among neighboring objects in the feature space are used to constrain the memberships of neighboring objects in the fuzzy membership space.

Description of the FLAME Algorithm

The FLAME algorithm is mainly divided into three steps:

1. Extraction of the structure information from the dataset:

   1. Construct a neighborhood graph to connect each object to its K-Nearest Neighbors (KNN);

   2. Estimate a density for each object based on its proximities to its KNN;

   3. Objects are classified into 3 types:

      1. Cluster Supporting Object (CSO): object with density higher than all its neighbors;

      2. Cluster Outliers: object with density lower than all its neighbors, and lower than a predefined threshold;

      3. the rest.

2. Local/Neighborhood approximation of fuzzy memberships:

1. Initialization of fuzzy membership:

    1. Each CSO is assigned with fixed and full membership to itself to represent one cluster;

    2. All outliers are assigned with fixed and full membership to the outlier group;

    3. The rest are assigned with equal memberships to all clusters and the outlier group;

2. Then the fuzzy memberships of all type 3 objects are updated by a converging iterative procedure called *Local/Neighborhood Approximation of Fuzzy Memberships*, in which the fuzzy membership of each object is updated by a linear combination of the fuzzy memberships of its nearest neighbors.

3. Cluster construction from fuzzy memberships in two possible ways:

    1. One-to-one object-cluster assignment, to assign each object to the cluster in which it has the highest membership;

    2. One-to-multiple object-clusters assignment, to assign each object to the cluster in which it has a membership higher than a threshold.

The Optimization Problem in FLAME

The Local/Neighborhood Approximation of Fuzzy Memberships is a procedure to minimize the Local/Neighborhood Approximation Error (LAE/NAE) defined as the following:

$$E(\{\mathbf{p}\}) = \sum_{\mathbf{x} \in \mathbf{X}} \left\| \mathbf{p}(\mathbf{x}) - \sum_{\mathbf{y} \in \mathcal{N}(\mathbf{x})} w_{\mathbf{xy}} \mathbf{p}(\mathbf{y}) \right\|^2$$

where $\mathbf{X}$ is the set of all type 3 objects, $\mathbf{p}(\mathbf{x})$ is the fuzzy membership vector of object $\mathbf{x}$, $\mathcal{N}(x)$ is the set of nearest neighbors of $\mathbf{x}$, , and $w_{\mathbf{xy}}$ with $\sum_{\mathbf{y} \in \mathcal{N}(\mathbf{x})} w_{\mathbf{xy}} = 1$ are the coefficients reflecting the relative proximities of the nearest neighbors.

The NAE can be minimized by solving the following linear equations with unique solution which is the unique global minimum of NAE with value zero:

$$p_k(\mathbf{x}) - \sum_{\mathbf{y} \in \mathcal{N}(\mathbf{x})} w_{\mathbf{xy}} p_k(\mathbf{y}) = 0, \quad \forall \mathbf{x} \in \mathbf{X}, \quad k = 1, ..., M$$

where M is the number of CSOs plus one (for the outlier group). The following iterative procedure can be used to solve these linear equations:

$$\mathbf{p}^{t+1}(\mathbf{x}) = \sum_{\mathbf{y} \in \mathcal{N}(\mathbf{x})} w_{\mathbf{xy}} \mathbf{p}^t(\mathbf{y})$$

A Simple Illustration on a 2-Dimension Testing Dataset

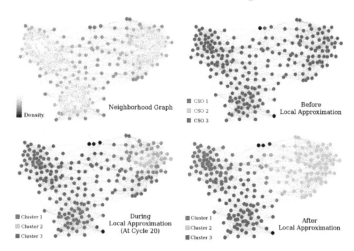

k-means Clustering

k-means clustering is a method of vector quantization, originally from signal processing, that is popular for cluster analysis in data mining. *k*-means clustering aims to partition *n* observations into *k* clusters in which each observation belongs to the cluster with the nearest mean, serving as a prototype of the cluster. This results in a partitioning of the data space into Voronoi cells.

The problem is computationally difficult (NP-hard); however, there are efficient heuristic algorithms that are commonly employed and converge quickly to a local optimum. These are usually similar to the expectation-maximization algorithm for mixtures of Gaussian distributions via an iterative refinement approach employed by both algorithms. Additionally, they both use cluster centers to model the data; however, *k*-means clustering tends to find clusters of comparable spatial extent, while the expectation-maximization mechanism allows clusters to have different shapes.

The algorithm has a loose relationship to the *k*-nearest neighbor classifier, a popular machine learning technique for classification that is often confused with *k*-means because of the *k* in the name. One can apply the 1-nearest neighbor classifier on the cluster centers obtained by *k*-means to classify new data into the existing clusters. This is known as nearest centroid classifier or Rocchio algorithm.

Description

Given a set of observations (x_1, x_2, ..., x_n), where each observation is a *d*-dimensional real vector, *k*-means clustering aims to partition the *n* observations into *k* ($\leq n$) sets S = {S_1, S_2, ..., S_k} so as to minimize the within-cluster sum of squares (WCSS) (sum of distance functions of each point in the cluster to the K center). In other words, its objective is to find:

$$\underset{S}{\arg\min} \sum_{i=1}^{k} \sum_{x \in S_i} \left\| x - \mu_i \right\|^2$$

where μ_i is the mean of points in S_i.

History

The term "k-means" was first used by James MacQueen in 1967, though the idea goes back to Hugo Steinhaus in 1957. The standard algorithm was first proposed by Stuart Lloyd in 1957 as a technique for pulse-code modulation, though it wasn't published outside of Bell Labs until 1982. In 1965, E. W. Forgy published essentially the same method, which is why it is sometimes referred to as Lloyd-Forgy. A more efficient version was later proposed and published in FORTRAN by Hartigan and Wong.

Algorithms

Standard Algorithm

The most common algorithm uses an iterative refinement technique. Due to its ubiquity it is often called the **k**-means algorithm; it is also referred to as Lloyd's algorithm, particularly in the computer science community.

Given an initial set of k means $m_1^{(1)},...,m_k^{(1)}$, the algorithm proceeds by alternating between two steps:

Assignment step: Assign each observation to the cluster whose mean yields the least within-cluster sum of squares (WCSS). Since the sum of squares is the squared Euclidean distance, this is intuitively the "nearest" mean. (Mathematically, this means partitioning the observations according to the Voronoi diagram generated by the means).

$$S_i^{(t)} = \left\{ x_p : \left\| x_p - m_i^{(t)} \right\|^2 \le \ \left\| x_p - m_j^{(t)} \right\|^2 \ \forall j, 1 \le j \le k \right\},$$

where each x_p is assigned to exactly one $S^{(t)}$, even if it could be assigned to two or more of them.

Update step: Calculate the new means to be the centroids of the observations in the new clusters.

$$m_i^{(t+1)} = \frac{1}{|S_i^{(t)}|} \sum_{x_j \in S_i^{(t)}} x_j$$

Since the arithmetic mean is a least-squares estimator, this also minimizes the within-cluster sum of squares (WCSS) objective.

The algorithm has converged when the assignments no longer change. Since both steps optimize the WCSS objective, and there only exists a finite number of such partitionings, the algorithm must converge to a (local) optimum. There is no guarantee that the global optimum is found using this algorithm.

The algorithm is often presented as assigning objects to the nearest cluster by distance. The standard algorithm aims at minimizing the WCSS objective, and thus assigns by "least sum of squares", which is exactly equivalent to assigning by the smallest Euclidean distance. Using a different distance function other than (squared) Euclidean distance may stop the algorithm from converging.

Various modifications of k-means such as spherical k-means and k-medoids have been proposed to allow using other distance measures.

Initialization Methods

Commonly used initialization methods are Forgy and Random Partition. The Forgy method randomly chooses k observations from the data set and uses these as the initial means. The Random Partition method first randomly assigns a cluster to each observation and then proceeds to the update step, thus computing the initial mean to be the centroid of the cluster's randomly assigned points. The Forgy method tends to spread the initial means out, while Random Partition places all of them close to the center of the data set. According to Hamerly et al., the Random Partition method is generally preferable for algorithms such as the k-harmonic means and fuzzy k-means. For expectation maximization and standard k-means algorithms, the Forgy method of initialization is preferable.

- Demonstration of the standard algorithm

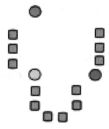

1. k initial "means" (in this case k=3) are randomly generated within the data domain (shown in color).

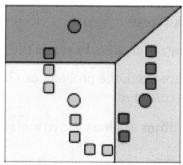

2. k clusters are created by associating every observation with the nearest mean. The partitions here represent the Voronoi diagram generated by the means.

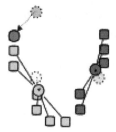

3. The centroid of each of the k clusters becomes the new mean.

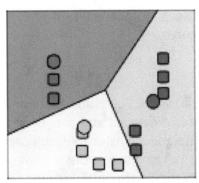

4. Steps 2 and 3 are repeated until convergence has been reached.

As it is a heuristic algorithm, there is no guarantee that it will converge to the global optimum, and the result may depend on the initial clusters. As the algorithm is usually very fast, it is common to run it multiple times with different starting conditions. However, in the worst case, k-means can be very slow to converge: in particular it has been shown that there exist certain point sets, even in 2 dimensions, on which k-means takes exponential time, that is $2^{\Omega(n)}$, to converge. These point sets do not seem to arise in practice: this is corroborated by the fact that the smoothed running time of k-means is polynomial.

The "assignment" step is also referred to as expectation step, the "update step" as maximization step, making this algorithm a variant of the *generalized* expectation-maximization algorithm.

Complexity

Regarding computational complexity, finding the optimal solution to the k-means clustering problem for observations in d dimensions is:

- NP-hard in general Euclidean space d even for 2 clusters

- NP-hard for a general number of clusters k even in the plane

- If k and d (the dimension) are fixed, the problem can be exactly solved in time where n is the number of entities to be clustered

Thus, a variety of heuristic algorithms such as Lloyd's algorithm given above are generally used.

The running time of Lloyd's algorithm is often given as $O(nkdi)$, where n is the number of d-dimensional vectors, k the number of clusters and i the number of iterations needed until convergence. On data that does have a clustering structure, the number of iterations until convergence is often small, and results only improve slightly after the first dozen iterations. Lloyd's algorithm is therefore often considered to be of "linear" complexity in practice.

Following are some recent insights into this algorithm complexity behavior.

- Lloyd's k-means algorithm has polynomial smoothed running time. It is shown that for arbitrary set of n points in $[0,1]^d$, if each point is independently perturbed by a normal distribution with mean 0 and variance σ^2, then the expected running time of k-means algorithm is bounded by $O(n^{34}k^{34}d^8 \log^4(n)/\sigma^6)$,, which is a polynomial in n, k, d and $1/\sigma$.

- Better bounds are proved for simple cases. For example, showed that the running time of k-means algorithm is bounded by $O(dn^4 M^2)$ for n points in an integer lattice $\{1,\ldots,M\}^d$.

Lloyd's algorithm is the standard approach for this problem, However, it spends a lot of processing time computing the distances between each of the k cluster centers and the n data points. Since points usually stay in the same clusters after a few iterations, much of this work is unnecessary, making the naive implementation very inefficient. Some implementations use the triangle inequality in order to create bounds and accelerate Lloyd's algorithm.

Variations

- Jenks natural breaks optimization: k-means applied to univariate data

- k-medians clustering uses the median in each dimension instead of the mean, and this way minimizes L_1 norm (Taxicab geometry).

- k-medoids (also: Partitioning Around Medoids, PAM) uses the medoid instead of the mean, and this way minimizes the sum of distances for *arbitrary* distance functions.

- Fuzzy C-Means Clustering is a soft version of K-means, where each data point has a fuzzy degree of belonging to each cluster.

- Gaussian mixture models trained with expectation-maximization algorithm (EM algorithm) maintains probabilistic assignments to clusters, instead of deterministic assignments, and multivariate Gaussian distributions instead of means.

- k-means++ chooses initial centers in a way that gives a provable upper bound on the WCSS objective.

- The filtering algorithm uses kd-trees to speed up each k-means step.

- Some methods attempt to speed up each k-means step using the triangle inequality.

- Escape local optima by swapping points between clusters.

- The Spherical k-means clustering algorithm is suitable for textual data.

- Hierarchical variants such as Bisecting k-means, X-means clustering and G-means clustering repeatedly split clusters to build a hierarchy, and can also try to automatically determine the optimal number of clusters in a dataset.

- Internal cluster evaluation measures such as cluster silhouette can be helpful at determining the number of clusters.

- Minkowski weighted k-means automatically calculates cluster specific feature weights, supporting the intuitive idea that a feature may have different degrees of relevance at different features. These weights can also be used to re-scale a given data set, increasing the likelihood of a cluster validity index to be optimized at the expected number of clusters.

Discussion

A typical example of the k-means convergence to a local minimum. In this example, the result of k-means clustering (the right figure) contradicts the obvious cluster structure of the data set. The small circles are the data points, the four ray stars are the centroids (means). The initial configuration is on the left figure. The algorithm converges after five iterations presented on the figures, from the left to the right. The illustration was prepared with the Mirkes Java applet.

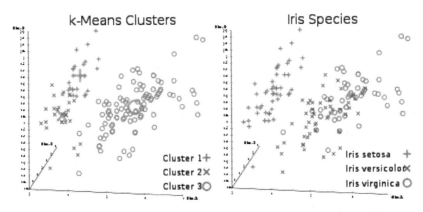

k-means clustering result for the Iris flower data set and actual species visualized using ELKI. Cluster means are marked using larger, semi-transparent symbols.

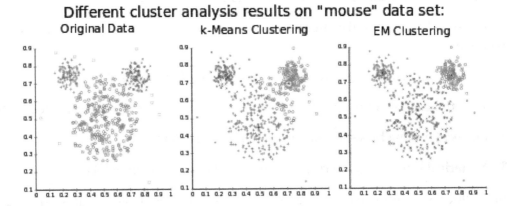

k-means clustering and EM clustering on an artificial dataset ("mouse"). The tendency of *k*-means to produce equi-sized clusters leads to bad results, while EM benefits from the Gaussian distribution present in the data set

Three key features of *k*-means which make it efficient are often regarded as its biggest drawbacks:

- Euclidean distance is used as a metric and variance is used as a measure of cluster scatter.

- The number of clusters *k* is an input parameter: an inappropriate choice of *k* may yield poor results. That is why, when performing k-means, it is important to run diagnostic checks for determining the number of clusters in the data set.

- Convergence to a local minimum may produce counterintuitive ("wrong") results.

A key limitation of k-means is its cluster model. The concept is based on spherical clusters that are separable in a way so that the mean value converges towards the cluster center. The clusters are expected to be of similar size, so that the assignment to the nearest cluster center is the correct assignment. When for example applying k-means with a value of $k = 3$ onto the well-known Iris flower data set, the result often fails to separate the three Iris species contained in the data set. With $k = 2$, the two visible clusters (one containing two species) will be discovered, whereas with $k = 3$ one of the two clusters will be split into two even parts. In fact, $k = 2$ is more appropriate for this data set, despite the data set containing 3 *classes*. As with any other clustering algorithm, the k-means result relies on the data set to satisfy the assumptions made by the clustering algorithms. It works well on some data sets, while failing on others.

The result of k-means can also be seen as the Voronoi cells of the cluster means. Since data is split halfway between cluster means, this can lead to suboptimal splits as can be seen in the "mouse" example. The Gaussian models used by the Expectation-maximization algorithm (which can be seen as a generalization of k-means) are more flexible here by having both variances and covariances. The EM result is thus able to accommodate clusters of variable size much better than k-means as well as correlated clusters (not in this example).

Applications

k-means clustering, in particular when using heuristics such as Lloyd's algorithm, is rather easy to implement and apply even on large data sets. As such, it has been successfully used in various topics, including market segmentation, computer vision, geostatistics, astronomy and agriculture. It often is used as a preprocessing step for other algorithms, for example to find a starting configuration.

Vector Quantization

Two-channel (for illustration purposes -- red and green only) color image.

k-means originates from signal processing, and still finds use in this domain. For example, in computer graphics, color quantization is the task of reducing the color palette of an image to a fixed number of colors k. The k-means algorithm can easily be used for this task and produces competitive results. A use case for this approach is image segmentation. Other uses of vector quantization include non-random sampling, as k-means can easily be used to choose k different but prototypical objects from a large data set for further analysis.

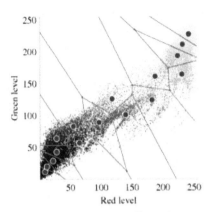

Vector quantization of colors present in the image above into Voronoi cells using k-means.

Cluster Analysis

In cluster analysis, the k-means algorithm can be used to partition the input data set into k partitions (clusters).

However, the pure k-means algorithm is not very flexible, and as such is of limited use (except for when vector quantization as above is actually the desired use case!). In particular, the parameter k is known to be hard to choose (as discussed above) when not given by external constraints. Another limitation of the algorithm is that it cannot be used with arbitrary distance functions or on non-numerical data. For these use cases, many other algorithms have been developed since.

Feature Learning

k-means clustering has been used as a feature learning (or dictionary learning) step, in either (semi-) supervised learning or unsupervised learning. The basic approach is first to train a k-means clustering representation, using the input training data (which need not be labelled). Then, to project any input datum into the new feature space, we have a choice of "encoding" functions, but we can use for example the thresholded matrix-product of the datum with the centroid locations, the distance from the datum to each centroid, or simply an indicator function for the nearest centroid, or some smooth transformation of the distance. Alternatively, by transforming the sample-cluster distance through a Gaussian RBF, one effectively obtains the hidden layer of a radial basis function network.

This use of k-means has been successfully combined with simple, linear classifiers for semi-supervised learning in NLP (specifically for named entity recognition) and in computer vision. On an object recognition task, it was found to exhibit comparable performance with more sophisticated feature learning approaches such as autoencoders and restricted Boltzmann machines. However, it generally requires more data than the sophisticated methods, for equivalent performance, because each data point only contributes to one "feature" rather than multiple.

Relation to other Statistical Machine Learning Algorithms

Gaussian Mixture Model

k-means clustering, and its associated expectation-maximization algorithm, is a special case of a

Gaussian mixture model, specifically, the limit of taking all covariances as diagonal, equal, and small. It is often easy to generalize a k-means problem into a Gaussian mixture model. Another generalization of the k-means algorithm is the K-SVD algorithm, which estimates data points as a sparse linear combination of "codebook vectors". K-means corresponds to the special case of using a single codebook vector, with a weight of 1.

Principal Component Analysis (PCA)

It was proved   that the relaxed solution of k-means clustering, specified by the cluster indicators, is given by principal component analysis (PCA), and the PCA subspace spanned by the principal directions is identical to the cluster centroid subspace. The intuition is that k-means describe spherically shaped (ball-like) clusters. If the data have 2 clusters, the line connecting the two centroids is the best 1-dimensional projection direction, which is also the 1st PCA direction. Cutting the line at the center of mass separate the clusters (this is the continuous relaxation of the discreet cluster indicator). If the data have 3 clusters, the 2-dimensional plane spanned by 3 cluster centroids is the best 2-D projection. This plane is also the first 2 PCA dimensions. Well-separated clusters are effectively modeled by ball-shape clusters and thus discovered by K-means. Non-ball-shaped clusters are hard to separate when they are close-by. For example, two half-moon shaped cluters intertwined in space does not separate well when projected to PCA subspace. But neither is k-means supposed to do well on this data. However, that PCA is a useful relaxation of k-means clustering was not a new result, and it is straightforward to uncover counterexamples to the statement that the cluster centroid subspace is spanned by the principal directions.

Mean Shift Clustering

Basic mean shift clustering algorithms maintain a set of data points the same size as the input data set. Initially, this set is copied from the input set. Then this set is iteratively replaced by the mean of those points in the set that are within a given distance of that point. By contrast, k-means restricts this updated set to k points usually much less than the number of points in the input data set, and replaces each point in this set by the mean of all points in the *input set* that are closer to that point than any other (e.g. within the Voronoi partition of each updating point). A mean shift algorithm that is similar then to k-means, called *likelihood mean shift*, replaces the set of points undergoing replacement by the mean of all points in the input set that are within a given distance of the changing set. One of the advantages of mean shift over k-means is that there is no need to choose the number of clusters, because mean shift is likely to find only a few clusters if indeed only a small number exist. However, mean shift can be much slower than k-means, and still requires selection of a bandwidth parameter. Mean shift has soft variants much as k-means does.

Independent Component Analysis (ICA)

It has been shown in that under sparsity assumptions and when input data is pre-processed with the whitening transformation k-means produces the solution to the linear Independent component analysis task. This aids in explaining the successful application of k-means to feature learning.

Bilateral Filtering

k-means implicitly assumes that the ordering of the input data set does not matter. The bilateral filter is similar to K-means and mean shift in that it maintains a set of data points that are iteratively replaced by means. However, the bilateral filter restricts the calculation of the (kernel weighted) mean to include only points that are close in the ordering of the input data. This makes it applicable to problems such as image denoising, where the spatial arrangement of pixels in an image is of critical importance.

Similar Problems

The set of squared error minimizing cluster functions also includes the k-medoids algorithm, an approach which forces the center point of each cluster to be one of the actual points, i.e., it uses medoids in place of centroids.

Software Implementations

Free Software/Open Source

the following implementations are available under Free/Open Source Software licenses, with publicly available source code.

- Accord.NET contains C# implementations for k-means, k-means++ and k-modes.

- CrimeStat implements two spatial k-means algorithms, one of which allows the user to define the starting locations.

- ELKI contains k-means (with Lloyd and MacQueen iteration, along with different initializations such as k-means++ initialization) and various more advanced clustering algorithms.

- Julia contains a k-means implementation in the JuliaStats Clustering package.

- Mahout contains a MapReduce based k-means.

- MLPACK contains a C++ implementation of k-means.

- Octave contains k-means.

- OpenCV contains a k-means implementation.

- PSPP contains k-means, The QUICK CLUSTER command performs k-means clustering on the dataset.

- R contains three k-means variations.

- SciPy and scikit-learn contain multiple k-means implementations.

- Spark MLlib implements a distributed k-means algorithm.

- Torch contains an *unsup* package that provides k-means clustering.

- Weka contains k-means and x-means.

Proprietary

The following implementations are available under proprietary license terms, and may not have publicly available source code.

- Ayasdi

- MATLAB

- Mathematica

- RapidMiner

- SAP HANA

- SAS

1. SPSS

k-medians Clustering

In statistics and data mining, *k*-medians clustering is a cluster analysis algorithm. It is a variation of *k*-means clustering where instead of calculating the mean for each cluster to determine its centroid, one instead calculates the median. This has the effect of minimizing error over all clusters with respect to the 1-norm distance metric, as opposed to the square of the 2-norm distance metric (which *k*-means does.)

This relates directly to the *k*-median problem which is the problem of finding *k* centers such that the clusters formed by them are the most compact. Formally, given a set of data points *x*, the *k* centers c_i are to be chosen so as to minimize the sum of the distances from each *x* to the nearest c_i.

The criterion function formulated in this way is sometimes a better criterion than that used in the *k*-means clustering algorithm, in which the sum of the squared distances is used. The sum of distances is widely used in applications such as facility location.

The proposed algorithm uses Lloyd-style iteration which alternates between an expectation (E) and maximization (M) step, making this an Expectation–maximization algorithm. In the E step, all objects are assigned to their nearest median. In the M step, the medians are recomputed by using the median in each single dimension.

Medians and Medoids

The median is computed in each single dimension in the Manhattan-distance formulation of the *k*-medians problem, so the individual attributes will come from the dataset. This makes the algorithm more reliable for discrete or even binary data sets. In contrast, the use of means or Euclidean-distance medians will not necessarily yield individual attributes from the dataset. Even with the Manhattan-distance formulation, the individual attributes may come from different instances in the dataset; thus, the resulting median may not be a member of the input dataset.

This algorithm is often confused with the *k*-medoids algorithm. However, a medoid has to be an actual instance from the dataset, while for the multivariate Manhattan-distance median this only holds for single attribute values. The actual median can thus be a combination of multiple instances. For example, given the vectors (0,1), (1,0) and (2,2), the Manhattan-distance median is (1,1), which does not exist in the original data, and thus cannot be a medoid.

Software

- ELKI includes various k-means variants, including k-medians.

- FORTRAN kmedians

- GNU R includes k-medians in the "flexclust" package.

- Stata kmedians

Single-linkage Clustering

In statistics, single-linkage clustering is one of several methods of hierarchical clustering. It is based on grouping clusters in bottom-up fashion (agglomerative clustering), at each step combining two clusters that contain the closest pair of elements not yet belonging to the same cluster as each other.

A drawback of this method is that it tends to produce long thin clusters in which nearby elements of the same cluster have small distances, but elements at opposite ends of a cluster may be much farther from each other than to elements of other clusters. This may lead to difficulties in defining classes that could usefully subdivide the data.

Overview of Agglomerative Clustering Methods

In the beginning of the agglomerative clustering process, each element is in a cluster of its own. The clusters are then sequentially combined into larger clusters, until all elements end up being in the same cluster. At each step, the two clusters separated by the shortest distance are combined. The definition of 'shortest distance' is what differentiates between the different agglomerative clustering methods.

In single-linkage clustering, the distance between two clusters is determined by a single element pair, namely those two elements (one in each cluster) that are closest to each other. The shortest of these links that remains at any step causes the fusion of the two clusters whose elements are involved. The method is also known as nearest neighbour clustering. The result of the clustering can be visualized as a dendrogram, which shows the sequence of cluster fusion and the distance at which each fusion took place.

Mathematically, the linkage function – the distance $D(X,Y)$ between clusters X and Y – is described by the expression

$$D(X,Y) = \min_{x \in X, y \in Y} d(x,y),$$

where X and Y are any two sets of elements considered as clusters, and $d(x,y)$ denotes the distance between the two elements x and y.

Naive Algorithm

The following algorithm is an agglomerative scheme that erases rows and columns in a proximity matrix as old clusters are merged into new ones. The $N \times N$ proximity matrix D contains all distances $d(i,j)$. The clusterings are assigned sequence numbers $0,1,......, (n-1)$ and $L(k)$ is the level of the kth clustering. A cluster with sequence number m is denoted (m) and the proximity between clusters (r) and (s) is denoted $d[(r),(s)]$.

The algorithm is composed of the following steps:

1. Begin with the disjoint clustering having level $L(0) = 0$ and sequence number m = 0.

2. Find the most similar pair of clusters in the current clustering, say pair (r), (s), according to $d[(r),(s)] = \min d[(i),(j)]$ where the minimum is over all pairs of clusters in the current clustering.

3. Increment the sequence number: $m = m + 1$. Merge clusters (r) and (s) into a single cluster to form the next clustering m. Set the level of this clustering to $L(m) = d[(r),(s)]$

4. Update the proximity matrix, D, by deleting the rows and columns corresponding to clusters (r) and (s) and adding a row and column corresponding to the newly formed cluster. The proximity between the new cluster, denoted (r,s) and old cluster (k) is defined as $d[(k), (r,s)] = \min \boldsymbol{d[(k),(r)], d[(k),(s)]}$.

5. If all objects are in one cluster, stop. Else, go to step 2.

Other Linkages

The naive algorithm for single linkage clustering is essentially the same as Kruskal's algorithm for minimum spanning trees. However, in single linkage clustering, the order in which clusters are formed is important, while for minimum spanning trees what matters is the set of pairs of points that form distances chosen by the algorithm.

Alternative linkage schemes include complete linkage clustering, average linkage clustering, and Ward's method. In the naive algorithm for agglomerative clustering, implementing a different linkage scheme may be accomplished simply by using a different formula to calculate inter-cluster distances in the algorithm.. The formula that should be adjusted has been highlighted using bold text. However, more efficient algorithms such as the one described below do not generalize to all linkage schemes in the same way.

Faster Algorithms

The naive algorithm for single-linkage clustering is easy to understand but slow, with time complexity $O(n^3)$. In 1973, R. Sibson proposed an algorithm with time complexity $O(n^2)$ and space complexity $O(n)$(both optimal) known as SLINK. The slink algorithm represents a clustering on a set of n numbered items by two functions. These functions are both determined by finding the smallest cluster C that contains both item i and at least one larger-numbered item. The first function, π, maps item i to the largest-numbered item in cluster C. The second function, λ, maps item i to the distance associated with the creation of cluster C. Storing these functions in two arrays that map each item number to its function value takes space $O(n)$, , and this information is sufficient to determine the clustering itself. As Sibson shows, when a new item is added to the set of items, the updated functions representing the new single-linkage clustering for the augmented set, represented in the same way, can be constructed from the old clustering in time $O(n)$. The SLINK algorithm then loops over the items, one by one, adding them to the representation of the clustering.

An alternative algorithm, running in the same optimal time and space bounds, is based on the equivalence between the naive algorithm and Kruskal's algorithm for minimum spanning trees. Instead of using Kruskal's algorithm, one can use Prim's algorithm, in a variation without binary heaps that takes time $O(n^2)$ and space $O(n)$ to construct the minimum spanning tree (but not the clustering) of the given items and distances. Then, applying Kruskal's algorithm to the sparse graph formed by the edges of the minimum spanning tree produces the clustering itself in an additional time $O(n \log n)$ and space $O(n)$.

Spectral Clustering

In multivariate statistics and the clustering of data, spectral clustering techniques make use of the spectrum (eigenvalues) of the similarity matrix of the data to perform dimensionality reduction before clustering in fewer dimensions. The similarity matrix is provided as an input and consists of a quantitative assessment of the relative similarity of each pair of points in the dataset.

In application to image segmentation, spectral clustering is known as segmentation-based object categorization.

Algorithms

Given an enumerated set of data points, the similarity matrix may be defined as a symmetric matrix A, where $A_{ij} \geq 0$ represents a measure of the similarity between data points with indexes i and j. The general approach to spectral clustering is to use a standard clustering method (there are many such methods, k-means is discussed below) on relevant eigenvectors of a Laplacian matrix of A. There are many different ways to define a Laplacian which have different mathematical interpretations, and so the clustering will also have different interpretations. The eigenvectors that are relevant are the ones that correspond to smallest several eigenvalues of the Laplacian except for the smallest eigenvalue which will have a value of 0. For computational efficiency, these eigenvectors are often computed as the eigenvectors corresponding to the largest several eigenvalues of a function of the Laplacian.

One spectral clustering technique is the normalized cuts algorithm or *Shi–Malik algorithm* introduced by Jianbo Shi and Jitendra Malik, commonly used for image segmentation. It partitions points into two sets (B_1, B_2) based on the eigenvector v corresponding to the second-smallest eigenvalue of the symmetric normalized Laplacian defined as

$$L^{norm} := I - D^{-1/2} A D^{-1/2}$$

where D is the diagonal matrix

$$D_{ii} = \sum_j A_{ij}.$$

A mathematically equivalent algorithm takes the eigenvector corresponding to the largest eigen-value of the random walk normalized Laplacian matrix $P = D^{-1}A$..

Another possibility is to use the Laplacian matrix defined as

$$L := D - A$$

rather than the symmetric normalized Laplacian matrix.

Partitioning may be done in various ways, such as by computing the median m of the components of the second smallest eigenvector v, and placing all points whose component in v is greater than m in B_1, and the rest in B_2. The algorithm can be used for hierarchical clustering by repeatedly partitioning the subsets in this fashion.

If the similarity matrix A has not already been explicitly constructed, the efficiency of spectral clustering may be improved if the solution to the corresponding eigenvalue problem is performed in a matrix-free fashion (without explicitly manipulating or even computing the similarity matrix), as in the Lanczos algorithm.

For large-sized graphs, the second eigenvalue of the (normalized) graph Laplacian matrix is often ill-conditioned, leading to slow convergence of iterative eigenvalue solvers. Preconditioning is a key technology accelerating the convergence, e.g., in the matrix-free LOBPCG method. Spectral clustering has been successfully applied on large graphs by first identifying their community struc-ture, and then clustering communities.

Spectral clustering is closely related to Nonlinear dimensionality reduction, and dimension re-duction techniques such as locally-linear embedding can be used to reduce errors from noise or outliers.

Free software to implement spectral clustering is available in large open source projects like Scikit-learn, MLlib for pseudo-eigenvector clustering using the power iteration method, and R.

Relationship with k-means

The kernel k-means problem is an extension of the k-means problem where the input data points are mapped non-linearly into a higher-dimensional feature space via a kernel function $k(x_i, x_j) = \phi^T(x_i)\phi(x_j)$. The weighted kernel k-means problem further extends this problem by defining a weight w_r for each cluster as the reciprocal of the number of elements in the cluster,

$$\max_{\{C_s\}} \sum_{r=1}^{k} w_r \sum_{x_i, x_j \in C_r} k(x_i, x_j).$$

Suppose F is a matrix of the normalizing coefficients for each point for each cluster $F_{ij} = w_r$ if $i, j \in C_r$ and zero otherwise. Suppose K is the kernel matrix for all points. The weighted kernel

k-means problem with n points and k clusters is given as,

$$\max_{F} \ \text{trace}\left(KF\right)$$

such that,

$$F = G_{n\times k}G^{T}_{k\times n}$$

$$G^{T}G = I$$

such that $\text{rank}(G) = k$. In addition, there are identity constrains on F given by,

$$F \cdot \mathbb{I} = \mathbb{I}$$

where $\mathbb{I}$ represents a vector of ones.

$$F^{T}\mathbb{I} = \mathbb{I}$$

This problem can be recast as,

$$\max_{G} \ \text{trace}\left(G^{T}G\right).$$

This problem is equivalent to the spectral clustering problem when the identity constraints on F are relaxed. In particular, the weighted kernel k-means problem can be reformulated as a spectral clustering (graph partitioning) problem and vice versa. The output of the algorithms are eigenvectors which do not satisfy the identity requirements for indicator variables defined by F. Hence, post-processing of the eigenvectors is required for the equivalence between the problems. Transforming the spectral clustering problem into a weighted kernel k-means problem greatly reduces the computational burden.

Measures to Compare Clusterings

Ravi Kannan, Santosh Vempala and Adrian Vetta in the following paper proposed a bicriteria measure to define the quality of a given clustering. They said that a clustering was an (α, ε)-clustering if the conductance of each cluster(in the clustering) was at least α and the weight of the inter-cluster edges was at most ε fraction of the total weight of all the edges in the graph. They also look at two approximation algorithms in the very same paper.

Hierarchical Clustering

In data mining and statistics, hierarchical clustering (also called hierarchical cluster analysis or HCA) is a method of cluster analysis which seeks to build a hierarchy of clusters. Strategies for hierarchical clustering generally fall into two types:

- Agglomerative: This is a "bottom up" approach: each observation starts in its own cluster, and pairs of clusters are merged as one moves up the hierarchy.

- Divisive: This is a "top down" approach: all observations start in one cluster, and splits are performed recursively as one moves down the hierarchy.

In general, the merges and splits are determined in a greedy manner. The results of hierarchical clustering are usually presented in a dendrogram.

In the general case, the complexity of agglomerative clustering is $O(n^2 \log(n))$, which makes them too slow for large data sets. Divisive clustering with an exhaustive search is $O(2^n)$, which is even worse. However, for some special cases, optimal efficient agglomerative methods (of complexity $O(n^2)$) are known: SLINK for single-linkage and CLINK for complete-linkage clustering.

Cluster Dissimilarity

In order to decide which clusters should be combined (for agglomerative), or where a cluster should be split (for divisive), a measure of dissimilarity between sets of observations is required. In most methods of hierarchical clustering, this is achieved by use of an appropriate metric (a measure of distance between pairs of observations), and a linkage criterion which specifies the dissimilarity of sets as a function of the pairwise distances of observations in the sets.

Metric

The choice of an appropriate metric will influence the shape of the clusters, as some elements may be close to one another according to one distance and farther away according to another. For example, in a 2-dimensional space, the distance between the point (1,0) and the origin (0,0) is always 1 according to the usual norms, but the distance between the point (1,1) and the origin (0,0) can be 2 under Manhattan distance, $\sqrt{2}$ under Euclidean distance, or 1 under maximum distance.

Some commonly used metrics for hierarchical clustering are:

Names	Formula
Euclidean distance	$\|a - b\|_2 = \sqrt{\sum_i (a_i - b_i)^2}$
Squared Euclidean distance	$\|a - b\|_2^2 = \sum_i (a_i - b_i)^2$
Manhattan distance	$\|a - b\|_1 = \sum_i |a_i - b_i|$
maximum distance	$\|a - b\|_\infty = \max_i |a_i - b_i|$
Mahalanobis distance	$\sqrt{(a - b)^\top S^{-1} (a - b)}$ where S is the Covariance matrix

For text or other non-numeric data, metrics such as the Hamming distance or Levenshtein distance are often used.

A review of cluster analysis in health psychology research found that the most common distance measure in published studies in that research area is the Euclidean distance or the squared Euclidean distance.

Linkage Criteria

The linkage criterion determines the distance between sets of observations as a function of the pairwise distances between observations.

Some commonly used linkage criteria between two sets of observations A and B are:

Names	Formula
Maximum or complete-linkage clustering	$\max\{d(a,b) : a \in A, b \in B\}$.
Minimum or single-linkage clustering	$\min\{d(a,b) : a \in A, b \in B\}$.
Mean or average linkage clustering, or UPGMA	$\dfrac{1}{|A||B|}\displaystyle\sum_{a \in A}\sum_{b \in B} d(a,b)$.
Centroid linkage clustering, or UPGMC	$\|c_s - c_t\|$ where c_s and c_t are the centroids of clusters s and t, respectively.
Minimum energy clustering	$\dfrac{2}{nm}\displaystyle\sum_{i,j=1}^{n,m}\|a_i - b_j\|_2 - \dfrac{1}{n^2}\sum_{i,j=1}^{n}\|a_i - a_j\|_2 - \dfrac{1}{m^2}\sum_{i,j=1}^{m}\|b_i - b_j\|_2$

where d is the chosen metric. Other linkage criteria include:

- The sum of all intra-cluster variance.

- The decrease in variance for the cluster being merged (Ward's criterion).

- The probability that candidate clusters spawn from the same distribution function (V-linkage).

- The product of in-degree and out-degree on a k-nearest-neighbour graph (graph degree linkage).

- The increment of some cluster descriptor (i.e., a quantity defined for measuring the quality of a cluster) after merging two clusters.

Discussion

Hierarchical clustering has the distinct advantage that any valid measure of distance can be used. In fact, the observations themselves are not required: all that is used is a matrix of distances.

Agglomerative Clustering Example

For example, suppose this data is to be clustered, and the Euclidean distance is the distance metric.

Cutting the tree at a given height will give a partitioning clustering at a selected precision. In this example, cutting after the second row of the dendrogram will yield clusters {a} {b c} {d e} {f}.

Cutting after the third row will yield clusters {a} {b c} {d e f}, which is a coarser clustering, with a smaller number but larger clusters.

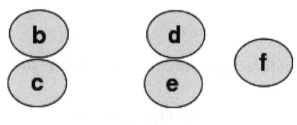

Raw data

The hierarchical clustering dendrogram would be as such:

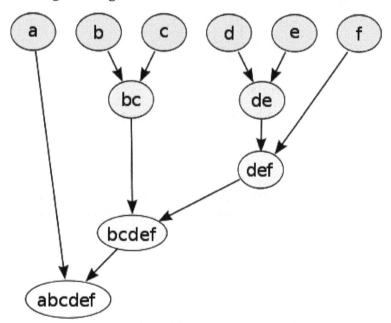

Traditional representation

This method builds the hierarchy from the individual elements by progressively merging clusters. In our example, we have six elements {a} {b} {c} {d} {e} and {f}. The first step is to determine which elements to merge in a cluster. Usually, we want to take the two closest elements, according to the chosen distance.

Optionally, one can also construct a distance matrix at this stage, where the number in the i-th row j-th column is the distance between the i-th and j-th elements. Then, as clustering progresses, rows and columns are merged as the clusters are merged and the distances updated. This is a common way to implement this type of clustering, and has the benefit of caching distances between clusters. A simple agglomerative clustering algorithm is described in the single-linkage clustering page; it can easily be adapted to different types of linkage.

Suppose we have merged the two closest elements b and c, we now have the following clusters $\{a\}$, $\{b, c\}$, $\{d\}$, $\{e\}$ and $\{f\}$, and want to merge them further. To do that, we need to take the distance between $\{a\}$ and $\{b\,c\}$, and therefore define the distance between two clusters. Usually the distance between two clusters $\mathcal{A}$ and $\mathcal{B}$ is one of the following:

- The maximum distance between elements of each cluster (also called complete-linkage clustering):

$$\max\{d(x, y): x \in \mathcal{A}, y \in \mathcal{B}\}.$$

- The minimum distance between elements of each cluster (also called single-linkage clustering):

$$\min\{d(x, y): x \in \mathcal{A}, y \in \mathcal{B}\}.$$

- The mean distance between elements of each cluster (also called average linkage clustering, used e.g. in UPGMA):

$$\frac{1}{|\mathcal{A}| \cdot |\mathcal{B}|} \sum_{x \in \mathcal{A}} \sum_{y \in \mathcal{B}} d(x, y).$$

- The sum of all intra-cluster variance.

- The decrease in variance for the cluster being merged (Ward's method)

- The probability that candidate clusters spawn from the same distribution function (V-linkage).

Each agglomeration occurs at a greater distance between clusters than the previous agglomeration, and one can decide to stop clustering either when the clusters are too far apart to be merged (distance criterion) or when there is a sufficiently small number of clusters (number criterion).

Divisive Clustering

The basic principle of divisive clustering was published as the DIANA (DIvisive ANAlysis Clustering) algorithm. Initially, all data is in the same cluster, and the largest cluster is split until every object is separate. Because there exist $O(2^n)$ ways of splitting each cluster, heuristics are needed. DIANA chooses the object with the maximum average dissimilarity and then moves all objects to this cluster that are more similar to the new cluster than to the remainder. An obvious alternate choice is k-means clustering with $k = 2$, but any other clustering algorithm can be used that always produces at least two clusters.

Software

Open Source Implementations

Hierarchical clustering dendrogram of the Iris dataset (using R). Source

- Cluster 3.0 provides a Graphical User Interface to access to different clustering routines and is available for Windows, Mac OS X, Linux, Unix.

- ELKI includes multiple hierarchical clustering algorithms, various linkage strategies and also includes the efficient SLINK, CLINK and Anderberg algorithms, flexible cluster extraction from dendrograms and various other cluster analysis algorithms.

- Octave, the GNU analog to MATLAB implements hierarchical clustering in linkage function

- Orange, a free data mining software suite, module orngClustering for scripting in Python, or cluster analysis through visual programming.

- R has several functions for hierarchical clustering.

- SCaViS computing environment in Java that implements this algorithm.

- scikit-learn implements a hierarchical clustering.

- Weka includes hierarchical cluster analysis.

Commercial

- MATLAB includes hierarchical cluster analysis.

- SAS includes hierarchical cluster analysis in PROC CLUSTER.

- Mathematica includes a Hierarchical Clustering Package.

- NCSS (statistical software) includes hierarchical cluster analysis.

- SPSS includes hierarchical cluster analysis.

- Qlucore Omics Explorer includes hierarchical cluster analysis.

- Stata includes hierarchical cluster analysis.

References

- Bailey, Ken (1994). "Numerical Taxonomy and Cluster Analysis". Typologies and Taxonomies. p. 34. ISBN 9780803952591.

- Meilă, Marina (2003). "Comparing Clusterings by the Variation of Information". Learning Theory and Kernel Machines. Lecture Notes in Computer Science. 2777: 173–187. doi:10.1007/978-3-540-45167-9_14. ISBN 978-3-540-40720-1.

- Manning, Christopher D.; Raghavan, Prabhakar; Schütze, Hinrich. Introduction to Information Retrieval. Cambridge University Press. ISBN 978-0-521-86571-5.

- MacKay, David (2003). "Chapter 20. An Example Inference Task: Clustering" (PDF). Information Theory, Inference and Learning Algorithms. Cambridge University Press. pp. 284–292. ISBN 0-521-64298-1.

- Press, WH; Teukolsky, SA; Vetterling, WT; Flannery, BP (2007). "Section 16.1. Gaussian Mixture Models and k-Means Clustering". Numerical Recipes: The Art of Scientific Computing (3rd ed.). New York: Cambridge University Press. ISBN 978-0-521-88068-8.

- Drake, Jonathan (2012). "Accelerated k-means with adaptive distance bounds" (PDF). the 5th NIPS Workshop on Optimization for Machine Learning, OPT2012.

7

Common Data Mining Software

The common data mining software are H2O, SAS, Orange, Massive Online Analysis, Natural Language Toolkit and General Architecture for Text Engineering. H2O is a software that is used for analysis of data. The speed of H2O allows users to fit thousands of models in order to discover patterns in data. This section is an overview of the subject matter, incorporating all the aspects of common data mining software.

H2O (Software)

H2O is open-source software for big-data analysis. It is produced by the start-up *H2O.ai* (formerly *oxdata*), which launched in 2011 in Silicon Valley. The speed and flexibility of H2O allow users to fit hundreds or thousands of potential models as part of discovering patterns in data. With H2O, users can throw models at data to find usable information, allowing H2O to discover patterns. Using H2O, Cisco estimates each month 20 thousand models of its customers' propensities to buy.

H2O's mathematical core is developed with the leadership of Arno Candel; after H2O was rated as the best "open-source Java machine learning project" by GitHub's programming members, Candel was named to the first class of "Big Data All Stars" by *Fortune* in 2014. The firm's scientific advisors are experts on statistical learning theory and mathematical optimization.

The H2O software runs can be called from the statistical package *R* and other environments. It is used for exploring and analyzing datasets held in cloud computing systems and in the Apache Hadoop Distributed File System as well as in the conventional operating-systems Linux, macOS, and Microsoft Windows. The H2O software is written in Java, Python, and *R*. Its graphical-user interface is compatible with four popular browsers: Chrome, Safari, Firefox, and Internet Explorer.

H2O

The H2O project aims to develop an analytical interface for cloud computing, providing users with intuitive tools for data analysis.

Leadership

H2O's chief executive, SriSatish Ambati, had helped to start Platfora, a big-data firm that develops software for the Apache Hadoop distributed file system. Ambati was frustrated with the performance of the *R* programming language on large data-sets and started the development of H2O software with encouragement from John Chambers, who created the *S* programming language at Bell Labs and who is a member of *R*'s core team (which leads the development of *R*).

Ambati co-founded oxdata with Cliff Click, who served as the chief technical officer of H2O and helped create much of H2O's product. Click helped to write the HotSpot Server Compiler and worked with Azul Systems to construct a big-data Java virtual machine (JVM). Click left H2O in February 2016.

H2O.ai was co-founded by Cliff Click and SriSatish Ambati. (Photograph by H2O.ai released under Creative Commons BY 2.0 license.)

Mathematical leadership is provided by the Dr. Arno Candel, who has the title "physicist and hacker". Candel was a founding engineer at Skytree, where he implemented methods for machine learning, before he developed the mathematical core of H2O. After H2O was rated as the best "open-source Java machine learning project" by GitHub's programming members, Candel (with 19 others) was named to the first class of "Big Data All Stars" by *Fortune*.

Scientific Advisory Council

Stanford University professor Trevor J. Hastie serves as an advisor to H2O.ai.

H2O's Scientific Advisory Council lists three mathematical scientists, who are all professors at Stanford University: Professor Stephen P. Boyd is an expert in convex minimization and applications in statistics and electrical engineering. Robert Tibshirani, a collaborator with Bradley Efron on bootstrapping, is an expert on generalized additive models and statistical learning theory. Trevor Hastie, a collaborator of John Chambers on *S*, is an expert on generalized additive models and statistical learning theory.

H2o.ai: A Silicon Valley Start-Up

The software is open-source and freely distributed. The company receives fees for providing customer service and customized extensions. In November 2014, its twenty clients included Cisco, eBay, Nielsen, and PayPal, according to *VentureBeat*. The speed and flexibility of H2O allow users to fit hundreds or thousands of potential models as part of discovering patterns in data. With H2O, users can throw models at data to find usable information, according to Tye Rattenbury at Trifacta. Using H2O, Cisco estimates each month 20 thousand models of its customers' propensities to buy while Google fits different models for each client according to the time of day.

Mining of Big Data

Big datasets are too large to be analyzed using traditional software like R. The H2O software provides data structures and methods suitable for big data.

H2O allow users to analyze and visualize whole sets of data without using the Procrustean strategy of studying only a small subset with a conventional statistical package. H2O's statistical repertoire includes generalized linear models and K-means clustering.

Iterative Methods for Real-time Problems

H2O uses iterative methods that provide quick answers using all of the client's data. When a client cannot wait for an optimal solution, the client can interrupt the computations and use an approximate solution.

In its approach to deep learning, H2O divides all the data into subsets and then analyzing each subset simultaneously using the same method. These processes are combined to estimate parameters by using the Hogwild scheme, a parallel stochastic gradient method. These methods allow H2O to provide answers that use all the client's data, rather than throwing away most of it and analyzing a subset with conventional software.

Software

Programming Languages

The H2O software has an interface to the following programming languages: Java (6 or later), Python (2.7.x, 3.5.x), R (3.0.0 or later) and Scala (1.4-1.6).

Operating Systems

The H2O software can be run on conventional operating-systems: Microsoft Windows (7 or later), Mac OS X (10.9 or later), and Linux (Ubuntu 12.04 ; RHEL/CentOS 6 or later), It also runs on big-data systems, particularly Apache Hadoop Distributed File System (HDFS), several popular versions: Cloudera (5.1 or later), MapR (3.0 or later), and Hortonworks (HDP 2.1 or later). It also operates on cloud computing environments, for example using Amazon EC2, Google Compute Engine, and Microsoft Azure. The H2O Sparkling Water software is Databricks-certified on Apache Spark.

Graphical user Interface and Browsers

Its graphical user interface is compatible with four browsers (unless specified, in their latest versions as of 1 June 2015): Chrome, Safari, Firefox, Internet Explorer (IE10).

SAS (Software)

SAS (Statistical Analysis System) is a software suite developed by SAS Institute for advanced analytics, multivariate analyses, business intelligence, data management, and predictive analytics.

SAS was developed at North Carolina State University from 1966 until 1976, when SAS Institute was incorporated. SAS was further developed in the 1980s and 1990s with the addition of new statistical procedures, additional components and the introduction of JMP. A point-and-click interface was added in version 9 in 2004. A social media analytics product was added in 2010.

Technical Overview and Terminology

SAS is a software suite that can mine, alter, manage and retrieve data from a variety of sources and perform statistical analysis on it. SAS provides a graphical point-and-click user interface for non-technical users and more advanced options through the SAS language. In order to use Statistical Analysis System, Data should be in an spreadsheet table format or SAS format. SAS programs have a DATA step, which retrieves and manipulates data, usually creating a SAS data set, and a PROC step, which analyzes the data.

Each step consists of a series of statements. The DATA step has executable statements that result in the software taking an action, and declarative statements that provide instructions to read a data set or alter the data's appearance. The DATA step has two phases, compilation and execution. In the compilation phase, declarative statements are processed and syntax errors are identified. Afterwards, the execution phase processes each executable statement sequentially. Data sets are organized into tables with rows called "observations" and columns called "variables". Additionally, each piece of data has a descriptor and a value.

The PROC step consists of PROC statements that call upon named procedures. Procedures perform analysis and reporting on data sets to produce statistics, analyses and graphics. There are more than 300 procedures and each one contains a substantial body of programming and statistical work. PROC statements can also display results, sort data or perform other operations. SAS Macros are pieces of code or variables that are coded once and referenced to perform repetitive tasks.

SAS data can be published in HTML, PDF, Excel and other formats using the Output Delivery System, which was first introduced in 2007. The SAS Enterprise Guide is SAS' point-and-click interface. It generates code to manipulate data or perform analysis automatically and does not require SAS programming experience to use.

The SAS software suite has more than 200 components Some of the SAS components include:

- Base SAS – Basic procedures and data management
- SAS/STAT – Statistical analysis
- SAS/GRAPH – Graphics and presentation
- SAS/OR – Operations research
- SAS/ETS – Econometrics and Time Series Analysis
- SAS/IML – Interactive matrix language
- SAS/AF – Applications facility
- SAS/QC – Quality control
- SAS/INSIGHT – Data mining
- SAS/PH – Clinical trial analysis
- Enterprise Miner – data mining
- Enterprise Guide - GUI based code editor & project manager
- SAS EBI - Suite of Business Intelligence Applications
- SAS Grid Manager - Manager of SAS grid computing environment

History

Origins

The development of SAS began in 1966 after North Carolina State University re-hired Anthony Barr to program his analysis of variance and regression software so that it would run on IBM System/360 computers. The project was funded by the National Institute of Health and was originally intended to analyze agricultural data to improve crop yields. Barr was joined by student James Goodnight, who developed the software's statistical routines, and the two became project-leaders. In 1968, Barr and Goodnight integrated new multiple regression and analysis of variance routines. In 1972, after issuing the first release of SAS, the project lost its funding. According to Goodnight, this was because NIH only wanted to fund projects with medical applications. Goodnight continued teaching at the university for a salary of $1 and access to mainframe computers for use with the project, until it was funded by the University Statisticians of the Southern Experiment Stations the following year. John Sall joined the project in 1973 and contributed to the software's econometrics, time series, and matrix algebra. Another early participant, Caroll G. Perkins, contributed to SAS' early programming. Jolayne W. Service and Jane T. Helwig created SAS' first documentation.

The first versions of SAS were named after the year in which they were released. In 1971, SAS 71 was published as a limited release. It was used only on IBM mainframes and had the main elements of SAS programming, such as the DATA step and the most common procedures in the PROC step. The following year a full version was released as SAS 72, which introduced the MERGE statement and added features for handling missing data or combining data sets. In 1976, Barr, Goodnight, Sall, and Helwig removed the project from North Carolina State and incorporated it into SAS Institute, Inc.

Development

SAS was re-designed in SAS 76 with an open architecture that allowed for compilers and procedures. The INPUT and INFILE statements were improved so they could read most data formats used by IBM mainframes. Generating reports was also added through the PUT and FILE statements. The ability to analyze general linear models was also added as was the FORMAT procedure, which allowed developers to customize the appearance of data. In 1979, SAS 79 added support for the CMS operating system and introduced the DATASETS procedure. Three years later, SAS 82 introduced an early macro language and the APPEND procedure.

SAS version 4 had limited features, but made SAS more accessible. Version 5 introduced a complete macro language, array subscripts, and a full-screen interactive user interface called Display Manager. In 1985, SAS was rewritten in the C programming language. This allowed for the SAS' Multivendor Architecture that allows the software to run on UNIX, MS-DOS, and Windows. It was previously written in PL/I, Fortran, and assembly language.

In the 1980s and 1990s, SAS released a number of components to complement Base SAS. SAS/GRAPH, which produces graphics, was released in 1980, as well as the SAS/ETS component, which supports econometric and time series analysis. A component intended for pharmaceutical users, SAS/PH-Clinical, was released in the 1990s. The Food and Drug Administration standardized on SAS/PH-Clinical for new drug applications in 2002. Vertical products like SAS Financial Management and SAS Human Capital Management (then called CFO Vision and HR Vision respectively) were also introduced. JMP was developed by SAS co-founder John Sall and a team of developers to take advantage of the graphical user interface introduced in the 1984 Apple Macintosh and shipped for the first time in 1989. Updated versions of JMP were released continuously after 2002 with the most recent release being from 2012.

SAS version 6 was used throughout the 1990s and was available on a wider range of operating systems, including Macintosh, OS/2, Silicon Graphics, and Primos. SAS introduced new features through dot-releases. From 6.06 to 6.09, a user interface based on the windows paradigm was introduced and support for SQL was added. Version 7 introduced the Output Delivery System (ODS) and an improved text editor. ODS was improved upon in successive releases. For example, more output options were added in version 8. The number of operating systems that were supported was reduced to UNIX, Windows and z/OS, and Linux was added. SAS version 8 and SAS Enterprise Miner were released in 1999.

Recent History

In 2002, the Text Miner software was introduced. Text Miner analyzes text data like emails for patterns in Business Intelligence applications. In 2004, SAS Version 9.0 was released, which was dubbed "Project Mercury" and was designed to make SAS accessible to a broader range of business users. Version 9.0 added custom user interfaces based on the user's role and established the point-and-click user interface of SAS Enterprise Guide as the software's primary graphical user interface (GUI). The Customer Relationship Management (CRM) features were improved in 2004 with SAS Interaction Management. In 2008 SAS announced Project Unity, designed to integrate data quality, data integration and master data management.

SAS sued World Programming, the developers of a competing implementation, World Programming System, alleging that they had infringed SAS's copyright in part by implementing the same functionality. This case was referred from the United Kingdom's High Court of Justice to the European Court of Justice on 11 August 2010. In May 2012, the European Court of Justice ruled in favor of World Programming, finding that "the functionality of a computer program and the programming language cannot be protected by copyright."

A free version was introduced for students in 2010. SAS Social Media Analytics, a tool for social media monitoring, engagement and sentiment analysis, was also released that year. SAS Rapid Predictive Modeler (RPM), which creates basic analytical models using Microsoft Excel, was introduced that same year. JMP 9 in 2010 added a new interface for using the R programming language from JMP and an add-in for Excel. The following year, a High Performance Computing appliance was made available in a partnership with Teradata and EMC Greenplum. In 2011, the company released Enterprise Miner 7.1. The company introduced 27 data management products from October 2013 to October 2014 and updates to 160 others. At the 2015 SAS Global Forum, it announced several new products that were specialized for different industries, as well as new training software.

Software Products

As of 2011 SAS's largest set of products is its line for customer intelligence. Numerous SAS modules for web, social media and marketing analytics may be used to profile customers and prospects, predict their behaviors and manage and optimize communications. SAS also provides the SAS Fraud Framework. The framework's primary functionality is to monitor transactions across different applications, networks and partners and use analytics to identify anomalies that are indicative of fraud. SAS Enterprise GRC (Governance, Risk and Compliance) provides risk modeling, scenario analysis and other functions in order to manage and visualize risk, compliance and corporate policies. There is also a SAS Enterprise Risk Management product-set designed primarily for banks and financial services organizations.

SAS' products for monitoring and managing the operations of IT systems are collectively referred to as SAS IT Management Solutions. SAS collects data from various IT assets on performance and utilization, then creates reports and analyses. SAS' Performance Management products consolidate and provide graphical displays for key performance indicators (KPIs) at the employee, department and organizational level. The SAS Supply Chain Intelligence product suite is offered for supply chain needs, such as forecasting product demand, managing distribution and inventory and optimizing pricing. There is also a "SAS for Sustainability Management" set of software to forecast environmental, social and economic effects and identify causal relationships between operations and an impact on the environmental or ecosystem.

SAS has product sets for specific industries, such as government, retail, telecommunications and aerospace and for marketing optimization or high-performance computing.

Comparison to Other Products

In a 2005 article for the *Journal of Marriage and Family* comparing statistical packages from SAS and its competitors Stata and SPSS, Alan C. Acock wrote that SAS programs provide "extraordinary range of data analysis and data management tasks," but were difficult to use and learn. SPSS and Stata, meanwhile, were both easier to learn (with better documentation) but had less capable analytic abilities, though these could be expanded with paid (in SPSS) or free (in Stata) add-ons.

Acock concluded that SAS was best for power users, while occasional users would benefit most from SPSS and Stata. A comparison by the University of California, Los Angeles, gave similar results.

Competitors such as Revolution Analytics and Alpine Data Labs advertise their products as considerably cheaper than SAS'. In a 2011 comparison, Doug Henschen of *InformationWeek* found that start-up fees for the three are similar, though he admitted that the starting fees were not necessarily the best basis for comparison. SAS' business model is not weighted as heavily on initial fees for its programs, instead focusing on revenue from annual subscription fees.

Adoption

According to IDC, SAS is the largest market-share holder in "advanced analytics" with 35.4 percent of the market as of 2013. It is the fifth largest market-share holder for business intelligence (BI) software with a 6.9% share and the largest independent vendor. It competes in the BI market against conglomerates, such as SAP BusinessObjects, IBM Cognos, SPSS Modeler, Oracle Hyperion, and Microsoft BI. SAS has been named in the Gartner Leader's Quadrant for Data Integration Tools and for Business Intelligence and Analytical Platforms. A study published in 2011 in *BMC Health Services Research* found that SAS was used in 42.6 percent of data analyses in health service research, based on a sample of 1,139 articles drawn from three journals.

Orange (Software)

Orange is a free software machine learning and data mining package (written in Python). It has a visual programming front-end for explorative data analysis and visualization, and can also be used as a Python library. The program is maintained and developed by the Bioinformatics Laboratory of the Faculty of Computer and Information Science at University of Ljubljana.

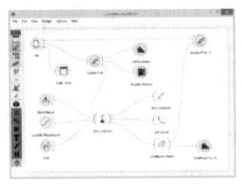

A typical workflow in Orange 3.

Description

Orange is a component-based visual programming software package for data mining, machine learning and data analysis.

Components are called widgets and they range from simple data visualization, subset selection and preprocessing, to empirical evaluation of learning algorithms and predictive modeling.

Visual programming is implemented through an interface in which workflows are created by linking predefined or user-designed widgets, while advanced users can use Orange as a Python library for data manipulation and widget alteration.

Software

Orange is an open-source software package released under GPL and available for use on github. Versions up to 3.0 include core components in C++ with wrappers in Python. From version 3.0 onwards, Orange uses common Python open-source libraries for scientific computing, such as numpy, scipy and scikit-learn, while its graphical user interface operates within the cross-platform Qt framework.

The default installation includes a number of machine learning, preprocessing and data visualization algorithms in 6 widget sets (data, visualize, classify, regression, evaluate and unsupervised). Additional functionalities are available as add-ons (bioinformatics, data fusion and text-mining).

Orange is supported on OS X, Windows and Linux and can also be installed from the Python Package Index repository (*pip install Orange*). As of 2016 the stable version is 3.3 and runs with Python 3, while the legacy version 2.7 that runs with Python 2.7 is still available.

Features

Orange consists of a canvas interface onto which the user places widgets and creates a data analysis workflow. Widgets offer basic functionalities such as reading the data, showing a data table, selecting features, training predictors, comparing learning algorithms, visualizing data elements, etc. The user can interactively explore visualizations or feed the selected subset into other widgets.

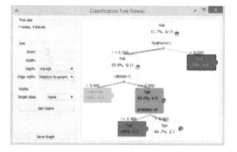

Classification Tree widget in Orange 3.0

- Canvas: graphical front-end for data analysis

- Widgets:

    - Data: widgets for data input, data filtering, sampling, imputation, feature manipulation and feature selection

    - Visualize: widgets for common visualization (box plot, histograms, scatter plot) and multivariate visualization (mosaic display, sieve diagram).

- Classify: a set of supervised machine learning algorithms for classification

- Regression: a set of supervised machine learning algorithms for regression

- Evaluate: cross-validation, sampling-based procedures, reliability estimation and scoring of prediction methods

- Unsupervised: unsupervised learning algorithms for clustering (k-means, hierarchical clustering) and data projection techniques (multidimensional scaling, principal component analysis, correspondence analysis).

- Add-ons:

- Associate: widgets for mining frequent itemsets and association rule learning

- Bioinformatics: widgets for gene set analysis, enrichment, and access to pathway libraries

- Data fusion: widgets for fusing different data sets, collective matrix factorization, and exploration of latent factors

- Educational: widgets for teaching machine learning concepts, such as k-means clustering, polynomial regression, stochastic gradient descent, ...

- Image analytics: widgets for working with images and ImageNet embeddings

- Network: widgets for graph and network analysis

- Text mining: widgets for natural language processing and text mining

- Time series: widgets for time series analysis and modeling

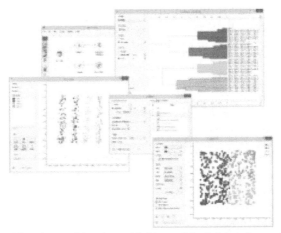

Paint Data widget in combination with hierarchical clustering and k-Means.

Objectives

The program provides a platform for experiment selection, recommendation systems and predictive modeling and is used in biomedicine, bioinformatics, genomic research, and teaching. In science, it is used as a platform for testing new machine learning algorithms and for implementing new techniques in genetics and bioinformatics. In education, it was used for teaching machine learning and data mining methods to students of biology, biomedicine and informatics.

History

- In 1996, the University of Ljubljana and Jožef Stefan Institute started development of ML*, a machine learning framework in C++.

- In 1997, Python bindings were developed for ML*, which together with emerging Python modules formed a joint framework called Orange.

- During the following years most major algorithms for data mining and machine learning have been developed either in C++ (Orange's core) or in Python modules.

- In 2002, first prototypes to create a flexible graphical user interface were designed, using Pmw Python megawidgets.

- In 2003, graphical user interface was redesigned and re-developed for Qt framework using PyQt Python bindings. The visual programming framework was defined, and development of widgets (graphical components of data analysis pipeline) has begun.

- In 2005, extensions for data analysis in bioinformatics was created.

- In 2008, Mac OS X DMG and Fink-based installation packages were developed.

- In 2009, over 100 widgets were created and maintained.

- From 2009, Orange is in 2.0 beta and web site offers installation packages based on daily compiling cycle.

- In 2012, new object hierarchy was imposed, replacing the old module-based structure.

- In 2013, a major GUI redesign.

- In 2015, Orange 3.0 is released.

- In 2016, Orange is in version 3.3. The development uses monthly stable release cycle.

Massive Online Analysis

MOA (Massive Online Analysis) is a free open-source software specific for Data stream mining with Concept drift. It is written in Java and developed at the University of Waikato, New Zealand.

Description

MOA is an open-source framework software that allows to build and run experiments of machine learning or data mining on evolving data streams. It includes a set of learners and stream generators that can be used from the Graphical User Interface (GUI), the command-line, and the Java API. MOA contains several collections of machine learning algorithms:

- Classification

    - Bayesian classifiers

- Naive Bayes

- Naive Bayes Multinomial
    - Decision trees classifiers
- Decision Stump
- Hoeffding Tree
- Hoeffding Option Tree
- Hoeffding Adaptive Tree
    - Meta classifiers
- Bagging
- Boosting
- Bagging using ADWIN
- Bagging using Adaptive-Size Hoeffding Trees.
- Perceptron Stacking of Restricted Hoeffding Trees
- Leveraging Bagging
- Online Accuracy Updated Ensemble
    - Function classifiers
- Perceptron
- Stochastic gradient descent (SGD)
- Pegasos
    - Drift classifiers
    - Multi-label classifiers
    - Active learning classifiers
- Regression
    - FIMTDD
    - AMRules
- Clustering
    - StreamKM++
    - CluStream
    - ClusTree
    - D-Stream
    - CobWeb.

- Outlier detection

    - STORM

    - Abstract-C

    - COD

    - MCOD

    - AnyOut

- Recommender systems

    - BRISMFPredictor

- Frequent pattern mining

    - Itemsets

    - Graphs

- Change detection algorithms

These algorithms are designed for large scale machine learning, dealing with concept drift, and big data streams in real time.

MOA supports bi-directional interaction with Weka (machine learning). MOA is free software released under the GNU GPL.

Natural Language Toolkit

Parse tree generated with NLTK

The Natural Language Toolkit, or more commonly NLTK, is a suite of libraries and programs for symbolic and statistical natural language processing (NLP) for English written in the Python programming language. It was developed by Steven Bird and Edward Loper in the Department of Computer and Information Science at the University of Pennsylvania. NLTK includes graphical demonstrations and sample data. It is accompanied by a book that explains the underlying concepts behind the language processing tasks supported by the toolkit, plus a cookbook.

NLTK is intended to support research and teaching in NLP or closely related areas, including empirical linguistics, cognitive science, artificial intelligence, information retrieval, and machine learning. NLTK has been used successfully as a teaching tool, as an individual study tool, and as a platform for prototyping and building research systems.There are 32 universities in the US and 25 countries using NLTK in their courses. NLTK supports classification, tokenization, stemming, tagging, parsing, and semantic reasoning functionalities.

Library Highlights

- Lexical analysis: Word and text tokenizer

- n-gram and collocations

- Part-of-speech tagger

- Tree model and Text chunker for capturing

- Named-entity recognition

OpenNN

OpenNN (Open Neural Networks Library) is a software library written in the C++ programming language which implements neural networks, a main area of deep learning research. The library is open source, licensed under the GNU Lesser General Public License.

Characteristics

The software implements any number of layers of non-linear processing units for supervised learning. This deep architecture allows the design of neural networks with universal approximation properties. Additionally, it allows multiprocessing programming by means of OpenMP, in order to increase computer performance.

OpenNN contains data mining algorithms as a bundle of functions. These can be embedded in other software tools, using an application programming interface, for the integration of the predictive analytics tasks. In this regard, a graphical user interface is missing but some functions can be supported by specific visualization tools.

History

The development started in 2003 at the International Center for Numerical Methods in Engineering (CIMNE), within the research project funded by the European Union called RAMFLOOD. Then it continued as part of similar projects. At present, OpenNN is being developed by the startup company Artelnics.

In 2014, *Big Data Analytics Today* rated OpenNN as the #1 brain inspired artificial intelligence project. Also, during the same year, *ToppersWorld* selected OpenNN among the top 5 open source data mining tools.

Applications

OpenNN is a general purpose artificial intelligence software package. It uses machine learning techniques for solving data mining and predictive analytics tasks in different fields. For instance, the library has been applied in the engineering, energy, or chemistry sectors.

Related Libraries

- Deeplearning4j, a deep learning library written for Java and Scala which is open source.

- Torch, an open source framework written in Lua with wide support for machine learning algorithms.

General Architecture for Text Engineering

General Architecture for Text Engineering or GATE is a Java suite of tools originally developed at the University of Sheffield beginning in 1995 and now used worldwide by a wide community of scientists, companies, teachers and students for many natural language processing tasks, including information extraction in many languages.

GATE has been compared to NLTK, R and RapidMiner. As well as being widely used in its own right, it forms the basis of the KIM semantic platform.

GATE community and research has been involved in several European research projects including TAO, SEKT, NeOn, Media-Campaign, Musing, Service-Finder, LIRICS and KnowledgeWeb, as well as many other projects.

As of May 28, 2011, 881 people are on the gate-users mailing list at SourceForge.net, and 111,932 downloads from SourceForge are recorded since the project moved to SourceForge in 2005. The paper "GATE: A Framework and Graphical Development Environment for Robust NLP Tools and Applications" has received over 800 citations in the seven years since publication (according to Google Scholar). Books covering the use of GATE, in addition to the GATE User Guide, include "Building Search Applications: Lucene, LingPipe, and Gate", by Manu Konchady, and "Introduction to Linguistic Annotation and Text Analytics", by Graham Wilcock.

Features

GATE includes an information extraction system called ANNIE (A Nearly-New Information Extraction System) which is a set of modules comprising a tokenizer, a gazetteer, a sentence splitter, a part of speech tagger, a named entities transducer and a coreference tagger. ANNIE can be used as-is to provide basic information extraction functionality, or provide a starting point for more specific tasks.

Languages currently handled in GATE include English, Chinese, Arabic, Bulgarian, French, German, Hindi, Italian, Cebuano, Romanian, Russian, Danish.

Plugins are included for machine learning with Weka, RASP, MAXENT, SVM Light, as well as a LIBSVM integration and an in-house perceptron implementation, for managing ontologies like WordNet, for querying search engines like Google or Yahoo, for part of speech tagging with Brill or TreeTagger, and many more. Many external plugins are also available, for handling e.g. tweets.

GATE accepts input in various formats, such as TXT, HTML, XML, Doc, PDF documents, and Java Serial, PostgreSQL, Lucene, Oracle Databases with help of RDBMS storage over JDBC.

JAPE transducers are used within GATE to manipulate annotations on text. Documentation is provided in the GATE User Guide. A tutorial has also been written by Press Association Images.

GATE Developer

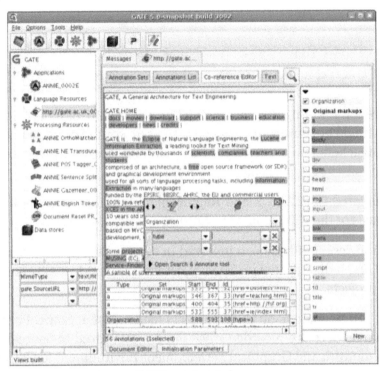

GATE 5 main window.

The screenshot shows the document viewer used to display a document and its annotations. In pink are <A> hyperlink annotations from an HTML file. The right list is the annotation sets list, and the bottom table is the annotation list. In the center is the annotation editor window.

GATE Mímir

Generate vast quantities of information including; natural language text, semantic annotations, and ontological information. Sometimes the data itself is the end product of an application but often the information would be more useful if it could be efficiently searched. GATE Mimir provides support for indexing and searching the linguistic and semantic information generated by such applications and allows for querying the information using arbitrary combinations of text, structural information, and SPARQL.

References

- Boyd, Stephen P.; Vandenberghe, Lieven (2004). Convex optimization. Cambridge University Press. ISBN 978-0-521-83378-3. Retrieved October 15, 2011. (Free download of PDF of corrected 7th printing, 2009)

- "Encyclopedia of Research Design Encyclopedia of research design". 2010. doi:10.4135/9781412961288. ISBN 9781412961271.

- Lora D. Delwiche; Susan J. Slaughter (2012). The Little SAS Book: A Primer : a Programming Approach. SAS Institute. p. 6. ISBN 978-1-61290-400-9.

- N. Jyoti Bass; K. Madhavi Lata & Kogent Solutions (1 September 2007). Base Sas Programming Black Book, 2007 Ed. Dreamtech Press. pp. 365–. ISBN 978-81-7722-769-7.

- Alan Agresti; Xiao-Li Meng (2 November 2012). Strength in Numbers: The Rising of Academic Statistics Departments in the U. S.: The Rising of Academic Statistics Departments in the U.S. Springer. p. 177. ISBN 978-1-4614-3649-2.

- Ian Cox; Marie A. Gaudard; Philip J. Ramsey; Mia L. Stephens; Leo Wright (21 December 2009). Visual Six Sigma: Making Data Analysis Lean. John Wiley & Sons. pp. 23–. ISBN 978-0-470-50691-2. Retrieved 16 November 2012.

- Bird, Steven; Klein, Ewan; Loper, Edward (2009). Natural Language Processing with Python. O'Reilly Media Inc. ISBN 0-596-51649-5.

- Gage, Deborah (15 April 2013). "Platfora founder goes in search of big-data answers". Wall Street Journal. Retrieved 2 June 2015.

- Hackett, Robert (3 August 2014), Nusca, Andrew; Hackett, Robert; Gupta, Shalene, eds., "Arno Candel, physicist and hacker, 0xdata", Fortune, Meet Fortune's 2014 Big Data All-Stars, retrieved 2 June 2015

- Harris, Derrick (14 August 2012). "How 0xdata wants to help everyone become data scientists". Gigaom Research. Retrieved 1 June 2015.

- Novet, Jordan (7 November 2014). "0xdata takes $8.9M and becomes H2O to match its open-source machine-learning project". VentureBeat. Retrieved 1 June 2015.

- Henschen, Dough (July 26, 2011). "Low-Cost Options For Predictive Analytics Challenge SAS, IBM". InformationWeek. Retrieved January 12, 2014.

- Ranii, David (January 20, 2012). "SAS' revenue up 12% in 2011". The News & Observer,. Raleigh, North Carolina. Retrieved January 12, 2014.

Applications of Data Mining

Predictive analytics is a technique that helps in analyzing current and historical facts. These facts help in making predictions for unknown events. Decision support system and web mining are the other applications of data mining. Data mining can best be understood in confluence with the major applications listed in the following chapter.

Predictive Analytics

Predictive analytics encompasses a variety of statistical techniques from predictive modeling, machine learning, and data mining that analyze current and historical facts to make predictions about future or otherwise unknown events.

In business, predictive models exploit patterns found in historical and transactional data to identify risks and opportunities. Models capture relationships among many factors to allow assessment of risk or potential associated with a particular set of conditions, guiding decision making for candidate transactions.

The defining functional effect of these technical approaches is that predictive analytics provides a predictive score (probability) for each individual (customer, employee, healthcare patient, product SKU, vehicle, component, machine, or other organizational unit) in order to determine, inform, or influence organizational processes that pertain across large numbers of individuals, such as in marketing, credit risk assessment, fraud detection, manufacturing, healthcare, and government operations including law enforcement.

Predictive analytics is used in actuarial science, marketing, financial services, insurance, telecommunications, retail, travel, healthcare, child protection, pharmaceuticals, capacity planning and other fields.

One of the most well known applications is credit scoring, which is used throughout financial services. Scoring models process a customer's credit history, loan application, customer data, etc., in order to rank-order individuals by their likelihood of making future credit payments on time.

Definition

Predictive analytics is an area of data mining that deals with extracting information from data and using it to predict trends and behavior patterns. Often the unknown event of interest is in the future, but predictive analytics can be applied to any type of unknown whether it be in the past, present or future. For example, identifying suspects after a crime has been committed, or credit card fraud as it occurs. The core of predictive analytics relies on capturing relationships between explanatory variables and the predicted variables from past occurrences, and exploiting them to predict the unknown outcome. It is important to note, however, that the accuracy and usability of results will depend greatly on the level of data analysis and the quality of assumptions.

Predictive analytics is often defined as predicting at a more detailed level of granularity, i.e., generating predictive scores (probabilities) for each individual organizational element. This distinguishes it from forecasting. For example, "Predictive analytics—Technology that learns from experience (data) to predict the future behavior of individuals in order to drive better decisions." In future industrial systems, the value of predictive analytics will be to predict and prevent potential issues to achieve near-zero break-down and further be integrated into prescriptive analytics for decision optimization. Furthermore, the converted data can be used for closed-loop product life cycle improvement which is the vision of Industrial Internet Consortium.

Types

Generally, the term predictive analytics is used to mean predictive modeling, "scoring" data with predictive models, and forecasting. However, people are increasingly using the term to refer to related analytical disciplines, such as descriptive modeling and decision modeling or optimization. These disciplines also involve rigorous data analysis, and are widely used in business for segmentation and decision making, but have different purposes and the statistical techniques underlying them vary.

Predictive Models

Predictive models are models of the relation between the specific performance of a unit in a sample and one or more known attributes or features of the unit. The objective of the model is to assess the likelihood that a similar unit in a different sample will exhibit the specific performance. This category encompasses models in many areas, such as marketing, where they seek out subtle data patterns to answer questions about customer performance, or fraud detection models. Predictive models often perform calculations during live transactions, for example, to evaluate the risk or opportunity of a given customer or transaction, in order to guide a decision. With advancements in computing speed, individual agent modeling systems have become capable of simulating human behaviour or reactions to given stimuli or scenarios.

The available sample units with known attributes and known performances is referred to as the "training sample". The units in other samples, with known attributes but unknown performances, are referred to as "out of [training] sample" units. The out of sample bear no chronological relation to the training sample units. For example, the training sample may consists of literary attributes of writings by Victorian authors, with known attribution, and the out-of sample unit may be newly found writing with unknown authorship; a predictive model may aid in attributing a work to a known author. Another example is given by analysis of blood splatter in simulated crime scenes in which the out of sample unit is the actual blood splatter pattern from a crime scene. The out of sample unit may be from the same time as the training units, from a previous time, or from a future time.

Descriptive Models

Descriptive models quantify relationships in data in a way that is often used to classify customers or prospects into groups. Unlike predictive models that focus on predicting a single customer behavior (such as credit risk), descriptive models identify many different relationships between customers or products. Descriptive models do not rank-order customers by their likelihood of taking a particular action the way predictive models do. Instead, descriptive models can be used, for example, to categorize customers by their product preferences and life stage. Descriptive modeling tools can be utilized to develop further models that can simulate large number of individualized agents and make predictions.

Decision Models

Decision models describe the relationship between all the elements of a decision—the known data (including results of predictive models), the decision, and the forecast results of the decision—in order to predict the results of decisions involving many variables. These models can be used in optimization, maximizing certain outcomes while minimizing others. Decision models are generally used to develop decision logic or a set of business rules that will produce the desired action for every customer or circumstance.

Applications

Although predictive analytics can be put to use in many applications, we outline a few examples where predictive analytics has shown positive impact in recent years.

Analytical Customer Relationship Management (CRM)

Analytical customer relationship management (CRM) is a frequent commercial application of predictive analysis. Methods of predictive analysis are applied to customer data to pursue CRM objectives, which involve constructing a holistic view of the customer no matter where their information resides in the company or the department involved. CRM uses predictive analysis in applications for marketing campaigns, sales, and customer services to name a few. These tools are required in order for a company to posture and focus their efforts effectively across the breadth of their customer base. They must analyze and understand the products in demand or have the potential for high demand, predict customers' buying habits in order to promote relevant products at multiple touch points, and proactively identify and mitigate issues that have the potential to lose customers or reduce their ability to gain new ones. Analytical customer relationship management can be applied throughout the customers lifecycle (acquisition, relationship growth, retention, and win-back). Several of the application areas described below (direct marketing, cross-sell, customer retention) are part of customer relationship management.

Child Protection

Over the last 5 years, some child welfare agencies have started using predictive analytics to flag high risk cases. The approach has been called "innovative" by the Commission to Eliminate Child Abuse and Neglect Fatalities (CECANF), and in Hillsborough County, Florida, where the lead child welfare agency uses a predictive modeling tool, there have been no abuse-related child deaths in the target population as of this writing.

Clinical Decision Support Systems

Experts use predictive analysis in health care primarily to determine which patients are at risk of developing certain conditions, like diabetes, asthma, heart disease, and other lifetime illnesses. Additionally, sophisticated clinical decision support systems incorporate predictive analytics to support medical decision making at the point of care. A working definition has been proposed by Jerome A. Osheroff and colleagues: *Clinical decision support (CDS) provides clinicians, staff, patients, or other individuals with knowledge and person-specific information, intelligently filtered or presented at appropriate times, to enhance health and health care. It encompasses a variety of tools and interventions such as computerized alerts and reminders, clinical guidelines, order sets, patient data reports and dashboards, documentation templates, diagnostic support, and clinical workflow tools.*

A 2016 study of neurodegenerative disorders provides a powerful example of a CDS platform to diagnose, track, predict and monitor the progression of Parkinson's disease. Using large and multi-source imaging, genetics, clinical and demographic data, these investigators developed a decision support system that can predict the state of the disease with high accuracy, consistency and precision. They employed classical model-based and machine learning model-free methods to discriminate between different patient and control groups. Similar approaches may be used for predictive diagnosis and disease progression forecasting in many neurodegenerative disorders like Alzheimer's, Huntington's, Amyotrophic Lateral Sclerosis, as well as for other clinical and biomedical applications where Big Data is available.

Collection Analytics

Many portfolios have a set of delinquent customers who do not make their payments on time. The financial institution has to undertake collection activities on these customers to recover the amounts due. A lot of collection resources are wasted on customers who are difficult or impossible to recover. Predictive analytics can help optimize the allocation of collection resources by identifying the most effective collection agencies, contact strategies, legal actions and other strategies to each customer, thus significantly increasing recovery at the same time reducing collection costs.

Cross-sell

Often corporate organizations collect and maintain abundant data (e.g. customer records, sale transactions) as exploiting hidden relationships in the data can provide a competitive advantage. For an organization that offers multiple products, predictive analytics can help analyze customers' spending, usage and other behavior, leading to efficient cross sales, or selling additional products to current customers. This directly leads to higher profitability per customer and stronger customer relationships.

Customer Retention

With the number of competing services available, businesses need to focus efforts on maintaining continuous customer satisfaction, rewarding consumer loyalty and minimizing customer attrition. In addition, small increases in customer retention have been shown to increase profits disproportionately. One study concluded that a 5% increase in customer retention rates will increase profits by 25% to 95%. Businesses tend to respond to customer attrition on a reactive basis, acting only after the customer has initiated the process to terminate service. At this stage, the chance of changing the customer's decision is almost zero. Proper application of predictive analytics can lead to a more proactive retention strategy. By a frequent examination of a customer's past service usage, service performance, spending and other behavior patterns, predictive models can determine the likelihood of a customer terminating service sometime soon. An intervention with lucrative offers can increase the chance of retaining the customer. Silent attrition, the behavior of a customer to slowly but steadily reduce usage, is another problem that many companies face. Predictive analytics can also predict this behavior, so that the company can take proper actions to increase customer activity.

Direct Marketing

When marketing consumer products and services, there is the challenge of keeping up with competing products and consumer behavior. Apart from identifying prospects, predictive analytics can also help to identify the most effective combination of product versions, marketing material, communication channels and timing that should be used to target a given consumer. The goal of predictive analytics is typically to lower the cost per order or cost per action.

Fraud Detection

Fraud is a big problem for many businesses and can be of various types: inaccurate credit applications, fraudulent transactions (both offline and online), identity thefts and false insurance claims. These problems plague firms of all sizes in many industries. Some examples of likely victims are credit card issuers, insurance companies, retail merchants, manufacturers, business-to-business suppliers and even services providers. A predictive model can help weed out the "bads" and reduce a business's exposure to fraud.

Predictive modeling can also be used to identify high-risk fraud candidates in business or the public sector. Mark Nigrini developed a risk-scoring method to identify audit targets. He describes the use of this approach to detect fraud in the franchisee sales reports of an international fast-food chain. Each location is scored using 10 predictors. The 10 scores are then weighted to give one final overall risk score for each location. The same scoring approach was also used to identify high-risk check kiting accounts, potentially fraudulent travel agents, and questionable vendors. A reasonably complex model was used to identify fraudulent monthly reports submitted by divisional controllers.

The Internal Revenue Service (IRS) of the United States also uses predictive analytics to mine tax returns and identify tax fraud.

Recent advancements in technology have also introduced predictive behavior analysis for web fraud detection. This type of solution utilizes heuristics in order to study normal web user behavior and detect anomalies indicating fraud attempts.

Portfolio, Product or Economy-level Prediction

Often the focus of analysis is not the consumer but the product, portfolio, firm, industry or even the economy. For example, a retailer might be interested in predicting store-level demand for inventory management purposes. Or the Federal Reserve Board might be interested in predicting the unemployment rate for the next year. These types of problems can be addressed by predictive analytics using time series techniques. They can also be addressed via machine learning approaches which transform the original time series into a feature vector space, where the learning algorithm finds patterns that have predictive power.

Project Risk Management

When employing risk management techniques, the results are always to predict and benefit from a future scenario. The capital asset pricing model (CAP-M) "predicts" the best portfolio to maximize return. Probabilistic risk assessment (PRA) when combined with mini-Delphi techniques and statistical approaches yields accurate forecasts. These are examples of approaches that can extend from project to market, and from near to long term. Underwriting and other business approaches identify risk management as a predictive method.

Underwriting

Many businesses have to account for risk exposure due to their different services and determine the cost needed to cover the risk. For example, auto insurance providers need to accurately determine the amount of premium to charge to cover each automobile and driver. A financial company needs to assess a borrower's potential and ability to pay before granting a loan. For a health insurance provider, predictive analytics can analyze a few years of past medical claims data, as well as lab, pharmacy and other records where available, to predict how expensive an enrollee is likely to be in the future. Predictive analytics can help underwrite these quantities by predicting the chances of illness, default, bankruptcy, etc. Predictive analytics can streamline the process of customer acquisition by predicting the future risk behavior of a customer using application level data. Predictive analytics in the form of credit scores have reduced the amount of time it takes for loan approvals, especially in the mortgage market where lending decisions are now made in a matter of hours rather than days or even weeks. Proper predictive analytics can lead to proper pricing decisions, which can help mitigate future risk of default.

Technology and Big Data Influences

Big data is a collection of data sets that are so large and complex that they become awkward to work with using traditional database management tools. The volume, variety and velocity of big data have introduced challenges across the board for capture, storage, search, sharing, analysis, and visualization. Examples of big data sources include web logs, RFID, sensor data, social networks, Internet search indexing, call detail records, military surveillance, and complex data in astronomic, biogeochemical, genomics, and atmospheric sciences. Big Data is the core of most predictive analytic services offered by IT organizations. Thanks to technological advances in computer hardware—faster CPUs, cheaper memory, and MPP architectures—and new technologies such as Hadoop, MapReduce, and in-database and text analytics for processing big data, it is now feasible to collect, analyze, and mine massive amounts of structured and unstructured data for new insights. It is also possible to run predictive algorithms on streaming data. Today, exploring big data and using predictive analytics is within reach of more organizations than ever before and new methods that are capable for handling such datasets are proposed

Analytical Techniques

The approaches and techniques used to conduct predictive analytics can broadly be grouped into regression techniques and machine learning techniques.

Regression Techniques

Regression models are the mainstay of predictive analytics. The focus lies on establishing a mathematical equation as a model to represent the interactions between the different variables in consideration. Depending on the situation, there are a wide variety of models that can be applied while performing predictive analytics. Some of them are briefly discussed below.

Linear Regression Model

The linear regression model analyzes the relationship between the response or dependent variable and a set of independent or predictor variables. This relationship is expressed as an equation that predicts the response variable as a linear function of the parameters. These parameters are adjusted so that a measure of fit is optimized. Much of the effort in model fitting is focused on minimizing the size of the residual, as well as ensuring that it is randomly distributed with respect to the model predictions.

The goal of regression is to select the parameters of the model so as to minimize the sum of the squared residuals. This is referred to as ordinary least squares (OLS) estimation and results in best linear unbiased estimates (BLUE) of the parameters if and only if the Gauss-Markov assumptions are satisfied.

Once the model has been estimated we would be interested to know if the predictor variables belong in the model—i.e. is the estimate of each variable's contribution reliable? To do this we can check the statistical significance of the model's coefficients which can be measured using the t-statistic. This amounts to testing whether the coefficient is significantly different from zero. How well the model predicts the dependent variable based on the value of the independent variables can be assessed by using the R^2 statistic. It measures predictive power of the model i.e. the proportion of the total variation in the dependent variable that is "explained" (accounted for) by variation in the independent variables.

Discrete Choice Models

Multiple regression (above) is generally used when the response variable is continuous and has an unbounded range. Often the response variable may not be continuous but rather discrete. While mathematically it is feasible to apply multiple regression to discrete ordered dependent variables, some of the assumptions behind the theory of multiple linear regression no longer hold, and there are other techniques such as discrete choice models which are better suited for this type of analysis. If the dependent variable is discrete, some of those superior methods are logistic regression, multinomial logit and probit models. Logistic regression and probit models are used when the dependent variable is binary.

Logistic Regression

In a classification setting, assigning outcome probabilities to observations can be achieved through the use of a logistic model, which is basically a method which transforms information about the binary dependent variable into an unbounded continuous variable and estimates a regular multivariate model.

The Wald and likelihood-ratio test are used to test the statistical significance of each coefficient b in the model. A test assessing the goodness-of-fit of a classification model is the "percentage correctly predicted".

Multinomial Logistic Regression

An extension of the binary logit model to cases where the dependent variable has more than 2 categories is the multinomial logit model. In such cases collapsing the data into two categories might not make good sense or may lead to loss in the richness of the data. The multinomial logit model is the appropriate technique in these cases, especially when the dependent variable categories are not ordered (for examples colors like red, blue, green). Some authors have extended multinomial regression to include feature selection/importance methods such as random multinomial logit.

Probit Regression

Probit models offer an alternative to logistic regression for modeling categorical dependent variables. Even though the outcomes tend to be similar, the underlying distributions are different. Probit models are popular in social sciences like economics.

A good way to understand the key difference between probit and logit models is to assume that the dependent variable is driven by a latent variable z, which is a sum of a linear combination of explanatory variables and a random noise term.

We do not observe z but instead observe y which takes the value 0 (when z < 0) or 1 (otherwise). In the logit model we assume that the random noise term follows a logistic distribution with mean zero. In the probit model we assume that it follows a normal distribution with mean zero. Note that in social sciences (e.g. economics), probit is often used to model situations where the observed variable y is continuous but takes values between 0 and 1.

Logit Versus Probit

The probit model has been around longer than the logit model. They behave similarly, except that the logistic distribution tends to be slightly flatter tailed. One of the reasons the logit model was formulated was that the probit model was computationally difficult due to the requirement of numerically calculating integrals. Modern computing however has made this computation fairly simple. The coefficients obtained from the logit and probit model are fairly close. However, the odds ratio is easier to interpret in the logit model.

Practical reasons for choosing the probit model over the logistic model would be:

- There is a strong belief that the underlying distribution is normal

- The actual event is not a binary outcome (*e.g.*, bankruptcy status) but a proportion (*e.g.*, proportion of population at different debt levels).

Time Series Models

Time series models are used for predicting or forecasting the future behavior of variables. These models account for the fact that data points taken over time may have an internal structure (such as autocorrelation, trend or seasonal variation) that should be accounted for. As a result, standard regression techniques cannot be applied to time series data and methodology has been developed to decompose the trend, seasonal and cyclical component of the series. Modeling the dynamic path of a variable can improve forecasts since the predictable component of the series can be projected into the future.

Time series models estimate difference equations containing stochastic components. Two commonly used forms of these models are autoregressive models (AR) and moving-average (MA) models. The Box–Jenkins methodology (1976) developed by George Box and G.M. Jenkins combines the AR and MA models to produce the ARMA (autoregressive moving average) model which is the cornerstone of stationary time series analysis. ARIMA (autoregressive integrated moving average models) on the other hand are used to describe non-stationary time series. Box and Jenkins suggest differencing a non stationary time series to obtain a stationary series to which an ARMA model can be applied. Non stationary time series have a pronounced trend and do not have a constant long-run mean or variance.

Box and Jenkins proposed a three-stage methodology which includes: model identification, estimation and validation. The identification stage involves identifying if the series is stationary or not and the presence of seasonality by examining plots of the series, autocorrelation and partial autocorrelation functions. In the estimation stage, models are estimated using non-linear time series or maximum likelihood estimation procedures. Finally the validation stage involves diagnostic checking such as plotting the residuals to detect outliers and evidence of model fit.

In recent years time series models have become more sophisticated and attempt to model conditional heteroskedasticity with models such as ARCH (autoregressive conditional heteroskedasticity) and GARCH (generalized autoregressive conditional heteroskedasticity) models frequently used for financial time series. In addition time series models are also used to understand inter-relationships among economic variables represented by systems of equations using VAR (vector autoregression) and structural VAR models.

Survival or Duration Analysis

Survival analysis is another name for time to event analysis. These techniques were primarily developed in the medical and biological sciences, but they are also widely used in the social sciences like economics, as well as in engineering (reliability and failure time analysis).

Censoring and non-normality, which are characteristic of survival data, generate difficulty when trying to analyze the data using conventional statistical models such as multiple linear regression. The normal distribution, being a symmetric distribution, takes positive as well as negative values, but duration by its very nature cannot be negative and therefore normality cannot be assumed when dealing with duration/survival data. Hence the normality assumption of regression models is violated.

The assumption is that if the data were not censored it would be representative of the population of interest. In survival analysis, censored observations arise whenever the dependent variable of interest represents the time to a terminal event, and the duration of the study is limited in time.

An important concept in survival analysis is the hazard rate, defined as the probability that the event will occur at time t conditional on surviving until time t. Another concept related to the hazard rate is the survival function which can be defined as the probability of surviving to time t.

Most models try to model the hazard rate by choosing the underlying distribution depending on the shape of the hazard function. A distribution whose hazard function slopes upward is said to have positive duration dependence, a decreasing hazard shows negative duration dependence whereas constant hazard is a process with no memory usually characterized by the exponential distribution. Some of the distributional choices in survival models are: F, gamma, Weibull, log normal, inverse normal, exponential etc. All these distributions are for a non-negative random variable.

Duration models can be parametric, non-parametric or semi-parametric. Some of the models commonly used are Kaplan-Meier and Cox proportional hazard model (non parametric).

Classification and Regression Trees (CART)

Globally-optimal classification tree analysis (GO-CTA) (also called hierarchical optimal discriminant analysis) is a generalization of optimal discriminant analysis that may be used to identify the statistical model that has maximum accuracy for predicting the value of a categorical dependent variable for a dataset consisting of categorical and continuous variables. The output of HODA is a non-orthogonal tree that combines categorical variables and cut points for continuous variables that yields maximum predictive accuracy, an assessment of the exact Type I error rate, and an evaluation of potential cross-generalizability of the statistical model. Hierarchical optimal discriminant analysis may be thought of as a generalization of Fisher's linear discriminant analysis. Optimal discriminant analysis is an alternative to ANOVA (analysis of variance) and regression analysis, which attempt to express one dependent variable as a linear combination of other features or measurements. However, ANOVA and regression analysis give a dependent variable that is a numerical variable, while hierarchical optimal discriminant analysis gives a dependent variable that is a class variable.

Classification and regression trees (CART) are a non-parametric decision tree learning technique that produces either classification or regression trees, depending on whether the dependent variable is categorical or numeric, respectively.

Decision trees are formed by a collection of rules based on variables in the modeling data set:

- Rules based on variables' values are selected to get the best split to differentiate observations based on the dependent variable

- Once a rule is selected and splits a node into two, the same process is applied to each "child" node (i.e. it is a recursive procedure)

- Splitting stops when CART detects no further gain can be made, or some pre-set stopping rules are met. (Alternatively, the data are split as much as possible and then the tree is later pruned.)

Each branch of the tree ends in a terminal node. Each observation falls into one and exactly one terminal node, and each terminal node is uniquely defined by a set of rules.

A very popular method for predictive analytics is Leo Breiman's Random forests.

Multivariate Adaptive Regression Splines

Multivariate adaptive regression splines (MARS) is a non-parametric technique that builds flexible models by fitting piecewise linear regressions.

An important concept associated with regression splines is that of a knot. Knot is where one local regression model gives way to another and thus is the point of intersection between two splines.

In multivariate and adaptive regression splines, basis functions are the tool used for generalizing the search for knots. Basis functions are a set of functions used to represent the information contained in one or more variables. Multivariate and Adaptive Regression Splines model almost always creates the basis functions in pairs.

Multivariate and adaptive regression spline approach deliberately overfits the model and then prunes to get to the optimal model. The algorithm is computationally very intensive and in practice we are required to specify an upper limit on the number of basis functions.

Machine Learning Techniques

Machine learning, a branch of artificial intelligence, was originally employed to develop techniques to enable computers to learn. Today, since it includes a number of advanced statistical methods for regression and classification, it finds application in a wide variety of fields including medical diagnostics, credit card fraud detection, face and speech recognition and analysis of the stock market. In certain applications it is sufficient to directly predict the dependent variable without focusing on the underlying relationships between variables. In other cases, the underlying relationships can be very complex and the mathematical form of the dependencies unknown. For such cases, machine learning techniques emulate human cognition and learn from training examples to predict future events.

A brief discussion of some of these methods used commonly for predictive analytics is provided below. A detailed study of machine learning can be found in Mitchell (1997).

Neural Networks

Neural networks are nonlinear sophisticated modeling techniques that are able to model complex functions. They can be applied to problems of prediction, classification or control in a wide spectrum of fields such as finance, cognitive psychology/neuroscience, medicine, engineering, and physics.

Neural networks are used when the exact nature of the relationship between inputs and output is not known. A key feature of neural networks is that they learn the relationship between inputs and output through training. There are three types of training in neural networks used by different networks, supervised and unsupervised training, reinforcement learning, with supervised being the most common one.

Some examples of neural network training techniques are backpropagation, quick propagation, conjugate gradient descent, projection operator, Delta-Bar-Delta etc. Some unsupervised network architectures are multilayer perceptrons, Kohonen networks, Hopfield networks, etc.

Multilayer Perceptron (MLP)

The multilayer perceptron (MLP) consists of an input and an output layer with one or more hidden layers of nonlinearly-activating nodes or sigmoid nodes. This is determined by the weight vector and it is necessary to adjust the weights of the network. The backpropagation employs gradient fall to minimize the squared error between the network output values and desired values for those outputs. The weights adjusted by an iterative process of repetitive present of attributes. Small changes in the weight to get the desired values are done by the process called training the net and is done by the training set (learning rule).

Radial Basis Functions

A radial basis function (RBF) is a function which has built into it a distance criterion with respect to a center. Such functions can be used very efficiently for interpolation and for smoothing of data. Radial basis functions have been applied in the area of neural networks where they are used as a replacement for the sigmoidal transfer function. Such networks have 3 layers, the input layer, the hidden layer with the RBF non-linearity and a linear output layer. The most popular choice for the non-linearity is the Gaussian. RBF networks have the advantage of not being locked into local minima as do the feed-forward networks such as the multilayer perceptron.

Support Vector Machines

support vector machines (SVM) are used to detect and exploit complex patterns in data by clustering, classifying and ranking the data. They are learning machines that are used to perform binary classifications and regression estimations. They commonly use kernel based methods to apply linear classification techniques to non-linear classification problems. There are a number of types of SVM such as linear, polynomial, sigmoid etc.

Naïve Bayes

Naïve Bayes based on Bayes conditional probability rule is used for performing classification tasks. Naïve Bayes assumes the predictors are statistically independent which makes it an effective classification tool that is easy to interpret. It is best employed when faced with the problem of 'curse of dimensionality' i.e. when the number of predictors is very high.

k-nearest Neighbours

The nearest neighbour algorithm (KNN) belongs to the class of pattern recognition statistical methods. The method does not impose a priori any assumptions about the distribution from which the modeling sample is drawn. It involves a training set with both positive and negative values. A new sample is classified by calculating the distance to the nearest neighbouring training case. The sign of that point will determine the classification of the sample. In the k-nearest neighbour classifier, the k nearest points are considered and the sign of the majority is used to classify the sample. The performance of the kNN algorithm is influenced by three main factors: (1) the distance measure used to locate the nearest neighbours; (2) the decision rule used to derive a classification from the k-nearest neighbours; and (3) the number of neighbours used to classify the new sample. It can be proved that, unlike other methods, this method is universally asymptotically convergent, i.e.: as the size of the training set increases, if the observations are independent and identically distributed (i.i.d.), regardless of the distribution from which the sample is drawn, the predicted class will converge to the class assignment that minimizes misclassification error.

Geospatial Predictive Modeling

Conceptually, geospatial predictive modeling is rooted in the principle that the occurrences of events being modeled are limited in distribution. Occurrences of events are neither uniform nor random in distribution—there are spatial environment factors (infrastructure, sociocultural, topographic, etc.) that constrain and influence where the locations of events occur. Geospatial predictive modeling attempts to describe those constraints and influences by spatially correlating occurrences of historical geospatial locations with environmental factors that represent those constraints and influences. Geospatial predictive modeling is a process for analyzing events through a geographic filter in order to make statements of likelihood for event occurrence or emergence.

Tools

Historically, using predictive analytics tools—as well as understanding the results they delivered—required advanced skills. However, modern predictive analytics tools are no longer restricted to IT specialists. As more organizations adopt predictive analytics into decision-making processes and integrate it into their operations, they are creating a shift in the market toward business users as the primary consumers of the information. Business users want tools they can use on their own. Vendors are responding by creating new software that removes the mathematical complexity, provides user-friendly graphic interfaces and/or builds in short cuts that can, for example, recognize the kind of data available and suggest an appropriate predictive model. Predictive analytics tools have become sophisticated enough to adequately present and dissect data problems, so that any data-savvy information worker can utilize them to analyze data and retrieve meaningful, useful results. For example, modern tools present findings using simple charts, graphs, and scores that indicate the likelihood of possible outcomes.

There are numerous tools available in the marketplace that help with the execution of predictive analytics. These range from those that need very little user sophistication to those that are designed for the expert practitioner. The difference between these tools is often in the level of customization and heavy data lifting allowed.

Notable open source predictive analytic tools include:

- Apache Mahout

- GNU Octave

- KNIME

- OpenNN

- Orange

- R

- scikit-learn

- Weka

Notable commercial predictive analytic tools include:

- Alpine Data Labs

- Alteryx

- Angoss KnowledgeSTUDIO

- BIRT Analytics

- IBM SPSS Statistics and IBM SPSS Modeler

- KXEN Modeler

- Mathematica

- MATLAB

- Minitab

- LabVIEW

- Neural Designer

- Oracle Advanced Analytics

- Pervasive

- Predixion Software

- RapidMiner

- RCASE

- Revolution Analytics

- SAP HANA and SAP BusinessObjects Predictive Analytics

- SAS and SAS Enterprise Miner

- STATA

- Statgraphics

- STATISTICA

- TeleRetail

- TIBCO

Beside these software packages, specific tools have also been developed for industrial applications. For example, Watchdog Agent Toolbox has been developed and optimized for predictive analysis in prognostics and health management applications and is available for MATLAB and LabVIEW.

The most popular commercial predictive analytics software packages according to the Rexer Analytics Survey for 2013 are IBM SPSS Modeler, SAS Enterprise Miner, and Dell Statistica.

PMML

In an attempt to provide a standard language for expressing predictive models, the Predictive Model Markup Language (PMML) has been proposed. Such an XML-based language provides a way for the different tools to define predictive models and to share these between PMML compliant applications. PMML 4.0 was released in June, 2009.

Criticism

There are plenty of skeptics when it comes to computers and algorithms abilities to predict the future, including Gary King, a professor from Harvard University and the director of the Institute for Quantitative Social Science. People are influenced by their environment in innumerable ways. Trying to understand what people will do next assumes that all the influential variables can be known and measured accurately. "People's environments change even more quickly than they themselves do. Everything from the weather to their relationship with their mother can change the way people think and act. All of those variables are unpredictable. How they will impact a person is even less predictable. If put in the exact same situation tomorrow, they may make a completely different decision. This means that a statistical prediction is only valid in sterile laboratory conditions, which suddenly isn't as useful as it seemed before."

Decision Support System

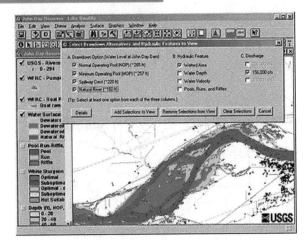

Example of a Decision Support System for John Day Reservoir.

A decision support system (DSS) is a computer-based information system that supports business or organizational decision-making activities. DSSs serve the management, operations, and planning levels of an organization (usually mid and higher management) and help people make decisions about problems that may be rapidly changing and not easily specified in advance—i.e. Unstructured and Semi-Structured decision problems. Decision support systems can be either fully computerized, human-powered or a combination of both.

While academics have perceived DSS as a tool to support decision making process, DSS users see DSS as a tool to facilitate organizational processes. Some authors have extended the definition of DSS to include any system that might support decision making; Sprague (1980) defines a properly termed DSS as follows:

1. DSS tends to be aimed at the less well structured, underspecified problem that upper level managers typically face;

2. DSS attempts to combine the use of models or analytic techniques with traditional data access and retrieval functions;

3. DSS specifically focuses on features which make them easy to use by non-computer-proficient people in an interactive mode; and

4. DSS emphasizes flexibility and adaptability to accommodate changes in the environment and the decision making approach of the user.

DSSs include knowledge-based systems. A properly designed DSS is an interactive software-based system intended to help decision makers compile useful information from a combination of raw data, documents, and personal knowledge, or business models to identify and solve problems and make decisions.

Typical information that a decision support application might gather and present includes:

*   inventories of information assets (including legacy and relational data sources, cubes, data warehouses, and data marts),

*   comparative sales figures between one period and the next,

*   projected revenue figures based on product sales assumptions.

DSSs are often contrasted with more automated decision-making systems known as Decision Management Systems.

History

The concept of decision support has evolved mainly from the theoretical studies of organizational decision making done at the Carnegie Institute of Technology during the late 1950s and early 1960s, and the implementation work done in the 1960s. DSS became an area of research of its own in the middle of the 1970s, before gaining in intensity during the 1980s. In the middle and late 1980s, executive information systems (EIS), group decision support systems (GDSS), and organizational decision support systems (ODSS) evolved from the single user and model-oriented DSS.

According to Sol (1987) the definition and scope of DSS has been migrating over the years: in the 1970s DSS was described as "a computer-based system to aid decision making"; in the late 1970s the DSS movement started focusing on "interactive computer-based systems which help decision-makers utilize data bases and models to solve ill-structured problems"; in the 1980s DSS should provide systems "using suitable and available technology to improve effectiveness of managerial and professional activities", and towards the end of 1980s DSS faced a new challenge towards the design of intelligent workstations.

In 1987, Texas Instruments completed development of the Gate Assignment Display System (GADS) for United Airlines. This decision support system is credited with significantly reducing travel delays by aiding the management of ground operations at various airports, beginning with O'Hare International Airport in Chicago and Stapleton Airport in Denver Colorado. Beginning in about 1990, data warehousing and on-line analytical processing (OLAP) began broadening the realm of DSS. As the turn of the millennium approached, new Web-based analytical applications were introduced.

The advent of more and better reporting technologies has seen DSS start to emerge as a critical component of management design. Examples of this can be seen in the intense amount of discussion of DSS in the education environment.

DSS also have a weak connection to the user interface paradigm of hypertext. Both the University of Vermont PROMIS system (for medical decision making) and the Carnegie Mellon ZOG/KMS system (for military and business decision making) were decision support systems which also were major breakthroughs in user interface research. Furthermore, although hypertext researchers have generally been concerned with information overload, certain researchers, notably Douglas Engelbart, have been focused on decision makers in particular.

Taxonomies

Using the relationship with the user as the criterion, Haettenschwiler differentiates *passive*, *active*, and *cooperative DSS*. A *passive DSS* is a system that aids the process of decision making, but that cannot bring out explicit decision suggestions or solutions. An *active DSS* can bring out such decision suggestions or solutions. A *cooperative DSS* allows for an iterative process between human and system towards the achievement of a consolidated solution: the decision maker (or its advisor) can modify, complete, or refine the decision suggestions provided by the system, before sending them back to the system for validation, and likewise the system again improves, completes, and refines the suggestions of the decision maker and sends them back to them for validation.

Another taxonomy for DSS, according to the mode of assistance, has been created by Daniel Power: he differentiates *communication-driven DSS*, *data-driven DSS*, *document-driven DSS*, *knowledge-driven DSS*, and *model-driven DSS*.

- A communication-driven DSS enables cooperation, supporting more than one person working on a shared task; examples include integrated tools like Google Docs or Microsoft Groove.

- A data-driven DSS (or data-oriented DSS) emphasizes access to and manipulation of a time series of internal company data and, sometimes, external data.

- A document-driven DSS manages, retrieves, and manipulates unstructured information in a variety of electronic formats.

- A knowledge-driven DSS provides specialized problem-solving expertise stored as facts, rules, procedures, or in similar structures.

- A model-driven DSS emphasizes access to and manipulation of a statistical, financial, optimization, or simulation model. Model-driven DSS use data and parameters provided by users to assist decision makers in analyzing a situation; they are not necessarily data-intensive. Dicodess is an example of an open source model-driven DSS generator.

Using scope as the criterion, Power differentiates *enterprise-wide DSS* and *desktop DSS*. An *enterprise-wide DSS* is linked to large data warehouses and serves many managers in the company. A *desktop, single-user DSS* is a small system that runs on an individual manager's PC.

Components

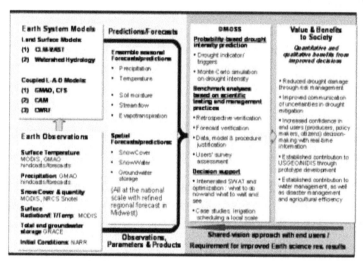

Design of a drought mitigation decision support system

Three fundamental components of a DSS architecture are:

1. the database (or knowledge base),

2. the model (i.e., the decision context and user criteria)

3. the user interface.

The users themselves are also important components of the architecture.

Development Frameworks

Similarly to other systems, DSS systems require a structured approach. Such a framework includes people, technology, and the development approach.

The Early Framework of Decision Support System consists of four phases:

- Intelligence – Searching for conditions that call for decision;

- Design – Developing and analyzing possible alternative actions of solution;

- Choice – Selecting a course of action among those;

- Implementation – Adopting the selected course of action in decision situation.

DSS technology levels (of hardware and software) may include:

1. The actual application that will be used by the user. This is the part of the application that allows the decision maker to make decisions in a particular problem area. The user can act upon that particular problem.

2. Generator contains Hardware/software environment that allows people to easily develop specific DSS applications. This level makes use of case tools or systems such as Crystal, Analytica and iThink.

3. Tools include lower level hardware/software. DSS generators including special languages, function libraries and linking modules

An iterative developmental approach allows for the DSS to be changed and redesigned at various intervals. Once the system is designed, it will need to be tested and revised where necessary for the desired outcome.

Classification

There are several ways to classify DSS applications. Not every DSS fits neatly into one of the categories, but may be a mix of two or more architectures.

Holsapple and Whinston classify DSS into the following six frameworks: text-oriented DSS, database-oriented DSS, spreadsheet-oriented DSS, solver-oriented DSS, rule-oriented DSS, and compound DSS. A compound DSS is the most popular classification for a DSS; it is a hybrid system that includes two or more of the five basic structures.

The support given by DSS can be separated into three distinct, interrelated categories: Personal Support, Group Support, and Organizational Support.

DSS components may be classified as:

1. Inputs: Factors, numbers, and characteristics to analyze

2. User Knowledge and Expertise: Inputs requiring manual analysis by the user

3. Outputs: Transformed data from which DSS "decisions" are generated

4. Decisions: Results generated by the DSS based on user criteria

DSSs which perform selected cognitive decision-making functions and are based on artificial intelligence or intelligent agents technologies are called Intelligent Decision Support Systems (IDSS)

The nascent field of Decision engineering treats the decision itself as an engineered object, and applies engineering principles such as Design and Quality assurance to an explicit representation of the elements that make up a decision.

Applications

DSS can theoretically be built in any knowledge domain.

One example is the clinical decision support system for medical diagnosis. There are four stages in the evolution of clinical decision support system (CDSS): the primitive version is standalone and does not support integration; the second generation supports integration with other medical systems; the third is standard-based, and the fourth is service model-based.

DSS is extensively used in business and management. Executive dashboard and other business performance software allow faster decision making, identification of negative trends, and better allocation of business resources. Due to DSS all the information from any organization is represented in the form of charts, graphs i.e. in a summarized way, which helps the management to take strategic decision. For example, one of the DSS applications is the management and development of complex anti-terrorism systems. Other examples include a bank loan officer verifying the credit of a loan applicant or an engineering firm that has bids on several projects and wants to know if they can be competitive with their costs.

A growing area of DSS application, concepts, principles, and techniques is in agricultural production, marketing for sustainable development. For example, the DSSAT4 package, developed through financial support of USAID during the 80s and 90s, has allowed rapid assessment of several agricultural production systems around the world to facilitate decision-making at the farm and policy levels. Precision agriculture seeks to tailor decisions to particular portions of farm fields. There are, however, many constraints to the successful adoption on DSS in agriculture.

DSS are also prevalent in forest management where the long planning horizon and the spatial dimension of planning problems demands specific requirements. All aspects of Forest management, from log transportation, harvest scheduling to sustainability and ecosystem protection have been addressed by modern DSSs. In this context the consideration of single or multiple management objectives related to the provision of goods and services that traded or non-traded and often subject to resource constraints and decision problems. The Community of Practice of Forest Management Decision Support Systems provides a large repository on knowledge about the construction and use of forest Decision Support Systems.

A specific example concerns the Canadian National Railway system, which tests its equipment on a regular basis using a decision support system. A problem faced by any railroad is worn-out or defective rails, which can result in hundreds of derailments per year. Under a DSS, the Canadian National Railway system managed to decrease the incidence of derailments at the same time other companies were experiencing an increase.

Web Mining

Web mining - is the application of data mining techniques to discover patterns from the World Wide Web. Web mining can be divided into three different types – Web usage mining, Web content mining and Web structure mining.

Web Usage Mining

Web Usage Mining is the application of data mining techniques to discover interesting usage patterns from Web data in order to understand and better serve the needs of Web-based applications. Usage data captures the identity or origin of Web users along with their browsing behavior at a Web site. Web usage mining itself can be classified further depending on the kind of usage data considered:

- Web Server Data: The user logs are collected by the Web server. Typical data includes IP address, page reference and access time.

- Application Server Data: Commercial application servers have significant features to enable e-commerce applications to be built on top of them with little effort. A key feature is the ability to track various kinds of business events and log them in application server logs.

- Application Level Data: New kinds of events can be defined in an application, and logging can be turned on for them thus generating histories of these specially defined events. It must be noted, however, that many end applications require a combination of one or more of the techniques applied in the categories above.

Studies related to work [Weichbroth et al.] are concerned with two areas: constraint-based data mining algorithms applied in Web Usage Mining and developed software tools (systems). Costa and Seco demonstrated that web log mining can be used to extract semantic information (hyponymy relationships in particular) about the user and a given community.

Pros

Web usage mining essentially has many advantages which makes this technology attractive to corporations including the government agencies. This technology has enabled e-commerce to do personalized marketing, which eventually results in higher trade volumes. Government agencies are using this technology to classify threats and fight against terrorism. The predicting capability of mining applications can benefit society by identifying criminal activities. The companies can establish better customer relationship by giving them exactly what they need. Companies can understand the needs of the customer better and they can react to customer needs faster. The companies can find, attract and retain customers; they can save on production costs by utilizing the acquired insight of customer requirements. They can increase profitability by target pricing based on the profiles created. They can even find the customer who might default to a competitor the company will try to retain the customer by providing promotional offers to the specific customer, thus reducing the risk of losing a customer or customers.

Cons

Web usage mining by itself does not create issues, but this technology when used on data of personal nature might cause concerns. The most criticized ethical issue involving web usage mining is the invasion of privacy. Privacy is considered lost when information concerning an individual is obtained, used, or disseminated, especially if this occurs without their knowledge or consent. The obtained data will be analyzed, and clustered to form profiles; the data will be made anonymous before clustering so that there are no personal profiles. Thus these applications de-individualize the users by judging them by their mouse clicks. De-individualization, can be defined as a tendency of judging and treating people on the basis of group characteristics instead of on their own individual characteristics and merits.

Another important concern is that the companies collecting the data for a specific purpose might use the data for a totally different purpose, and this essentially violates the user's interests.

The growing trend of selling personal data as a commodity encourages website owners to trade personal data obtained from their site. This trend has increased the amount of data being captured and traded increasing the likeliness of one's privacy being invaded. The companies which buy the data are obliged make it anonymous and these companies are considered authors of any specific release of mining patterns. They are legally responsible for the contents of the release; any inaccuracies in the release will result in serious lawsuits, but there is no law preventing them from trading the data.

Some mining algorithms might use controversial attributes like sex, race, religion, or sexual orientation to categorize individuals. These practices might be against the anti-discrimination legislation. The applications make it hard to identify the use of such controversial attributes, and there is no strong rule against the usage of such algorithms with such attributes. This process could result in denial of service or a privilege to an individual based on his race, religion or sexual orientation. Right now this situation can be avoided by the high ethical standards maintained by the data mining company. The collected data is being made anonymous so that, the obtained data and the obtained patterns cannot be traced back to an individual. It might look as if this poses no threat to one's privacy, however additional information can be inferred by the application by combining two separate unscrupulous data from the user.

Web Structure Mining

Web structure mining is the process of using graph theory to analyze the node and connection structure of a web site. According to the type of web structural data, web structure mining can be divided into two kinds:

1. Extracting patterns from hyperlinks in the web: a hyperlink is a structural component that connects the web page to a different location.

2. Mining the document structure: analysis of the tree-like structure of page structures to describe HTML or XML tag usage.

Web structure mining Terminologies:

1. web graph: directed graph representing web.

2. node: web page in graph.

3. edge: hyperlinks.

4. in degree: number of links pointing to particular node.

5. out degree: Number of links generated from particular node.

Techniques of web structure mining:

1. PageRank: this algorithm is used by Google to rank search results. The name of this algo-

rithm is given by Google-founder Larry Page. The rank of a page is decided by the number of links pointing to the target node.

Web Content Mining

Web content mining is the mining, extraction and integration of useful data, information and knowledge from Web page content. The heterogeneity and the lack of structure that permits much of the ever-expanding information sources on the World Wide Web, such as hypertext documents, makes automated discovery, organization, and search and indexing tools of the Internet and the World Wide Web such as Lycos, Alta Vista, WebCrawler, Aliweb, MetaCrawler, and others provide some comfort to users, but they do not generally provide structural information nor categorize, filter, or interpret documents. In recent years these factors have prompted researchers to develop more intelligent tools for information retrieval, such as intelligent web agents, as well as to extend database and data mining techniques to provide a higher level of organization for semi-structured data available on the web. The agent-based approach to web mining involves the development of sophisticated AI systems that can act autonomously or semi-autonomously on behalf of a particular user, to discover and organize web-based information.

Web content mining is differentiated from two different points of view: Information Retrieval View and Database View. summarized the research works done for unstructured data and semi-structured data from information retrieval view. It shows that most of the researches use bag of words, which is based on the statistics about single words in isolation, to represent unstructured text and take single word found in the training corpus as features. For the semi-structured data, all the works utilize the HTML structures inside the documents and some utilized the hyperlink structure between the documents for document representation. As for the database view, in order to have the better information management and querying on the web, the mining always tries to infer the structure of the web site to transform a web site to become a database.

There are several ways to represent documents; vector space model is typically used. The documents constitute the whole vector space. This representation does not realize the importance of words in a document. To resolve this, tf-idf (Term Frequency Times Inverse Document Frequency) is introduced.

By multi-scanning the document, we can implement feature selection. Under the condition that the category result is rarely affected, the extraction of feature subset is needed. The general algorithm is to construct an evaluating function to evaluate the features. As feature set, Information Gain, Cross Entropy, Mutual Information, and Odds Ratio are usually used. The classifier and pattern analysis methods of text data mining are very similar to traditional data mining techniques. The usual evaluative merits are Classification Accuracy, Precision, Recall and Information Score.

Web mining is an important component of content pipeline for web portals. It is used in data confirmation and validity verification, data integrity and building taxonomies, content management, content generation and opinion mining.

Web Mining in Foreign Languages

It should be noted that the language code of Chinese words is very complicated compared to that of English. The GB code, BIG5 code and HZ code are common Chinese word codes in web documents. Before text mining, one needs to identify the code standard of the HTML documents and transform it into inner code, then use other data mining techniques to find useful knowledge and useful patterns.

References

- Coker, Frank (2014). Pulse: Understanding the Vital Signs of Your Business (1st ed.). Bellevue, WA: Ambient Light Publishing. pp. 30, 39, 42,more. ISBN 978-0-9893086-0-1.

- Finlay, Steven (2014). Predictive Analytics, Data Mining and Big Data. Myths, Misconceptions and Methods (1st ed.). Basingstoke: Palgrave Macmillan. p. 237. ISBN 1137379278.

- Siegel, Eric (2013). Predictive Analytics: The Power to Predict Who Will Click, Buy, Lie, or Die (1st ed.). Wiley. ISBN 978-1-1183-5685-2.

- Nigrini, Mark (June 2011). "Forensic Analytics: Methods and Techniques for Forensic Accounting Investigations". Hoboken, NJ: John Wiley & Sons Inc. ISBN 978-0-470-89046-2.

- Keen, P. G. W. (1978). Decision support systems: an organizational perspective. Reading, Mass., Addison-Wesley Pub. Co. ISBN 0-201-03667-3

- Henk G. Sol et al. (1987). Expert systems and artificial intelligence in decision support systems: proceedings of the Second Mini Euroconference, Lunteren, The Netherlands, 17–20 November 1985. Springer, 1987. ISBN 90-277-2437-7. p.1-2.

- Holsapple, C.W., and A. B. Whinston. (1996). Decision Support Systems: A Knowledge-Based Approach. St. Paul: West Publishing. ISBN 0-324-03578-0

- Lindert, Bryan (October 2014). "Eckerd Rapid Safety Feedback Bringing Business Intelligence to Child Welfare" (PDF). Policy & Practice. Retrieved March 3, 2016.

- "Florida Leverages Predictive Analytics to Prevent Child Fatalities -- Other States Follow". The Huffington Post. Retrieved 2016-03-25.

- "New Strategies Long Overdue on Measuring Child Welfare Risk - The Chronicle of Social Change". The Chronicle of Social Change. Retrieved 2016-04-04.

- "Eckerd Rapid Safety Feedback® Highlighted in National Report of Commission to Eliminate Child Abuse and Neglect Fatalities". Eckerd Kids. Retrieved 2016-04-04.

- "A National Strategy to Eliminate Child Abuse and Neglect Fatalities" (PDF). Commission to Eliminate Child Abuse and Neglect Fatalities. (2016). Retrieved April 4, 2016.

- "Predictive Big Data Analytics: A Study of Parkinson's Disease using Large, Complex, Heterogeneous, Incongruent, Multi-source and Incomplete Observations". PLoS ONE. Retrieved 2016-08-10.

- Reichheld, Frederick; Schefter, Phil. "The Economics of E-Loyalty". Havard Business School Working Knowledge. Retrieved 10 November 2014.

Allied Fields of Data Mining

Data mining is an interdisciplinary subject. It is a part of other fields as well. Fields such as artificial intelligence, machine learning, statistics and database make use of data mining. This subject helps in discovering patterns in the data sets and these data sets are involved in the joining of subjects such as artificial intelligence, statistics and database. This section will provide a glimpse of the related fields of data mining.

Artificial Intelligence

Artificial intelligence (AI) is intelligence exhibited by machines. In computer science, an ideal "intelligent" machine is a flexible rational agent that perceives its environment and takes actions that maximize its chance of success at some goal. Colloquially, the term "artificial intelligence" is applied when a machine mimics "cognitive" functions that humans associate with other human minds, such as "learning" and "problem solving". As machines become increasingly capable, mental facilities once thought to require intelligence are removed from the definition. For example, optical character recognition is no longer perceived as an exemplar of "artificial intelligence", having become a routine technology. Capabilities currently classified as AI include successfully understanding human speech, competing at a high level in strategic game systems (such as Chess and Go), self-driving cars, and interpreting complex data. Some people also consider AI a danger to humanity if it progresses unabatedly. AI research is divided into subfields that focus on specific problems or on specific approaches or on the use of a particular tool or towards satisfying particular applications.

The central problems (or goals) of AI research include reasoning, knowledge, planning, learning, natural language processing (communication), perception and the ability to move and manipulate objects. General intelligence is among the field's long-term goals. Approaches include statistical methods, computational intelligence, soft computing (e.g. machine learning), and traditional symbolic AI. Many tools are used in AI, including versions of search and mathematical optimization, logic, methods based on probability and economics. The AI field draws upon computer science, mathematics, psychology, linguistics, philosophy, neuroscience and artificial psychology.

The field was founded on the claim that human intelligence "can be so precisely described that a machine can be made to simulate it." This raises philosophical arguments about the nature of the mind and the ethics of creating artificial beings endowed with human-like intelligence, issues which have been explored by myth, fiction and philosophy since antiquity. Attempts to create artificial intelligence have experienced many setbacks, including the ALPAC report of 1966, the abandonment of perceptrons in 1970, the Lighthill Report of 1973, the second AI winter 1987–1993 and the collapse of the Lisp machine market in 1987. In the twenty-first century AI techniques became an essential part of the technology industry, helping to solve many challenging problems in computer science.

History

While thought-capable artificial beings appeared as storytelling devices in antiquity, the idea of actually trying to build a machine to perform useful reasoning may have begun with Ramon Llull (c. 1300 CE). With his Calculus ratiocinator, Gottfried Leibniz extended the concept of the calculating machine (Wilhelm Schickard engineered the first one around 1623), intending to perform operations on concepts rather than numbers. Since the 19th century, artificial beings are common in fiction, as in Mary Shelley's *Frankenstein* or Karel Čapek's *R.U.R. (Rossum's Universal Robots)*.

The study of mechanical or "formal" reasoning began with philosophers and mathematicians in antiquity. In the 19th century, George Boole refined those ideas into propositional logic and Gottlob Frege developed a notational system for mechanical reasoning (a *"predicate calculus"*). Around the 1940s, Alan Turing's theory of computation suggested that a machine, by shuffling symbols as simple as "0" and "1", could simulate any conceivable act of mathematical deduction. This insight, that digital computers can simulate any process of formal reasoning, is known as the Church–Turing thesis. Along with concurrent discoveries in neurology, information theory and cybernetics, this led researchers to consider the possibility of building an electronic brain. The first work that is now generally recognized as AI was McCullouch and Pitts' 1943 formal design for Turing-complete "artificial neurons".

The field of AI research was founded at a conference at Dartmouth College in 1956. The attendees, including John McCarthy, Marvin Minsky, Allen Newell, Arthur Samuel and Herbert Simon, became the leaders of AI research. They and their students wrote programs that were, to most people, simply astonishing: computers were winning at checkers, solving word problems in algebra, proving logical theorems and speaking English. By the middle of the 1960s, research in the U.S. was heavily funded by the Department of Defense and laboratories had been established around the world. AI's founders were optimistic about the future: Herbert Simon predicted that "machines will be capable, within twenty years, of doing any work a man can do". Marvin Minsky agreed, writing that "within a generation ... the problem of creating 'artificial intelligence' will substantially be solved".

They failed to recognize the difficulty of some of the remaining tasks. Progress slowed and in 1974, in response to the criticism of Sir James Lighthill and ongoing pressure from the US Congress to fund more productive projects, both the U.S. and British governments cut off exploratory research in AI. The next few years would later be called an "AI winter", a period when funding for AI projects was hard to find.

In the early 1980s, AI research was revived by the commercial success of expert systems, a form of AI program that simulated the knowledge and analytical skills of human experts. By 1985 the market for AI had reached over a billion dollars. At the same time, Japan's fifth generation computer project inspired the U.S and British governments to restore funding for academic research. However, beginning with the collapse of the Lisp Machine market in 1987, AI once again fell into disrepute, and a second, longer-lasting hiatus began.

In the late 1990s and early 21st century, AI began to be used for logistics, data mining, medical diagnosis and other areas. The success was due to increasing computational power, greater emphasis on solving specific problems, new ties between AI and other fields and a commitment by researchers to mathematical methods and scientific standards. Deep Blue became the first computer chess-playing system to beat a reigning world chess champion, Garry Kasparov on 11 May 1997.

Advanced statistical techniques (loosely known as deep learning), access to large amounts of data and faster computers enabled advances in machine learning and perception. By the mid 2010s, machine learning applications were used throughout the world. In a *Jeopardy!* quiz show exhibition match, IBM's question answering system, Watson, defeated the two greatest Jeopardy champions, Brad Rutter and Ken Jennings, by a significant margin. The Kinect, which provides a 3D body–motion interface for the Xbox 360 and the Xbox One use algorithms that emerged from lengthy AI research as do intelligent personal assistants in smartphones. In March 2016, AlphaGo won 4 out of 5 games of Go in a match with Go champion Lee Sedol, becoming the first computer Go-playing system to beat a professional Go player without handicaps.

According to Bloomberg's Jack Clark, 2015 was a landmark year for artificial intelligence, with the number of software projects that use AI within Google increasing from a "sporadic usage" in 2012 to more than 2,700 projects. Clark also presents factual data indicating that error rates in image processing tasks have fallen significantly since 2011. He attributes this to an increase in affordable neural networks, due to a rise in cloud computing infrastructure and to an increase in research tools and datasets. Other cited examples include Microsoft's development of a Skype system that can automatically translate from one language to another and Facebook's system that can describe images to blind people.

Research

Goals

The general problem of simulating (or creating) intelligence has been broken down into sub-problems. These consist of particular traits or capabilities that researchers expect an intelligent system to display. The traits described below have received the most attention.

Deduction, Reasoning, Problem Solving

Early researchers developed algorithms that imitated step-by-step reasoning that humans use when they solve puzzles or make logical deductions (reason). By the late 1980s and 1990s, AI research had developed methods for dealing with uncertain or incomplete information, employing concepts from probability and economics.

For difficult problems, algorithms can require enormous computational resources—most experience a "combinatorial explosion": the amount of memory or computer time required becomes astronomical for problems of a certain size. The search for more efficient problem-solving algorithms is a high priority.

Human beings ordinarily use fast, intuitive judgments rather than step-by-step deduction that early AI research was able to model. AI has progressed using "sub-symbolic" problem solving: embodied agent approaches emphasize the importance of sensorimotor skills to higher reasoning; neural net research attempts to simulate the structures inside the brain that give rise to this skill; statistical approaches to AI mimic the human ability to guess.

Knowledge Representation

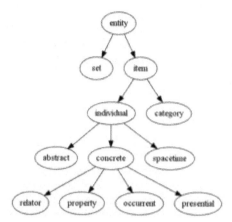

An ontology represents knowledge as a set of concepts within a domain and the relationships between those concepts.

Knowledge representation and knowledge engineering are central to AI research. Many of the problems machines are expected to solve will require extensive knowledge about the world. Among the things that AI needs to represent are: objects, properties, categories and relations between objects; situations, events, states and time; causes and effects; knowledge about knowledge (what we know about what other people know); and many other, less well researched domains. A representation of "what exists" is an ontology: the set of objects, relations, concepts and so on that the machine knows about. The most general are called upper ontologies, which attempt to provide a foundation for all other knowledge.

Among the most difficult problems in knowledge representation are:

Default reasoning and the qualification problem

> Many of the things people know take the form of "working assumptions." For example, if a bird comes up in conversation, people typically picture an animal that is fist sized, sings, and flies. None of these things are true about all birds. John McCarthy identified this problem in 1969 as the qualification problem: for any commonsense rule that AI researchers care to represent, there tend to be a huge number of exceptions. Almost nothing is simply true or false in the way that abstract logic requires. AI research has explored a number of solutions to this problem.

The breadth of commonsense knowledge

> The number of atomic facts that the average person knows is astronomical. Research projects that attempt to build a complete knowledge base of commonsense knowledge (e.g., Cyc) require enormous amounts of laborious ontological engineering—they must be built, by hand, one complicated concept at a time. A major goal is to have the computer understand enough concepts to be able to learn by reading from sources like the Internet, and thus be able to add to its own ontology.

The subsymbolic form of some commonsense knowledge

> Much of what people know is not represented as "facts" or "statements" that they could ex-

press verbally. For example, a chess master will avoid a particular chess position because it "feels too exposed" or an art critic can take one look at a statue and instantly realize that it is a fake. These are intuitions or tendencies that are represented in the brain non-consciously and sub-symbolically. Knowledge like this informs, supports and provides a context for symbolic, conscious knowledge. As with the related problem of sub-symbolic reasoning, it is hoped that situated AI, computational intelligence, or statistical AI will provide ways to represent this kind of knowledge.

Planning

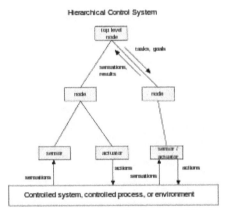

A hierarchical control system is a form of control system in which a set of devices and governing software is arranged in a hierarchy.

Intelligent agents must be able to set goals and achieve them. They need a way to visualize the future (they must have a representation of the state of the world and be able to make predictions about how their actions will change it) and be able to make choices that maximize the utility (or "value") of the available choices.

In classical planning problems, the agent can assume that it is the only thing acting on the world and it can be certain what the consequences of its actions may be. However, if the agent is not the only actor, it must periodically ascertain whether the world matches its predictions and it must change its plan as this becomes necessary, requiring the agent to reason under uncertainty.

Multi-agent planning uses the cooperation and competition of many agents to achieve a given goal. Emergent behavior such as this is used by evolutionary algorithms and swarm intelligence.

Learning

Machine learning is the study of computer algorithms that improve automatically through experience and has been central to AI research since the field's inception.

Unsupervised learning is the ability to find patterns in a stream of input. Supervised learning includes both classification and numerical regression. Classification is used to determine what category something belongs in, after seeing a number of examples of things from several categories. Regression is the attempt to produce a function that describes the relationship between inputs and outputs and predicts how the outputs should change as the inputs change. In reinforcement learning the agent is rewarded for good responses and punished for bad ones. The agent uses this sequence of rewards and punishments to form a strategy for operating in its problem space. These three types of learning can be analyzed in terms of decision theory, using concepts like utility. The mathematical analysis of machine learning algorithms and their performance is a branch of theoretical computer science known as computational learning theory.

Within developmental robotics, developmental learning approaches were elaborated for lifelong cumulative acquisition of repertoires of novel skills by a robot, through autonomous self-exploration and social interaction with human teachers, and using guidance mechanisms such as active learning, maturation, motor synergies, and imitation.

Natural Language Processing (Communication)

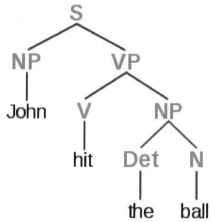

A parse tree represents the syntactic structure of a sentence according to some formal grammar.

Natural language processing gives machines the ability to read and understand the languages that humans speak. A sufficiently powerful natural language processing system would enable natural language user interfaces and the acquisition of knowledge directly from human-written sources, such as newswire texts. Some straightforward applications of natural language processing include information retrieval, text mining, question answering and machine translation.

A common method of processing and extracting meaning from natural language is through semantic indexing. Increases in processing speeds and the drop in the cost of data storage makes indexing large volumes of abstractions of the user's input much more efficient.

Perception

Machine perception is the ability to use input from sensors (such as cameras, microphones, tactile sensors, sonar and others more exotic) to deduce aspects of the world. Computer vision is the ability to analyze visual input. A few selected subproblems are speech recognition, facial recognition and object recognition.

Motion and Manipulation

The field of robotics is closely related to AI. Intelligence is required for robots to be able to handle such tasks as object manipulation and navigation, with sub-problems of localization (knowing where you are, or finding out where other things are), mapping (learning what is around you, building a map of the environment), and motion planning (figuring out how to get there) or path planning (going from one point in space to another point, which may involve compliant motion – where the robot moves while maintaining physical contact with an object).

Social Intelligence

Kismet, a robot with rudimentary social skills

Affective computing is the study and development of systems and devices that can recognize, interpret, process, and simulate human affects. It is an interdisciplinary field spanning computer sciences, psychology, and cognitive science. While the origins of the field may be traced as far back as to early philosophical inquiries into emotion, the more modern branch of computer science originated with Rosalind Picard's 1995 paper on affective computing. A motivation for the research is the ability to simulate empathy. The machine should interpret the emotional state of humans and adapt its behaviour to them, giving an appropriate response for those emotions.

Emotion and social skills play two roles for an intelligent agent. First, it must be able to predict the actions of others, by understanding their motives and emotional states. (This involves elements of game theory, decision theory, as well as the ability to model human emotions and the perceptual skills to detect emotions.) Also, in an effort to facilitate human-computer interaction, an intelligent machine might want to be able to *display* emotions—even if it does not actually experience them itself—in order to appear sensitive to the emotional dynamics of human interaction.

Creativity

A sub-field of AI addresses creativity both theoretically (from a philosophical and psychological perspective) and practically (via specific implementations of systems that generate outputs that can be considered creative, or systems that identify and assess creativity). Related areas of computational research are Artificial intuition and Artificial thinking.

General Intelligence

Many researchers think that their work will eventually be incorporated into a machine with artificial general intelligence, combining all the skills above and exceeding human abilities at most or all of them. A few believe that anthropomorphic features like artificial consciousness or an artificial brain may be required for such a project.

Many of the problems above may require general intelligence to be considered solved. For example, even a straightforward, specific task like machine translation requires that the machine read and write in both languages (NLP), follow the author's argument (reason), know what is being talked about (knowledge), and faithfully reproduce the author's intention (social intelligence). A problem like machine translation is considered "AI-complete". In order to for machines to reach human-level performance, one must solve all the problems.

Long-term Goals

Artificial Intelligence is accomplished from 3 viewpoints: computational psychology, computational philosophy, and computer science. Computational psychology is used to make computer programs that mimic human behavior. Computational philosophy, is used to develop an adaptive, free-flowing computer mind. Implementing computer science serves the goal of creating computers that can perform tasks that only people could previously accomplish. Together, the human-esque behavior, mind, and actions make up artificial intelligence.

The overall research goal of AI is to create technology that allows computers and machines to function in an intelligent manner. This can be done through developing and creating efficient methods for planning and learning in order for the outcomes to be relevant and applicable to the given situation. Short-term and long-term research goals have been created in order to develop AI technology. For example, some scientists from the Future of Life Institute described some short-term research goals to be how AI influences the economy, the laws and ethics that are involved with AI and how to minimize AI security risks. In the long-term, the scientists have proposed to continue optimizing function while minimizing possible security risks that come along with new technologies.

Approaches

There is no established unifying theory or paradigm that guides AI research. Researchers disagree about many issues. A few of the most long standing questions that have remained unanswered are these: should artificial intelligence simulate natural intelligence by studying psychology or neurology? Or is human biology as irrelevant to AI research as bird biology is to aeronautical engineering? Can intelligent behavior be described using simple, elegant principles (such as logic or optimization)? Or does it necessarily require solving a large number of completely unrelated problems? Can intelligence be reproduced using high-level symbols, similar to words and ideas? Or does it require "sub-symbolic" processing? John Haugeland, who coined the term GOFAI (Good Old-Fashioned Artificial Intelligence), also proposed that AI should more properly be referred to as synthetic intelligence, a term which has since been adopted by some non-GOFAI researchers.

Cybernetics and Brain Simulation

In the 1940s and 1950s, a number of researchers explored the connection between neurology, information theory, and cybernetics. Some of them built machines that used electronic networks to exhibit rudimentary intelligence, such as W. Grey Walter's turtles and the Johns Hopkins Beast. Many of these researchers gathered for meetings of the Teleological Society at Princeton University and the Ratio Club in England. By 1960, this approach was largely abandoned, although elements of it would be revived in the 1980s.

Symbolic

When access to digital computers became possible in the middle 1950s, AI research began to explore the possibility that human intelligence could be reduced to symbol manipulation. The research was centered in three institutions: Carnegie Mellon University, Stanford and MIT, and each one developed its own style of research. John Haugeland named these approaches to AI "good old fashioned AI" or "GOFAI". During the 1960s, symbolic approaches had achieved great success at simulating high-level thinking in small demonstration programs. Approaches based on cybernetics or neural networks were abandoned or pushed into the background. Researchers in the 1960s and the 1970s were convinced that symbolic approaches would eventually succeed in creating a machine with artificial general intelligence and considered this the goal of their field.

Cognitive simulation

Economist Herbert Simon and Allen Newell studied human problem-solving skills and attempted to formalize them, and their work laid the foundations of the field of artificial intelligence, as well as cognitive science, operations research and management science. Their research team used the results of psychological experiments to develop programs that simulated the techniques that people used to solve problems. This tradition, centered at Carnegie Mellon University would eventually culminate in the development of the Soar architecture in the middle 1980s.

Logic-based

Unlike Newell and Simon, John McCarthy felt that machines did not need to simulate human thought, but should instead try to find the essence of abstract reasoning and problem solving, regardless of whether people used the same algorithms. His laboratory at Stanford (SAIL) focused on using formal logic to solve a wide variety of problems, including knowledge representation, planning and learning. Logic was also the focus of the work at the University of Edinburgh and elsewhere in Europe which led to the development of the programming language Prolog and the science of logic programming.

"Anti-logic" or "scruffy"

Researchers at MIT (such as Marvin Minsky and Seymour Papert) found that solving difficult problems in vision and natural language processing required ad-hoc solutions – they argued that there was no simple and general principle (like logic) that would capture all the aspects of intelligent behavior. Roger Schank described their "anti-logic" approaches as "scruffy" (as opposed to the "neat" paradigms at CMU and Stanford). Commonsense knowledge bases (such as Doug Lenat's Cyc) are an example of "scruffy" AI, since they must be built by hand, one complicated concept at a time.

Knowledge-based

When computers with large memories became available around 1970, researchers from all three traditions began to build knowledge into AI applications. This "knowledge revolution" led to the development and deployment of expert systems (introduced by Edward Feigenbaum), the first truly successful form of AI software. The knowledge revolution was also driven by the realization that enormous amounts of knowledge would be required by many simple AI applications.

Sub-symbolic

By the 1980s progress in symbolic AI seemed to stall and many believed that symbolic systems would never be able to imitate all the processes of human cognition, especially perception, robotics, learning and pattern recognition. A number of researchers began to look into "sub-symbolic" approaches to specific AI problems. Sub-symbolic methods manage to approach intelligence without specific representations of knowledge.

Bottom-up, embodied, situated, behavior-based or nouvelle AI

> Researchers from the related field of robotics, such as Rodney Brooks, rejected symbolic AI and focused on the basic engineering problems that would allow robots to move and survive. Their work revived the non-symbolic viewpoint of the early cybernetics researchers of the 1950s and reintroduced the use of control theory in AI. This coincided with the development of the embodied mind thesis in the related field of cognitive science: the idea that aspects of the body (such as movement, perception and visualization) are required for higher intelligence.

Computational intelligence and soft computing

> Interest in neural networks and "connectionism" was revived by David Rumelhart and others in the middle of 1980s. Neural networks are an example of soft computing --- they are solutions to problems which cannot be solved with complete logical certainty, and where an approximate solution is often enough. Other soft computing approaches to AI include fuzzy systems, evolutionary computation and many statistical tools. The application of soft computing to AI is studied collectively by the emerging discipline of computational intelligence.

Statistical

In the 1990s, AI researchers developed sophisticated mathematical tools to solve specific subproblems. These tools are truly scientific, in the sense that their results are both measurable and verifiable, and they have been responsible for many of AI's recent successes. The shared mathematical language has also permitted a high level of collaboration with more established fields (like mathematics, economics or operations research). Stuart Russell and Peter Norvig describe this movement as nothing less than a "revolution" and "the victory of the neats." Critics argue that these techniques (with few exceptions) are too focused on particular problems and have failed to address the long-term goal of general intelligence. There is an ongoing debate about the relevance and validity of statistical approaches in AI, exemplified in part by exchanges between Peter Norvig and Noam Chomsky.

Integrating the Approaches

Intelligent agent paradigm

> An intelligent agent is a system that perceives its environment and takes actions which maximize its chances of success. The simplest intelligent agents are programs that solve specific problems. More complicated agents include human beings and organizations of

human beings (such as firms). The paradigm gives researchers license to study isolated problems and find solutions that are both verifiable and useful, without agreeing on one single approach. An agent that solves a specific problem can use any approach that works – some agents are symbolic and logical, some are sub-symbolic neural networks and others may use new approaches. The paradigm also gives researchers a common language to communicate with other fields—such as decision theory and economics—that also use concepts of abstract agents. The intelligent agent paradigm became widely accepted during the 1990s.

Agent architectures and cognitive architectures

Researchers have designed systems to build intelligent systems out of interacting intelligent agents in a multi-agent system. A system with both symbolic and sub-symbolic components is a hybrid intelligent system, and the study of such systems is artificial intelligence systems integration. A hierarchical control system provides a bridge between sub-symbolic AI at its lowest, reactive levels and traditional symbolic AI at its highest levels, where relaxed time constraints permit planning and world modelling. Rodney Brooks' subsumption architecture was an early proposal for such a hierarchical system.

Tools

In the course of 50 years of research, AI has developed a large number of tools to solve the most difficult problems in computer science. A few of the most general of these methods are discussed below.

Search and Optimization

Many problems in AI can be solved in theory by intelligently searching through many possible solutions: Reasoning can be reduced to performing a search. For example, logical proof can be viewed as searching for a path that leads from premises to conclusions, where each step is the application of an inference rule. Planning algorithms search through trees of goals and subgoals, attempting to find a path to a target goal, a process called means-ends analysis. Robotics algorithms for moving limbs and grasping objects use local searches in configuration space. Many learning algorithms use search algorithms based on optimization.

Simple exhaustive searches are rarely sufficient for most real world problems: the search space (the number of places to search) quickly grows to astronomical numbers. The result is a search that is too slow or never completes. The solution, for many problems, is to use "heuristics" or "rules of thumb" that eliminate choices that are unlikely to lead to the goal (called "pruning the search tree"). Heuristics supply the program with a "best guess" for the path on which the solution lies. Heuristics limit the search for solutions into a smaller sample size.

A very different kind of search came to prominence in the 1990s, based on the mathematical theory of optimization. For many problems, it is possible to begin the search with some form of a guess and then refine the guess incrementally until no more refinements can be made. These algorithms can be visualized as blind hill climbing: we begin the search at a random point on the landscape, and then, by jumps or steps, we keep moving our guess uphill, until we reach the top. Other optimization algorithms are simulated annealing, beam search and random optimization.

Evolutionary computation uses a form of optimization search. For example, they may begin with a population of organisms (the guesses) and then allow them to mutate and recombine, selecting only the fittest to survive each generation (refining the guesses). Forms of evolutionary computation include swarm intelligence algorithms (such as ant colony or particle swarm optimization) and evolutionary algorithms (such as genetic algorithms, gene expression programming, and genetic programming).

Logic

Logic is used for knowledge representation and problem solving, but it can be applied to other problems as well. For example, the satplan algorithm uses logic for planning and inductive logic programming is a method for learning.

Several different forms of logic are used in AI research. Propositional or sentential logic is the logic of statements which can be true or false. First-order logic also allows the use of quantifiers and predicates, and can express facts about objects, their properties, and their relations with each other. Fuzzy logic, is a version of first-order logic which allows the truth of a statement to be represented as a value between 0 and 1, rather than simply True (1) or False (0). Fuzzy systems can be used for uncertain reasoning and have been widely used in modern industrial and consumer product control systems. Subjective logic models uncertainty in a different and more explicit manner than fuzzy-logic: a given binomial opinion satisfies belief + disbelief + uncertainty = 1 within a Beta distribution. By this method, ignorance can be distinguished from probabilistic statements that an agent makes with high confidence.

Default logics, non-monotonic logics and circumscription are forms of logic designed to help with default reasoning and the qualification problem. Several extensions of logic have been designed to handle specific domains of knowledge, such as: description logics; situation calculus, event calculus and fluent calculus (for representing events and time); causal calculus; belief calculus; and modal logics.

Probabilistic Methods for Uncertain Reasoning

Many problems in AI (in reasoning, planning, learning, perception and robotics) require the agent to operate with incomplete or uncertain information. AI researchers have devised a number of powerful tools to solve these problems using methods from probability theory and economics.

Bayesian networks are a very general tool that can be used for a large number of problems: reasoning (using the Bayesian inference algorithm), learning (using the expectation-maximization algorithm), planning (using decision networks) and perception (using dynamic Bayesian networks). Probabilistic algorithms can also be used for filtering, prediction, smoothing and finding explanations for streams of data, helping perception systems to analyze processes that occur over time (e.g., hidden Markov models or Kalman filters).

A key concept from the science of economics is "utility": a measure of how valuable something is to an intelligent agent. Precise mathematical tools have been developed that analyze how an agent can make choices and plan, using decision theory, decision analysis, and information value theory. These tools include models such as Markov decision processes, dynamic decision networks, game theory and mechanism design.

Classifiers and Statistical Learning Methods

The simplest AI applications can be divided into two types: classifiers ("if shiny then diamond") and controllers ("if shiny then pick up"). Controllers do, however, also classify conditions before inferring actions, and therefore classification forms a central part of many AI systems. Classifiers are functions that use pattern matching to determine a closest match. They can be tuned according to examples, making them very attractive for use in AI. These examples are known as observations or patterns. In supervised learning, each pattern belongs to a certain predefined class. A class can be seen as a decision that has to be made. All the observations combined with their class labels are known as a data set. When a new observation is received, that observation is classified based on previous experience.

A classifier can be trained in various ways; there are many statistical and machine learning approaches. The most widely used classifiers are the neural network, kernel methods such as the support vector machine, k-nearest neighbor algorithm, Gaussian mixture model, naive Bayes classifier, and decision tree. The performance of these classifiers have been compared over a wide range of tasks. Classifier performance depends greatly on the characteristics of the data to be classified. There is no single classifier that works best on all given problems; this is also referred to as the "no free lunch" theorem. Determining a suitable classifier for a given problem is still more an art than science.

Neural Networks

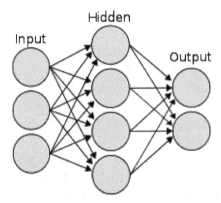

A neural network is an interconnected group of nodes, akin to the vast network of neurons in the human brain.

The study of non-learning artificial neural networks began in the decade before the field of AI research was founded, in the work of Walter Pitts and Warren McCullouch. Frank Rosenblatt invented the perceptron, a learning network with a single layer, similar to the old concept of linear regression. Early pioneers also include Alexey Grigorevich Ivakhnenko, Teuvo Kohonen, Stephen Grossberg, Kunihiko Fukushima, Christoph von der Malsburg, David Willshaw, Shun-Ichi Amari, Bernard Widrow, John Hopfield, Eduardo R. Caianiello, and others.

The main categories of networks are acyclic or feedforward neural networks (where the signal passes in only one direction) and recurrent neural networks (which allow feedback and short-term memories of previous input events). Among the most popular feedforward networks are perceptrons, multi-layer perceptrons and radial basis networks. Neural networks can be applied to the problem of intelligent control (for robotics) or learning, using such techniques as Hebbian learning, GMDH or competitive learning.

Today, neural networks are often trained by the backpropagation algorithm, which had been around since 1970 as the reverse mode of automatic differentiation published by Seppo Linnainmaa, and was introduced to neural networks by Paul Werbos.

Hierarchical temporal memory is an approach that models some of the structural and algorithmic properties of the neocortex.

Deep Feedforward Neural Networks

Deep learning in artificial neural networks with many layers has transformed many important subfields of artificial intelligence, including computer vision, speech recognition, natural language processing and others.

According to a survey, the expression "Deep Learning" was introduced to the Machine Learning community by Rina Dechter in 1986 and gained traction after Igor Aizenberg and colleagues introduced it to Artificial Neural Networks in 2000. The first functional Deep Learning networks were published by Alexey Grigorevich Ivakhnenko and V. G. Lapa in 1965. These networks are trained one layer at a time. Ivakhnenko's 1971 paper describes the learning of a deep feedforward multilayer perceptron with eight layers, already much deeper than many later networks. In 2006, a publication by Geoffrey Hinton and Ruslan Salakhutdinov introduced another way of pre-training many-layered feedforward neural networks (FNNs) one layer at a time, treating each layer in turn as an unsupervised restricted Boltzmann machine, then using supervised backpropagation for fine-tuning. Similar to shallow artificial neural networks, deep neural networks can model complex non-linear relationships. Over the last few years, advances in both machine learning algorithms and computer hardware have led to more efficient methods for training deep neural networks that contain many layers of non-linear hidden units and a very large output layer.

Deep learning often uses convolutional neural networks (CNNs), whose origins can be traced back to the Neocognitron introduced by Kunihiko Fukushima in 1980. In 1989, Yann LeCun and colleagues applied backpropagation to such an architecture. In the early 2000s, in an industrial application CNNs already processed an estimated 10% to 20% of all the checks written in the US. Since 2011, fast implementations of CNNs on GPUs have won many visual pattern recognition competitions.

Deep feedforward neural networks were used in conjunction with reinforcement learning by AlphaGo, Google Deepmind's program that was the first to beat a professional human player.

Deep Recurrent Neural Networks

Early on, deep learning was also applied to sequence learning with recurrent neural networks (RNNs) which are general computers and can run arbitrary programs to process arbitrary sequences of inputs. The depth of an RNN is unlimited and depends on the length of its input sequence. RNNs can be trained by gradient descent but suffer from the vanishing gradient problem. In 1992, it was shown that unsupervised pre-training of a stack of recurrent neural networks can speed up subsequent supervised learning of deep sequential problems.

Numerous researchers now use variants of a deep learning recurrent NN called the long short-term memory (LSTM) network published by Hochreiter & Schmidhuber in 1997. LSTM is often trained by Connectionist Temporal Classification (CTC). At Google, Microsoft and Baidu this approach has revolutionised speech recognition. For example, in 2015, Google's speech recognition experienced a dramatic performance jump of 49% through CTC-trained LSTM, which is now available through Google Voice to billions of smartphone users. Google also used LSTM to improve machine translation, Language Modeling and Multilingual Language Processing. LSTM combined with CNNs also improved automatic image captioning and a plethora of other applications.

Control Theory

Control theory, the grandchild of cybernetics, has many important applications, especially in robotics.

Languages

AI researchers have developed several specialized languages for AI research, including Lisp and Prolog.

Evaluating Progress

In 1950, Alan Turing proposed a general procedure to test the intelligence of an agent now known as the Turing test. This procedure allows almost all the major problems of artificial intelligence to be tested. However, it is a very difficult challenge and at present all agents fail.

Artificial intelligence can also be evaluated on specific problems such as small problems in chemistry, hand-writing recognition and game-playing. Such tests have been termed subject matter expert Turing tests. Smaller problems provide more achievable goals and there are an ever-increasing number of positive results.

One classification for outcomes of an AI test is:

1. Optimal: it is not possible to perform better.

2. Strong super-human: performs better than all humans.

3. Super-human: performs better than most humans.

4. Sub-human: performs worse than most humans.

For example, performance at draughts (i.e. checkers) is optimal, performance at chess is super-human and nearing strong super-human and performance at many everyday tasks (such as recognizing a face or crossing a room without bumping into something) is sub-human.

A quite different approach measures machine intelligence through tests which are developed from *mathematical* definitions of intelligence. Examples of these kinds of tests start in the late nineties devising intelligence tests using notions from Kolmogorov complexity and data compression. Two major advantages of mathematical definitions are their applicability to nonhuman intelligences and their absence of a requirement for human testers.

A derivative of the Turing test is the Completely Automated Public Turing test to tell Computers and Humans Apart (CAPTCHA). As the name implies, this helps to determine that a user is an actual person and not a computer posing as a human. In contrast to the standard Turing test, CAPTCHA administered by a machine and targeted to a human as opposed to being administered by a human and targeted to a machine. A computer asks a user to complete a simple test then generates a grade for that test. Computers are unable to solve the problem, so correct solutions are deemed to be the result of a person taking the test. A common type of CAPTCHA is the test that requires the typing of distorted letters, numbers or symbols that appear in an image undecipherable by a computer.

Applications

An automated online assistant providing customer service on a web page – one of many very primitive applications of artificial intelligence.

AI is relevant to any intellectual task. Modern artificial intelligence techniques are pervasive and are too numerous to list here. Frequently, when a technique reaches mainstream use, it is no longer considered artificial intelligence; this phenomenon is described as the AI effect.

High-profile examples of AI include autonomous vehicles (such as drones and self-driving cars), medical diagnosis, creating art (such as poetry), proving mathematical theorems, playing games (such as Chess or Go), search engines (such as Google search), online assistants (such as Siri), image recognition in photographs, spam filtering, prediction of judicial decisions and targeting online advertisements.

With social media sites overtaking TV as a source for news for young people and news organisations increasingly reliant on social media platforms for generating distribution, major publishers now use artificial intelligence (AI) technology to post stories more effectively and generate higher volumes of traffic.

Competitions and Prizes

There are a number of competitions and prizes to promote research in artificial intelligence. The main areas promoted are: general machine intelligence, conversational behavior, data-mining, robotic cars, robot soccer and games.

Shaping the Healthcare Industry

Artificial intelligence is breaking into the healthcare industry by assisting doctors. According to Bloomberg Technology, Microsoft has developed AI to help doctors find the right treatments for cancer. There is a great amount of research and drugs developed relating to cancer. In detail, there are more than 800 medicines and vaccines to treat cancer. This negatively affects the doctors because there are way too many options to choose the right drugs from, for the patients. Microsoft is working on a project to develop a machine called "Hanover". Its goal is to memorize all the papers necessary to cancer and help predict which combinations of drugs will be most effective for each patient. One project that is being worked on at the moment is fighting the myeloid leukemia, a fatal cancer where the treatment has not improved in decades.

According to CNN, there was a recent study by surgeons at the Children's National Medical Center in Washington. They successfully practiced a surgeon with a robot, rather than a human. The team supervised an autonomous robot performing a soft-tissue surgery, stitching together a pig's bowel during open surgery, and doing so better than a human surgeon.

Automotive Industry

Advancements in AI have contributed to the growth of the automotive industry through the creation and evolution of self-driving vehicles. As of 2016, there are over 30 companies utilizing AI into the creation of driverless cars. A few companies involved with AI include Tesla, Google, and Apple.

Many components contribute to the functioning of self-driving cars. These vehicles incorporate systems such as braking, lane changing, collision prevention, navigation and mapping. Together, these systems, as well as high performance computers are integrated into one complex vehicle.

One main factor that influences the ability for a driver-less car to function is mapping. In general, the vehicle would be pre-programmed with a map of the area being driven. This map would include data on the approximations of street light and curb heights in order for the vehicle to be aware of its surroundings. However, Google has been working on an algorithm with the purpose of eliminating the need for pre-programmed maps and instead, creating a device that would be able to adjust to a variety of new surroundings. Some self-driving cars are not equipped with steering wheels or brakes, so there has also been research focused on creating an algorithm that is capable of maintaining a safe environment for the passengers in the vehicle through awareness of speed and driving conditions.

Platforms

A platform (or "computing platform") is defined as "some sort of hardware architecture or software framework (including application frameworks), that allows software to run." As Rodney Brooks pointed out many years ago, it is not just the artificial intelligence software that defines the AI features of the platform, but rather the actual platform itself that affects the AI that results, i.e., there needs to be work in AI problems on real-world platforms rather than in isolation.

A wide variety of platforms has allowed different aspects of AI to develop, ranging from expert systems such as Cyc to deep-learning frameworks to robot platforms such as the Roomba with open interface. Recent advances in deep artificial neural networks and distributed computing have led to a proliferation of software libraries, including Deeplearning4j, TensorFlow, Theano and Torch.

Partnerships between Big 5 Companies to Improve AI

Amazon, Google, Facebook, IBM, and Microsoft have established a non-profit partnership to benefit people and society. The companies have established a partnership to formulate the best practices on artificial intelligence technologies, advance the public's understanding, and to serve as a platform about artificial intelligence. There will be 10 members on the board, one from each company. The remainder of the board will be filled with representatives from academia and the non-profit world, according to a press release. They stated: "This partnership on AI will conduct research, organize discussions, provide thought leadership, consult with relevant third parties, respond to questions from the public and media, and create educational material that advance the understanding of AI technologies including machine perception, learning, and automated reasoning."

There are concerns with the rise of artificial intelligence and the impacts it can have on humanity. In result, according to both Fortune and CNN technology news, the group's focus will be on ethics. According to the announcement by the groups, "The partnership will conduct research and recommend best practices relating to "ethics, fairness and inclusivity; transparency, privacy, and interoperability; collaboration between people and AI systems; and the trustworthiness, reliability and robustness of the technology." The corporate members will make financial and research contributions to the group, while engaging with the scientific community to bring academics onto the board.

Philosophy and Ethics

There are three philosophical questions related to AI:

1. Is artificial general intelligence possible? Can a machine solve any problem that a human being can solve using intelligence? Or are there hard limits to what a machine can accomplish?

2. Are intelligent machines dangerous? How can we ensure that machines behave ethically and that they are used ethically?

1. Can a machine have a mind, consciousness and mental states in exactly the same sense that human beings do? Can a machine be sentient, and thus deserve certain rights? Can a machine intentionally cause harm?

The Limits of Artificial General Intelligence

Can a machine be intelligent? Can it "think"?

Turing's "polite convention"

We need not decide if a machine can "think"; we need only decide if a machine can act as intelligently as a human being. This approach to the philosophical problems associated with artificial intelligence forms the basis of the Turing test.

The Dartmouth proposal

"Every aspect of learning or any other feature of intelligence can be so precisely described that a machine can be made to simulate it." This conjecture was printed in the proposal for the Dartmouth Conference of 1956, and represents the position of most working AI researchers.

Newell and Simon's physical symbol system hypothesis

"A physical symbol system has the necessary and sufficient means of general intelligent action." Newell and Simon argue that intelligence consists of formal operations on symbols. Hubert Dreyfus argued that, on the contrary, human expertise depends on unconscious instinct rather than conscious symbol manipulation and on having a "feel" for the situation rather than explicit symbolic knowledge.

Gödelian arguments

Gödel himself, John Lucas (in 1961) and Roger Penrose (in a more detailed argument from 1989 onwards) made highly technical arguments that human mathematicians can consistently see the truth of their own "Gödel statements" and therefore have computational abilities beyond that of mechanical Turing machines. However, the modern consensus in the scientific and mathematical community is that these "Gödelian arguments" fail.

The artificial brain argument

The brain can be simulated by machines and because brains are intelligent, simulated brains must also be intelligent; thus machines can be intelligent. Hans Moravec, Ray Kurzweil and others have argued that it is technologically feasible to copy the brain directly into hardware and software, and that such a simulation will be essentially identical to the original.

The AI effect

Machines are *already* intelligent, but observers have failed to recognize it. When Deep Blue beat Garry Kasparov in chess, the machine was acting intelligently. However, onlookers commonly discount the behavior of an artificial intelligence program by arguing that it is not "real" intelligence after all; thus "real" intelligence is whatever intelligent behavior people can do that machines still can not. This is known as the AI Effect: "AI is whatever hasn't been done yet."

Intelligent Behaviour and Machine Ethics

As a minimum, an AI system must be able to reproduce aspects of human intelligence. This raises the issue of how ethically the machine should behave towards both humans and other AI agents. This issue was addressed by Wendell Wallach in his book titled *Moral Machines* in which he introduced the concept of artificial moral agents (AMA). For Wallach, AMAs have become a part of the research landscape of artificial intelligence as guided by its two central questions which he identifies as "Does Humanity Want Computers Making Moral Decisions" and "Can (Ro)bots Really Be Moral". For Wallach the question is not centered on the issue of *whether* machines can demonstrate the equivalent of moral behavior in contrast to the *constraints* which society may place on the development of AMAs.

Machine Ethics

The field of machine ethics is concerned with giving machines ethical principles, or a procedure for discovering a way to resolve the ethical dilemmas they might encounter, enabling them to function in an ethically responsible manner through their own ethical decision making. The field was delineated in the AAAI Fall 2005 Symposium on Machine Ethics: "Past research concerning the relationship between technology and ethics has largely focused on responsible and irresponsible use of technology by human beings, with a few people being interested in how human beings ought to treat machines. In all cases, only human beings have engaged in ethical reasoning. The time has come for adding an ethical dimension to at least some machines. Recognition of the ethical ramifications of behavior involving machines, as well as recent and potential developments in machine autonomy, necessitate this. In contrast to computer hacking, software property issues, privacy issues and other topics normally ascribed to computer ethics, machine ethics is concerned with the behavior of machines towards human users and other machines. Research in machine ethics is key to alleviating concerns with autonomous systems—it could be argued that the notion of autonomous machines without such a dimension is at the root of all fear concerning machine intelligence. Further, investigation of machine ethics could enable the discovery of problems with current ethical theories, advancing our thinking about Ethics." Machine ethics is sometimes referred to as machine morality, computational ethics or computational morality. A variety of perspectives of this nascent field can be found in the collected edition "Machine Ethics" that stems from the AAAI Fall 2005 Symposium on Machine Ethics. Some suggest that to ensure that AI-equipped machines (sometimes called "smart machines") will act ethically requires a new kind of AI. This AI would be able to monitor, supervise, and if need be, correct the first order AI.

Malevolent and Friendly AI

Political scientist Charles T. Rubin believes that AI can be neither designed nor guaranteed to be benevolent. He argues that "any sufficiently advanced benevolence may be indistinguishable from malevolence." Humans should not assume machines or robots would treat us favorably, because there is no *a priori* reason to believe that they would be sympathetic to our system of morality, which has evolved along with our particular biology (which AIs would not share). Hyper-intelligent software may not necessarily decide to support the continued existence of mankind, and would be extremely difficult to stop. This topic has also recently begun to be discussed in academic publications as a real source of risks to civilization, humans, and planet Earth.

Physicist Stephen Hawking, Microsoft founder Bill Gates and SpaceX founder Elon Musk have expressed concerns about the possibility that AI could evolve to the point that humans could not control it, with Hawking theorizing that this could "spell the end of the human race".

One proposal to deal with this is to ensure that the first generally intelligent AI is 'Friendly AI', and will then be able to control subsequently developed AIs. Some question whether this kind of check could really remain in place.

Leading AI researcher Rodney Brooks writes, "I think it is a mistake to be worrying about us developing malevolent AI anytime in the next few hundred years. I think the worry stems from a fundamental error in not distinguishing the difference between the very real recent advances in a particular aspect of AI, and the enormity and complexity of building sentient volitional intelligence."

Devaluation of Humanity

Joseph Weizenbaum wrote that AI applications can not, by definition, successfully simulate genuine human empathy and that the use of AI technology in fields such as customer service or psychotherapy was deeply misguided. Weizenbaum was also bothered that AI researchers (and some philosophers) were willing to view the human mind as nothing more than a computer program (a position now known as computationalism). To Weizenbaum these points suggest that AI research devalues human life.

Decrease in Demand for Human Labor

Martin Ford, author of *The Lights in the Tunnel: Automation, Accelerating Technology and the Economy of the Future*, and others argue that specialized artificial intelligence applications, robotics and other forms of automation will ultimately result in significant unemployment as machines begin to match and exceed the capability of workers to perform most routine and repetitive jobs. Ford predicts that many knowledge-based occupations—and in particular entry level jobs—will be increasingly susceptible to automation via expert systems, machine learning and other AI-enhanced applications. AI-based applications may also be used to amplify the capabilities of low-wage offshore workers, making it more feasible to outsource knowledge work.

Machine Consciousness, Sentience and Mind

If an AI system replicates all key aspects of human intelligence, will that system also be sentient – will it have a mind which has conscious experiences? This question is closely related to the philosophical problem as to the nature of human consciousness, generally referred to as the hard problem of consciousness.

Consciousness

Computationalism

Computationalism is the position in the philosophy of mind that the human mind or the human brain (or both) is an information processing system and that thinking is a form of computing. Computationalism argues that the relationship between mind and body is similar or identical to the relationship between software and hardware and thus may be a solution to the mind-body problem. This philosophical position was inspired by the work of AI researchers and cognitive scientists in the 1960s and was originally proposed by philosophers Jerry Fodor and Hilary Putnam.

Strong AI Hypothesis

The philosophical position that John Searle has named "strong AI" states: "The appropriately programmed computer with the right inputs and outputs would thereby have a mind in exactly the same sense human beings have minds." Searle counters this assertion with his Chinese room argument, which asks us to look *inside* the computer and try to find where the "mind" might be.

Robot Rights

Mary Shelley's *Frankenstein* considers a key issue in the ethics of artificial intelligence: if a machine can be created that has intelligence, could it also *feel*? If it can feel, does it have the same rights as a human? The idea also appears in modern science fiction, such as the film *A.I.: Artificial Intelligence*, in which humanoid machines have the ability to feel emotions. This issue, now known as "robot rights", is currently being considered by, for example, California's Institute for the Future, although many critics believe that the discussion is premature. The subject is profoundly discussed in the 2010 documentary film *Plug & Pray*.

Superintelligence

Are there limits to how intelligent machines – or human-machine hybrids – can be? A superintelligence, hyperintelligence, or superhuman intelligence is a hypothetical agent that would possess intelligence far surpassing that of the brightest and most gifted human mind. "Superintelligence" may also refer to the form or degree of intelligence possessed by such an agent.

Technological Singularity

If research into Strong AI produced sufficiently intelligent software, it might be able to reprogram and improve itself. The improved software would be even better at improving itself, leading to recursive self-improvement. The new intelligence could thus increase exponentially and dramatically surpass humans. Science fiction writer Vernor Vinge named this scenario "singularity". Technological singularity is when accelerating progress in technologies will cause a runaway effect wherein artificial intelligence will exceed human intellectual capacity and control, thus radically changing or even ending civilization. Because the capabilities of such an intelligence may be impossible to comprehend, the technological singularity is an occurrence beyond which events are unpredictable or even unfathomable.

Ray Kurzweil has used Moore's law (which describes the relentless exponential improvement in digital technology) to calculate that desktop computers will have the same processing power as human brains by the year 2029, and predicts that the singularity will occur in 2045.

Transhumanism

You awake one morning to find your brain has another lobe functioning. Invisible, this auxiliary lobe answers your questions with information beyond the realm of your own memory, suggests plausible courses of action, and asks questions that help bring out relevant facts. You quickly come to rely on the new lobe so much that you stop wondering how it works. You just use it. This is the dream of artificial intelligence.

—BYTE, April 1985

Robot designer Hans Moravec, cyberneticist Kevin Warwick and inventor Ray Kurzweil have predicted that humans and machines will merge in the future into cyborgs that are more capable and powerful than either. This idea, called transhumanism, which has roots in Aldous Huxley and Robert Ettinger, has been illustrated in fiction as well, for example in the manga *Ghost in the Shell* and the science-fiction series *Dune*.

In the 1980s artist Hajime Sorayama's Sexy Robots series were painted and published in Japan depicting the actual organic human form with lifelike muscular metallic skins and later "the Gynoids" book followed that was used by or influenced movie makers including George Lucas and other creatives. Sorayama never considered these organic robots to be real part of nature but always unnatural product of the human mind, a fantasy existing in the mind even when realized in actual form.

Edward Fredkin argues that "artificial intelligence is the next stage in evolution", an idea first proposed by Samuel Butler's "Darwin among the Machines" (1863), and expanded upon by George Dyson in his book of the same name in 1998.

Existential Risk

The development of full artificial intelligence could spell the end of the human race. Once humans develop artificial intelligence, it will take off on its own and redesign itself at an ever-increasing rate. Humans, who are limited by slow biological evolution, couldn't compete and would be superseded.

—Stephen Hawking

A common concern about the development of artificial intelligence is the potential threat it could pose to mankind. This concern has recently gained attention after mentions by celebrities including Stephen Hawking, Bill Gates, and Elon Musk. A group of prominent tech titans including Peter Thiel, Amazon Web Services and Musk have committed $1billion to OpenAI a nonprofit company aimed at championing responsible AI development. The opinion of experts within the field of artificial intelligence is mixed, with sizable fractions both concerned and unconcerned by risk from eventual superhumanly-capable AI.

In his book *Superintelligence*, Nick Bostrom provides an argument that artificial intelligence will pose a threat to mankind. He argues that sufficiently intelligent AI, if it chooses actions based on achieving some goal, will exhibit convergent behavior such as acquiring resources or protecting itself from being shut down. If this AI's goals do not reflect humanity's - one example is an AI told to compute as many digits of pi as possible - it might harm humanity in order to acquire more resources or prevent itself from being shut down, ultimately to better achieve its goal.

For this danger to be realized, the hypothetical AI would have to overpower or out-think all of humanity, which a minority of experts argue is a possibility far enough in the future to not be worth researching. Other counterarguments revolve around humans being either intrinsically or convergently valuable from the perspective of an artificial intelligence.

Concern over risk from artificial intelligence has led to some high-profile donations and investments. In January 2015, Elon Musk donated ten million dollars to the Future of Life Institute to fund research on understanding AI decision making. The goal of the institute is to "grow wisdom with which we manage" the growing power of technology. Musk also funds companies developing artificial intelligence such as Google DeepMind and Vicarious to "just keep an eye on what's going on with artificial intelligence. I think there is potentially a dangerous outcome there."

Development of militarized artificial intelligence is a related concern. Currently, 50+ countries are researching battlefield robots, including the United States, China, Russia, and the United Kingdom. Many people concerned about risk from superintelligent AI also want to limit the use of artificial soldiers.

Moral Decision-making

To keep AI ethical, some have suggested teaching new technologies equipped with AI, such as driver-less cars, to render moral decisions on their own. Others argued that these technologies could learn to act ethically the way children do—by interacting with adults, in particular, with ethicists. Still others suggest these smart technologies can determine the moral preferences of those who use them (just the way one learns about consumer preferences) and then be programmed to heed these preferences.

In Fiction

Thought-capable artificial beings have appeared as storytelling devices since antiquity.

The implications of a constructed machine exhibiting artificial intelligence have been a persistent theme in science fiction since the twentieth century. Early stories typically revolved around intelligent robots. The word "robot" itself was coined by Karel Čapek in his 1921 play *R.U.R.*, the title standing for "Rossum's Universal Robots". Later, the SF writer Isaac Asimov developed the Three Laws of Robotics which he subsequently explored in a long series of robot stories. These laws have since gained some traction in genuine AI research.

The novel *Do Androids Dream of Electric Sheep?*, by Philip K. Dick, tells a science fiction story about Androids and humans clashing in a futuristic world. Elements of artificial intelligence include the empathy box, mood organ, and the androids themselves. Throughout the novel, Dick portrays the idea that human subjectivity is altered by technology created with artificial intelligence.

Other influential fictional intelligences include HAL, the computer in charge of the spaceship in *2001: A Space Odyssey*, released as both a film and a book in 1968 and written by Arthur C. Clarke.

AI has since become firmly rooted in popular culture and is in many films, such as *The Terminator* (1984) and *A.I. Artificial Intelligence* (2001).

Machine Learning

Machine learning is the subfield of computer science that "gives computers the ability to learn without being explicitly programmed" (Arthur Samuel, 1959). Evolved from the study of pattern recognition and computational learning theory in artificial intelligence, machine learning explores the study and construction of algorithms that can learn from and make predictions on data – such algorithms overcome following strictly static program instructions by making data driven predictions or decisions, through building a model from sample inputs. Machine learning is employed in a range of computing tasks where designing and programming explicit algorithms is unfeasible; example applications include spam filtering, detection of network intruders or malicious insiders working towards a data breach, optical character recognition (OCR), search engines and computer vision.

Machine learning is closely related to (and often overlaps with) computational statistics, which also focuses in prediction-making through the use of computers. It has strong ties to mathematical optimization, which delivers methods, theory and application domains to the field. Machine learning is sometimes conflated with data mining, where the latter subfield focuses more on exploratory data analysis and is known as unsupervised learning. Machine learning can also be unsupervised and be used to learn and establish baseline behavioral profiles for various entities and then used to find meaningful anomalies, such as in the way LightCyber detects active network attacks leading up to data or asset theft or damage.

Within the field of data analytics, machine learning is a method used to devise complex models and algorithms that lend themselves to prediction; in commercial use, this is known as predictive analytics. These analytical models allow researchers, data scientists, engineers, and analysts to "produce reliable, repeatable decisions and results" and uncover "hidden insights" through learning from historical relationships and trends in the data.

Overview

Tom M. Mitchell provided a widely quoted, more formal definition: "A computer program is said to learn from experience E with respect to some class of tasks T and performance measure P if its performance at tasks in T, as measured by P, improves with experience E." This definition is notable for its defining machine learning in fundamentally operational rather than cognitive terms, thus following Alan Turing's proposal in his paper "Computing Machinery and Intelligence", that the question "Can machines think?" be replaced with the question "Can machines do what we (as thinking entities) can do?". In the proposal he explores the various characteristics that could be possessed by a *thinking machine* and the various implications in constructing one.

Types of Problems and Tasks

Machine learning tasks are typically classified into three broad categories, depending on the nature of the learning "signal" or "feedback" available to a learning system. These are

- Supervised learning: The computer is presented with example inputs and their desired outputs, given by a "teacher", and the goal is to learn a general rule that maps inputs to outputs.

- Unsupervised learning: No labels are given to the learning algorithm, leaving it on its own to find structure in its input. Unsupervised learning can be a goal in itself (discovering hidden patterns in data) or a means towards an end (feature learning).

- Reinforcement learning: A computer program interacts with a dynamic environment in which it must perform a certain goal (such as driving a vehicle), without a teacher explicitly telling it whether it has come close to its goal. Another example is learning to play a game by playing against an opponent.

Between supervised and unsupervised learning is semi-supervised learning, where the teacher gives an incomplete training signal: a training set with some (often many) of the target outputs missing. Transduction is a special case of this principle where the entire set of problem instances is known at learning time, except that part of the targets are missing.

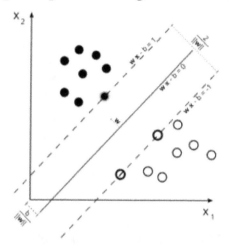

A support vector machine is a classifier that divides its input space into two regions, separated by a linear boundary. Here, it has learned to distinguish black and white circles.

Among other categories of machine learning problems, learning to learn learns its own inductive bias based on previous experience. Developmental learning, elaborated for robot learning, generates its own sequences (also called curriculum) of learning situations to cumulatively acquire repertoires of novel skills through autonomous self-exploration and social interaction with human teachers and using guidance mechanisms such as active learning, maturation, motor synergies, and imitation.

Another categorization of machine learning tasks arises when one considers the desired *output* of a machine-learned system:

- In classification, inputs are divided into two or more classes, and the learner must produce a model that assigns unseen inputs to one or more (multi-label classification) of these classes. This is typically tackled in a supervised way. Spam filtering is an example of classification, where the inputs are email (or other) messages and the classes are "spam" and "not spam".

- In regression, also a supervised problem, the outputs are continuous rather than discrete.

- In clustering, a set of inputs is to be divided into groups. Unlike in classification, the groups are not known beforehand, making this typically an unsupervised task.

- Density estimation finds the distribution of inputs in some space.

- Dimensionality reduction simplifies inputs by mapping them into a lower-dimensional space. Topic modeling is a related problem, where a program is given a list of human language documents and is tasked to find out which documents cover similar topics.

History and Relationships to other Fields

As a scientific endeavour, machine learning grew out of the quest for artificial intelligence. Already in the early days of AI as an academic discipline, some researchers were interested in having machines learn from data. They attempted to approach the problem with various symbolic methods, as well as what were then termed "neural networks"; these were mostly perceptrons and other models that were later found to be reinventions of the generalized linear models of statistics. Probabilistic reasoning was also employed, especially in automated medical diagnosis.

However, an increasing emphasis on the logical, knowledge-based approach caused a rift between AI and machine learning. Probabilistic systems were plagued by theoretical and practical problems of data acquisition and representation. By 1980, expert systems had come to dominate AI, and statistics was out of favor. Work on symbolic/knowledge-based learning did continue within AI, leading to inductive logic programming, but the more statistical line of research was now outside the field of AI proper, in pattern recognition and information retrieval. Neural networks research had been abandoned by AI and computer science around the same time. This line, too, was continued outside the AI/CS field, as "connectionism", by researchers from other disciplines including Hopfield, Rumelhart and Hinton. Their main success came in the mid-1980s with the reinvention of backpropagation.

Machine learning, reorganized as a separate field, started to flourish in the 1990s. The field changed its goal from achieving artificial intelligence to tackling solvable problems of a practical nature. It shifted focus away from the symbolic approaches it had inherited from AI, and toward methods and models borrowed from statistics and probability theory. It also benefited from the increasing availability of digitized information, and the possibility to distribute that via the Internet.

Machine learning and data mining often employ the same methods and overlap significantly, but while machine learning focuses on prediction, based on *known* properties learned from the training data, data mining focuses on the discovery of (previously) *unknown* properties in the data (this is the analysis step of Knowledge Discovery in Databases). Data mining uses many machine learning methods, but with different goals; on the other hand, machine learning also employs data mining methods as "unsupervised learning" or as a preprocessing step to improve learner accuracy. Much of the confusion between these two research communities (which do often have separate conferences and separate journals, ECML PKDD being a major exception) comes from the basic assumptions they work with: in machine learning, performance is usually evaluated with respect to the ability to *reproduce known* knowledge, while in Knowledge Discovery and Data Mining (KDD) the key task is the discovery of previously *unknown* knowledge. Evaluated with respect to known knowledge, an uninformed (unsupervised) method will easily be outperformed by other supervised methods, while in a typical KDD task, supervised methods cannot be used due to the unavailability of training data.

Machine learning also has intimate ties to optimization: many learning problems are formulated as minimization of some loss function on a training set of examples. Loss functions express the discrepancy between the predictions of the model being trained and the actual problem instances (for example, in classification, one wants to assign a label to instances, and models are trained to correctly predict the pre-assigned labels of a set examples). The difference between the two fields arises from the goal of generalization: while optimization algorithms can minimize the loss on a training set, machine learning is concerned with minimizing the loss on unseen samples.

Relation to Statistics

Machine learning and statistics are closely related fields. According to Michael I. Jordan, the ideas of machine learning, from methodological principles to theoretical tools, have had a long pre-history in statistics. He also suggested the term data science as a placeholder to call the overall field.

Leo Breiman distinguished two statistical modelling paradigms: data model and algorithmic model, wherein 'algorithmic model' means more or less the machine learning algorithms like Random forest.

Some statisticians have adopted methods from machine learning, leading to a combined field that they call *statistical learning*.

Theory

A core objective of a learner is to generalize from its experience. Generalization in this context is the ability of a learning machine to perform accurately on new, unseen examples/tasks after having experienced a learning data set. The training examples come from some generally unknown probability distribution (considered representative of the space of occurrences) and the learner has to build a general model about this space that enables it to produce sufficiently accurate predictions in new cases.

The computational analysis of machine learning algorithms and their performance is a branch of theoretical computer science known as computational learning theory. Because training sets are finite and the future is uncertain, learning theory usually does not yield guarantees of the performance of algorithms. Instead, probabilistic bounds on the performance are quite common. The bias–variance decomposition is one way to quantify generalization error.

For the best performance in the context of generalization, the complexity of the hypothesis should match the complexity of the function underlying the data. If the hypothesis is less complex than the function, then the model has underfit the data. If the complexity of the model is increased in response, then the training error decreases. But if the hypothesis is too complex, then the model is subject to overfitting and generalization will be poorer.

In addition to performance bounds, computational learning theorists study the time complexity and feasibility of learning. In computational learning theory, a computation is considered feasible if it can be done in polynomial time. There are two kinds of time complexity results. Positive results show that a certain class of functions can be learned in polynomial time. Negative results show that certain classes cannot be learned in polynomial time.

Approaches

Decision Tree Learning

Decision tree learning uses a decision tree as a predictive model, which maps observations about an item to conclusions about the item's target value.

Association Rule Learning

Association rule learning is a method for discovering interesting relations between variables in large databases.

Artificial Neural Networks

An artificial neural network (ANN) learning algorithm, usually called "neural network" (NN), is a learning algorithm that is inspired by the structure and functional aspects of biological neural networks. Computations are structured in terms of an interconnected group of artificial neurons, processing information using a connectionist approach to computation. Modern neural networks are non-linear statistical data modeling tools. They are usually used to model complex relationships between inputs and outputs, to find patterns in data, or to capture the statistical structure in an unknown joint probability distribution between observed variables.

Deep Learning

Falling hardware prices and the development of GPUs for personal use in the last few years have contributed to the development of the concept of Deep learning which consists of multiple hidden layers in an artificial neural network. This approach tries to model the way the human brain processes light and sound into vision and hearing. Some successful applications of deep learning are computer vision and speech recognition.

Inductive Logic Programming

Inductive logic programming (ILP) is an approach to rule learning using logic programming as a uniform representation for input examples, background knowledge, and hypotheses. Given an encoding of the known background knowledge and a set of examples represented as a logical database of facts, an ILP system will derive a hypothesized logic program that entails all positive and no negative examples. Inductive programming is a related field that considers any kind of programming languages for representing hypotheses (and not only logic programming), such as functional programs.

Support Vector Machines

Support vector machines (SVMs) are a set of related supervised learning methods used for classification and regression. Given a set of training examples, each marked as belonging to one of two categories, an SVM training algorithm builds a model that predicts whether a new example falls into one category or the other.

Clustering

Cluster analysis is the assignment of a set of observations into subsets (called *clusters*) so that observations within the same cluster are similar according to some predesignated criterion or criteria, while observations drawn from different clusters are dissimilar. Different clustering techniques make different assumptions on the structure of the data, often defined by some *similarity metric* and evaluated for example by *internal compactness* (similarity between members of the same cluster) and *separation* between different clusters. Other methods are based on *estimated density* and *graph connectivity*. Clustering is a method of unsupervised learning, and a common technique for statistical data analysis.

Bayesian Networks

A Bayesian network, belief network or directed acyclic graphical model is a probabilistic graphical model that represents a set of random variables and their conditional independencies via a directed acyclic graph (DAG). For example, a Bayesian network could represent the probabilistic relationships between diseases and symptoms. Given symptoms, the network can be used to compute the probabilities of the presence of various diseases. Efficient algorithms exist that perform inference and learning.

Reinforcement Learning

Reinforcement learning is concerned with how an *agent* ought to take *actions* in an *environment* so as to maximize some notion of long-term *reward*. Reinforcement learning algorithms attempt to find a *policy* that maps *states* of the world to the actions the agent ought to take in those states. Reinforcement learning differs from the supervised learning problem in that correct input/output pairs are never presented, nor sub-optimal actions explicitly corrected.

Representation Learning

Several learning algorithms, mostly unsupervised learning algorithms, aim at discovering better representations of the inputs provided during training. Classical examples include principal components analysis and cluster analysis. Representation learning algorithms often attempt to preserve the information in their input but transform it in a way that makes it useful, often as a pre-processing step before performing classification or predictions, allowing to reconstruct the inputs coming from the unknown data generating distribution, while not being necessarily faithful for configurations that are implausible under that distribution.

Manifold learning algorithms attempt to do so under the constraint that the learned representation is low-dimensional. Sparse coding algorithms attempt to do so under the constraint that the learned representation is sparse (has many zeros). Multilinear subspace learning algorithms aim to learn low-dimensional representations directly from tensor representations for multidimensional data, without reshaping them into (high-dimensional) vectors. Deep learning algorithms discover multiple levels of representation, or a hierarchy of features, with higher-level, more abstract features defined in terms of (or generating) lower-level features. It has been argued that an intelligent machine is one that learns a representation that disentangles the underlying factors of variation that explain the observed data.

Similarity and Metric Learning

In this problem, the learning machine is given pairs of examples that are considered similar and pairs of less similar objects. It then needs to learn a similarity function (or a distance metric function) that can predict if new objects are similar. It is sometimes used in Recommendation systems.

Sparse Dictionary Learning

In this method, a datum is represented as a linear combination of basis functions, and the coefficients are assumed to be sparse. Let x be a d-dimensional datum, D be a d by n matrix, where each column of D represents a basis function. r is the coefficient to represent x using D. Mathematically, sparse dictionary learning means solving where r is sparse. Generally speaking, n is assumed to be larger than d to allow the freedom for a sparse representation.

Learning a dictionary along with sparse representations is strongly NP-hard and also difficult to solve approximately. A popular heuristic method for sparse dictionary learning is K-SVD.

Sparse dictionary learning has been applied in several contexts. In classification, the problem is to determine which classes a previously unseen datum belongs to. Suppose a dictionary for each class has already been built. Then a new datum is associated with the class such that it's best sparsely represented by the corresponding dictionary. Sparse dictionary learning has also been applied in image de-noising. The key idea is that a clean image patch can be sparsely represented by an image dictionary, but the noise cannot.

Genetic Algorithms

A genetic algorithm (GA) is a search heuristic that mimics the process of natural selection, and uses methods such as mutation and crossover to generate new genotype in the hope of finding good solutions to a given problem. In machine learning, genetic algorithms found some uses in the 1980s and 1990s. Vice versa, machine learning techniques have been used to improve the performance of genetic and evolutionary algorithms.

Rule-based Machine Learning

Rule-based machine learning is a general term for any machine learning method that identifies, learns, or evolves `rules' to store, manipulate or apply, knowledge. The defining characteristic of a rule-based machine learner is the identification and utilization of a set of relational rules that collectively represent the knowledge captured by the system. This is in contrast to other machine learners that commonly identify a singular model that can be universally applied to any instance in order to make a prediction. Rule-based machine learning approaches include learning classifier systems, association rule learning, and artificial immune systems.

Learning Classifier Systems

Learning classifier systems (LCS) are a family of rule-based machine learning algorithms that combine a discovery component (e.g. typically a genetic algorithm) with a learning component (performing either supervised learning, reinforcement learning, or unsupervised learning). They seek to identify a set of context-dependent rules that collectively store and apply knowledge in a piecewise manner in order to make predictions.

Applications

Applications for machine learning include:

- Adaptive websites
- Affective computing
- Bioinformatics
- Brain-machine interfaces
- Cheminformatics
- Classifying DNA sequences
- Computational anatomy
- Computer vision, including object recognition
- Detecting credit card fraud
- Game playing
- Information retrieval
- Internet fraud detection
- Marketing
- Machine perception
- Medical diagnosis
- Economics
- Natural language processing
- Natural language understanding
- Optimization and metaheuristic
- Online advertising
- Recommender systems
- Robot locomotion
- Search engines
- Sentiment analysis (or opinion mining)
- Sequence mining
- Software engineering
- Speech and handwriting recognition
- Stock market analysis
- Structural health monitoring
- Syntactic pattern recognition

- User behavior analytics

In 2006, the online movie company Netflix held the first "Netflix Prize" competition to find a program to better predict user preferences and improve the accuracy on its existing Cinematch movie recommendation algorithm by at least 10%. A joint team made up of researchers from AT&T Labs-Research in collaboration with the teams Big Chaos and Pragmatic Theory built an ensemble model to win the Grand Prize in 2009 for $1 million. Shortly after the prize was awarded, Netflix realized that viewers' ratings were not the best indicators of their viewing patterns ("everything is a recommendation") and they changed their recommendation engine accordingly.

In 2010 The Wall Street Journal wrote about money management firm Rebellion Research's use of machine learning to predict economic movements. The article describes Rebellion Research's prediction of the financial crisis and economic recovery.

In 2012 co-founder of Sun Microsystems Vinod Khosla predicted that 80% of medical doctors jobs would be lost in the next two decades to automated machine learning medical diagnostic software.

In 2014 it has been reported that a machine learning algorithm has been applied in Art History to study fine art paintings, and that it may have revealed previously unrecognized influences between artists.

Model Assessments

Classification machine learning models can be validated by accuracy estimation techniques like the Holdout method, which splits the data in a training and test set (conventionally 2/3 training set and 1/3 test set designation) and evaluates the performance of the training model on the test set. In comparison, the N-fold-cross-validation method randomly splits the data in k subsets where the k-1 instances of the data are used to train the model while the kth instance is used to test the predictive ability of the training model. In addition to the holdout and cross-validation methods, bootstrap, which samples n instances with replacement from the dataset, can be used to assess model accuracy. In addition to accuracy, sensitivity and specificity (True Positive Rate: TPR and True Negative Rate: TNR, respectively) can provide modes of model assessment. Similarly False Positive Rate (FPR) as well as the False Negative Rate (FNR) can be computed. Receiver operating characteristic (ROC) along with the accompanying Area Under the ROC Curve (AUC) offer additional tools for classification model assessment. Higher AUC is associated with a better performing model.

Ethics

Machine Learning poses a host of ethical questions. Systems which are trained on datasets collected with biases may exhibit these biases upon use, thus digitizing cultural prejudices such as institutional racism and classism. Responsible collection of data thus is a critical part of machine learning.

Because language contains biases, machines trained on language corpora will necessarily also learn bias.

Software

Software suites containing a variety of machine learning algorithms include the following:

Free and Open-source Software

- dlib
- ELKI
- Encog
- GNU Octave
- H_2O
- Mahout
- Mallet (software project)
- mlpy
- MLPACK
- MOA (Massive Online Analysis)
- ND4J with Deeplearning4j
- NuPIC
- OpenAI
- OpenNN
- Orange
- R
- scikit-learn
- Shogun
- TensorFlow
- Torch (machine learning)
- Spark
- Yooreeka
- Weka

Proprietary Software with Free and Open-source Editions

- KNIME
- RapidMiner

Proprietary Software

- Amazon Machine Learning

- Angoss KnowledgeSTUDIO
- Ayasdi
- Databricks
- Google Prediction API
- IBM SPSS Modeler
- KXEN Modeler
- LIONsolver
- Mathematica
- MATLAB
- Microsoft Azure Machine Learning
- Neural Designer
- NeuroSolutions
- Oracle Data Mining
- RCASE
- SAS Enterprise Miner
- SequenceL
- Splunk
- STATISTICA Data Miner

Statistics

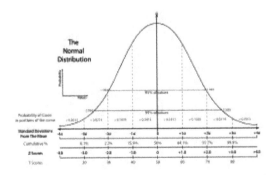

More probability density is found as one gets closer to the expected (mean) value in a normal distribution. Statistics used in standardized testing assessment are shown. The scales include *standard deviations, cumulative percentages, percentile equivalents, Z-scores, T-scores, standard nines,* and *percentages in standard nines.*

Statistics is the study of the collection, analysis, interpretation, presentation, and organization of data. In applying statistics to, e.g., a scientific, industrial, or social problem, it is conventional to begin with a statistical population or a statistical model process to be studied. Populations can be diverse topics such as "all people living in a country" or "every atom composing a crystal". Statistics deals with all aspects of data including the planning of data collection in terms of the design of surveys and experiments.

Scatter plots are used in descriptive statistics to show the observed relationships between different variables.

Some popular definitions are:

- Merriam-Webster dictionary defines statistics as "classified facts representing the conditions of a people in a state – especially the facts that can be stated in numbers or any other tabular or classified arrangement".

- Statistician Sir Arthur Lyon Bowley defines statistics as "Numerical statements of facts in any department of inquiry placed in relation to each other".

When census data cannot be collected, statisticians collect data by developing specific experiment designs and survey samples. Representative sampling assures that inferences and conclusions can safely extend from the sample to the population as a whole. An experimental study involves taking measurements of the system under study, manipulating the system, and then taking additional measurements using the same procedure to determine if the manipulation has modified the values of the measurements. In contrast, an observational study does not involve experimental manipulation.

Two main statistical methodologies are used in data analysis: descriptive statistics, which summarizes data from a sample using indexes such as the mean or standard deviation, and inferential statistics, which draws conclusions from data that are subject to random variation (e.g., observational errors, sampling variation). Descriptive statistics are most often concerned with two sets of properties of a *distribution* (sample or population): *central tendency* (or *location*) seeks to characterize the distribution's central or typical value, while *dispersion* (or *variability*) characterizes the extent to which members of the distribution depart from its center and each other. Inferences on mathematical statistics are made under the framework of probability theory, which deals with the analysis of random phenomena.

A standard statistical procedure involves the test of the relationship between two statistical data sets, or a data set and a synthetic data drawn from idealized model. A hypothesis is proposed for the statistical relationship between the two data sets, and this is compared as an alternative to an idealized null hypothesis of no relationship between two data sets. Rejecting or disproving the null hypothesis is done using statistical tests that quantify the sense in which the null can be proven false, given the data that are used in the test. Working from a null hypothesis, two basic forms of error are recognized: Type I errors (null hypothesis is falsely rejected giving a "false positive") and Type II errors (null hypothesis fails to be rejected and an actual difference between populations is missed giving a "false negative"). Multiple problems have come to be associated with this framework: ranging from obtaining a sufficient sample size to specifying an adequate null hypothesis.

Measurement processes that generate statistical data are also subject to error. Many of these errors are classified as random (noise) or systematic (bias), but other types of errors (e.g., blunder, such as when an analyst reports incorrect units) can also be important. The presence of missing data and/or censoring may result in biased estimates and specific techniques have been developed to address these problems.

Statistics can be said to have begun in ancient civilization, going back at least to the 5th century BC, but it was not until the 18th century that it started to draw more heavily from calculus and probability theory. Statistics continues to be an area of active research, for example on the problem of how to analyze Big data.

Scope

Statistics is a mathematical body of science that pertains to the collection, analysis, interpretation or explanation, and presentation of data, or as a branch of mathematics. Some consider statistics to be a distinct mathematical science rather than a branch of mathematics. While many scientific investigations make use of data, statistics is concerned with the use of data in the context of uncertainty and decision making in the face of uncertainty.

Mathematical Statistics

Mathematical statistics is the application of mathematics to statistics, which was originally conceived as the science of the state — the collection and analysis of facts about a country: its economy, land, military, population, and so forth. Mathematical techniques used for this include mathematical analysis, linear algebra, stochastic analysis, differential equations, and measure-theoretic probability theory.

Overview

In applying statistics to a problem, it is common practice to start with a population or process to be studied. Populations can be diverse topics such as "all persons living in a country" or "every atom composing a crystal".

Ideally, statisticians compile data about the entire population (an operation called census). This may be organized by governmental statistical institutes. Descriptive statistics can be used to summarize the population data. Numerical descriptors include mean and standard deviation for continuous data types (like income), while frequency and percentage are more useful in terms of describing categorical data (like race).

When a census is not feasible, a chosen subset of the population called a sample is studied. Once a sample that is representative of the population is determined, data is collected for the sample members in an observational or experimental setting. Again, descriptive statistics can be used to summarize the sample data. However, the drawing of the sample has been subject to an element of randomness, hence the established numerical descriptors from the sample are also due to uncertainty. To still draw meaningful conclusions about the entire population, inferential statistics is needed. It uses patterns in the sample data to draw inferences about the population represented, accounting for randomness. These inferences may take the form of: answering yes/no questions about the data (hypothesis testing), estimating numerical characteristics of the data (estimation), describing associations within the data (correlation) and modeling relationships within the data (for example, using regression analysis). Inference can extend to forecasting, prediction and estimation of unobserved values either in or associated with the population being studied; it can include extrapolation and interpolation of time series or spatial data, and can also include data mining.

Data Collection

Sampling

When full census data cannot be collected, statisticians collect sample data by developing specific experiment designs and survey samples. Statistics itself also provides tools for prediction and forecasting the use of data through statistical models. To use a sample as a guide to an entire population, it is important that it truly represents the overall population. Representative sampling assures that inferences and conclusions can safely extend from the sample to the population as a whole. A major problem lies in determining the extent that the sample chosen is actually representative. Statistics offers methods to estimate and correct for any bias within the sample and data collection procedures. There are also methods of experimental design for experiments that can lessen these issues at the outset of a study, strengthening its capability to discern truths about the population.

Sampling theory is part of the mathematical discipline of probability theory. Probability is used in mathematical statistics to study the sampling distributions of sample statistics and, more generally, the properties of statistical procedures. The use of any statistical method is valid when the system or population under consideration satisfies the assumptions of the method. The difference in point of view between classic probability theory and sampling theory is, roughly, that probability theory starts from the given parameters of a total population to deduce probabilities that pertain to samples. Statistical inference, however, moves in the opposite direction—inductively inferring from samples to the parameters of a larger or total population.

Experimental and Observational Studies

A common goal for a statistical research project is to investigate causality, and in particular to draw a conclusion on the effect of changes in the values of predictors or independent variables on dependent variables. There are two major types of causal statistical studies: experimental studies and observational studies. In both types of studies, the effect of differences of an independent variable (or variables) on the behavior of the dependent variable are observed. The difference between the two types lies in how the study is actually conducted. Each can be very effective. An experimental study involves taking measurements of the system under study, manipulating the system, and then taking additional measurements using the same procedure to determine if the manipulation has modified the values of the measurements. In contrast, an observational study does not involve experimental manipulation. Instead, data are gathered and correlations between predictors and response are investigated. While the tools of data analysis work best on data from randomized studies, they are also applied to other kinds of data – like natural experiments and observational studies – for which a statistician would use a modified, more structured estimation method (e.g., Difference in differences estimation and instrumental variables, among many others) that produce consistent estimators.

Experiments

The basic steps of a statistical experiment are:

1. Planning the research, including finding the number of replicates of the study, using the following information: preliminary estimates regarding the size of treatment effects, alternative hypotheses, and the estimated experimental variability. Consideration of the selection of experimental subjects and the ethics of research is necessary. Statisticians recommend that experiments compare (at least) one new treatment with a standard treatment or control, to allow an unbiased estimate of the difference in treatment effects.

2. Design of experiments, using blocking to reduce the influence of confounding variables, and randomized assignment of treatments to subjects to allow unbiased estimates of treatment effects and experimental error. At this stage, the experimenters and statisticians write the *experimental protocol* that will guide the performance of the experiment and which specifies the *primary analysis* of the experimental data.

3. Performing the experiment following the experimental protocol and analyzing the data following the experimental protocol.

4. Further examining the data set in secondary analyses, to suggest new hypotheses for future study.

5. Documenting and presenting the results of the study.

Experiments on human behavior have special concerns. The famous Hawthorne study examined changes to the working environment at the Hawthorne plant of the Western Electric Company. The researchers were interested in determining whether increased illumination would increase the productivity of the assembly line workers. The researchers first measured the productivity in the plant, then modified the illumination in an area of the plant and checked if the changes in illumination affected productivity. It turned out that productivity indeed improved (under the experimental conditions). However, the study is heavily criticized today for errors in experimental procedures, specifically for the lack of a control group and blindness. The Hawthorne effect refers to finding that an outcome (in this case, worker productivity) changed due to observation itself. Those in the Hawthorne study became more productive not because the lighting was changed but because they were being observed.

Observational Study

An example of an observational study is one that explores the association between smoking and lung cancer. This type of study typically uses a survey to collect observations about the area of interest and then performs statistical analysis. In this case, the researchers would collect observations of both smokers and non-smokers, perhaps through a cohort study, and then look for the number of cases of lung cancer in each group. A case-control study is another type of observational study in which people with and without the outcome of interest (e.g. lung cancer) are invited to participate and their exposure histories are collected.

Types of Data

Various attempts have been made to produce a taxonomy of levels of measurement. The psychophysicist Stanley Smith Stevens defined nominal, ordinal, interval, and ratio scales. Nominal measurements do not have meaningful rank order among values, and permit any one-to-one transformation. Ordinal measurements have imprecise differences between consecutive values, but have a meaningful order to those values, and permit any order-preserving transformation. Interval measurements have meaningful distances between measurements defined, but the zero value is arbitrary (as in the case with longitude and temperature measurements in Celsius or Fahrenheit), and permit any linear transformation. Ratio measurements have both a meaningful zero value and the distances between different measurements defined, and permit any rescaling transformation.

Because variables conforming only to nominal or ordinal measurements cannot be reasonably measured numerically, sometimes they are grouped together as categorical variables, whereas ratio and interval measurements are grouped together as quantitative variables, which can be either discrete or continuous, due to their numerical nature. Such distinctions can often be loosely correlated with data type in computer science, in that dichotomous categorical variables may be represented with the Boolean data type, polytomous categorical variables with arbitrarily assigned integers in the integral data type, and continuous variables with the real data type involving floating point computation. But the mapping of computer science data types to statistical data types depends on which categorization of the latter is being implemented.

Other categorizations have been proposed. For example, Mosteller and Tukey (1977) distinguished grades, ranks, counted fractions, counts, amounts, and balances. Nelder (1990) described continuous counts, continuous ratios, count ratios, and categorical modes of data..

The issue of whether or not it is appropriate to apply different kinds of statistical methods to data obtained from different kinds of measurement procedures is complicated by issues concerning the transformation of variables and the precise interpretation of research questions. "The relationship between the data and what they describe merely reflects the fact that certain kinds of statistical statements may have truth values which are not invariant under some transformations. Whether or not a transformation is sensible to contemplate depends on the question one is trying to answer" (Hand, 2004, p. 82).

Terminology and Theory of Inferential Statistics

Statistics, Estimators and Pivotal Quantities

Consider independent identically distributed (IID) random variables with a given probability distribution: standard statistical inference and estimation theory defines a random sample as the random vector given by the column vector of these IID variables. The population being examined is described by a probability distribution that may have unknown parameters.

A statistic is a random variable that is a function of the random sample, but *not a function of unknown parameters*. The probability distribution of the statistic, though, may have unknown parameters.

Consider now a function of the unknown parameter: an estimator is a statistic used to estimate such function. Commonly used estimators include sample mean, unbiased sample variance and sample covariance.

A random variable that is a function of the random sample and of the unknown parameter, but whose probability distribution *does not depend on the unknown parameter* is called a pivotal quantity or pivot. Widely used pivots include the z-score, the chi square statistic and Student's t-value.

Between two estimators of a given parameter, the one with lower mean squared error is said to be more efficient. Furthermore, an estimator is said to be unbiased if its expected value is equal to the true value of the unknown parameter being estimated, and asymptotically unbiased if its expected value converges at the limit to the true value of such parameter.

Other desirable properties for estimators include: UMVUE estimators that have the lowest variance for all possible values of the parameter to be estimated (this is usually an easier property to verify than efficiency) and consistent estimators which converges in probability to the true value of such parameter.

This still leaves the question of how to obtain estimators in a given situation and carry the computation, several methods have been proposed: the method of moments, the maximum likelihood method, the least squares method and the more recent method of estimating equations.

Null Hypothesis and Alternative Hypothesis

Interpretation of statistical information can often involve the development of a null hypothesis which is usually (but not necessarily) that no relationship exists among variables or that no change occurred over time.

The best illustration for a novice is the predicament encountered by a criminal trial. The null hypothesis, H_0, asserts that the defendant is innocent, whereas the alternative hypothesis, H_1, asserts that the defendant is guilty. The indictment comes because of suspicion of the guilt. The H_0 (status quo) stands in opposition to H_1 and is maintained unless H_1 is supported by evidence "beyond a reasonable doubt". However, "failure to reject H_0" in this case does not imply innocence, but merely that the evidence was insufficient to convict. So the jury does not necessarily *accept* H_0 but *fails to reject* H_0. While one can not "prove" a null hypothesis, one can test how close it is to being true with a power test, which tests for type II errors.

What statisticians call an alternative hypothesis is simply an hypothesis that contradicts the null hypothesis.

Error

Working from a null hypothesis, two basic forms of error are recognized:

- Type I errors where the null hypothesis is falsely rejected giving a "false positive".

- Type II errors where the null hypothesis fails to be rejected and an actual difference between populations is missed giving a "false negative".

Standard deviation refers to the extent to which individual observations in a sample differ from a central value, such as the sample or population mean, while Standard error refers to an estimate of difference between sample mean and population mean.

A statistical error is the amount by which an observation differs from its expected value, a residual is the amount an observation differs from the value the estimator of the expected value assumes on a given sample (also called prediction).

Mean squared error is used for obtaining efficient estimators, a widely used class of estimators. Root mean square error is simply the square root of mean squared error.

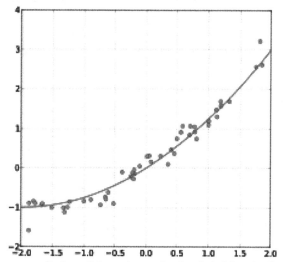

A least squares fit: in red the points to be fitted, in blue the fitted line.

Many statistical methods seek to minimize the residual sum of squares, and these are called "methods of least squares" in contrast to Least absolute deviations. The latter gives equal weight to small and big errors, while the former gives more weight to large errors. Residual sum of squares is also differentiable, which provides a handy property for doing regression. Least squares applied to linear regression is called ordinary least squares method and least squares applied to nonlinear regression is called non-linear least squares. Also in a linear regression model the non deterministic part of the model is called error term, disturbance or more simply noise. Both linear regression and non-linear regression are addressed in polynomial least squares, which also describes the variance in a prediction of the dependent variable (y axis) as a function of the independent variable (x axis) and the deviations (errors, noise, disturbances) from the estimated (fitted) curve.

Measurement processes that generate statistical data are also subject to error. Many of these errors are classified as random (noise) or systematic (bias), but other types of errors (e.g., blunder, such as when an analyst reports incorrect units) can also be important. The presence of missing data and/or censoring may result in biased estimates and specific techniques have been developed to address these problems.

Interval Estimation

Confidence intervals: the red line is true value for the mean in this example, the blue lines are random confidence intervals for 100 realizations.

Most studies only sample part of a population, so results don't fully represent the whole population. Any estimates obtained from the sample only approximate the population value. Confidence intervals allow statisticians to express how closely the sample estimate matches the true value in the whole population. Often they are expressed as 95% confidence intervals. Formally, a 95% confidence interval for a value is a range where, if the sampling and analysis were repeated under the same conditions (yielding a different dataset), the interval would include the true (population) value in 95% of all possible cases. This does *not* imply that the probability that the true value is in the confidence interval is 95%. From the frequentist perspective, such a claim does not even make sense, as the true value is not a random variable. Either the true value is or is not within the given interval. However, it is true that, before any data are sampled and given a plan for how to construct the confidence interval, the probability is 95% that the yet-to-be-calculated interval will cover the true value: at this point, the limits of the interval are yet-to-be-observed random variables. One approach that does yield an interval that can be interpreted as having a given probability of containing the true value is to use a credible interval from Bayesian statistics: this approach depends on a different way of interpreting what is meant by "probability", that is as a Bayesian probability.

In principle confidence intervals can be symmetrical or asymmetrical. An interval can be asymmetrical because it works as lower or upper bound for a parameter (left-sided interval or right sided interval), but it can also be asymmetrical because the two sided interval is built violating symmetry around the estimate. Sometimes the bounds for a confidence interval are reached asymptotically and these are used to approximate the true bounds.

Significance

Statistics rarely give a simple Yes/No type answer to the question under analysis. Interpretation often comes down to the level of statistical significance applied to the numbers and often refers to the probability of a value accurately rejecting the null hypothesis (sometimes referred to as the p-value).

The standard approach is to test a null hypothesis against an alternative hypothesis. A critical region is the set of values of the estimator that leads to refuting the null hypothesis. The probability of type I error is therefore the probability that the estimator belongs to the critical region given that null hypothesis is true (statistical significance) and the probability of type II error is the probability that the estimator doesn't belong to the critical region given that the alternative hypothesis is true. The statistical power of a test is the probability that it correctly rejects the null hypothesis when the null hypothesis is false.

Important:

Pr (observation | hypothesis) ≠ Pr (hypothesis | observation)

The probability of observing a result given that some hypothesis
is true is *not equivalent* to the probability that a hypothesis is true
given that some result has been observed.

Using the p-value as a "score" is committing an egregious logical error:
the transposed conditional fallacy.

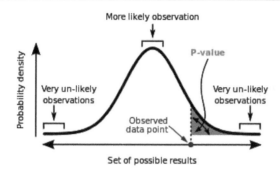

A p-value (shaded green area) is the probability of an observed
(or more extreme) result assuming that the null hypothesis is true.

In this graph the black line is probability distribution for the test statistic, the critical region is the set of values to the right of the observed data point (observed value of the test statistic) and the p-value is represented by the green area.

Referring to statistical significance does not necessarily mean that the overall result is significant in real world terms. For example, in a large study of a drug it may be shown that the drug has a statistically significant but very small beneficial effect, such that the drug is unlikely to help the patient noticeably.

While in principle the acceptable level of statistical significance may be subject to debate, the p-value is the smallest significance level that allows the test to reject the null hypothesis. This is logically equivalent to saying that the p-value is the probability, assuming the null hypothesis is true, of observing a result at least as extreme as the test statistic. Therefore, the smaller the p-value, the lower the probability of committing type I error.

Some problems are usually associated with this framework:

- A difference that is highly statistically significant can still be of no practical significance, but it is possible to properly formulate tests to account for this. One response involves going beyond reporting only the significance level to include the *p*-value when reporting whether a hypothesis is rejected or accepted. The p-value, however, does not indicate the size or importance of the observed effect and can also seem to exaggerate the importance of minor differences in large studies. A better and increasingly common approach is to report confidence intervals. Although these are produced from the same calculations as those of hypothesis tests or *p*-values, they describe both the size of the effect and the uncertainty surrounding it.

- Fallacy of the transposed conditional, aka prosecutor's fallacy: criticisms arise because the hypothesis testing approach forces one hypothesis (the null hypothesis) to be favored, since what is being evaluated is probability of the observed result given the null hypothesis and not probability of the null hypothesis given the observed result. An alternative to this approach is offered by Bayesian inference, although it requires establishing a prior probability.

- Rejecting the null hypothesis does not automatically prove the alternative hypothesis.

- As everything in inferential statistics it relies on sample size, and therefore under fat tails p-values may be seriously mis-computed.

Examples

Some well-known statistical tests and procedures are:

- Analysis of variance (ANOVA)
- Chi-squared test
- Correlation
- Factor analysis
- Mann–Whitney U
- Mean square weighted deviation (MSWD)
- Pearson product-moment correlation coefficient
- Regression analysis
- Spearman's rank correlation coefficient
- Student's t-test
- Time series analysis
- Conjoint Analysis

Misuse

Misuse of statistics can produce subtle, but serious errors in description and interpretation—subtle in the sense that even experienced professionals make such errors, and serious in the sense that they can lead to devastating decision errors. For instance, social policy, medical practice, and the reliability of structures like bridges all rely on the proper use of statistics.

Even when statistical techniques are correctly applied, the results can be difficult to interpret for those lacking expertise. The statistical significance of a trend in the data—which measures the extent to which a trend could be caused by random variation in the sample—may or may not agree with an intuitive sense of its significance. The set of basic statistical skills (and skepticism) that people need to deal with information in their everyday lives properly is referred to as statistical literacy.

There is a general perception that statistical knowledge is all-too-frequently intentionally misused by finding ways to interpret only the data that are favorable to the presenter. A mistrust and misunderstanding of statistics is associated with the quotation, "There are three kinds of lies: lies, damned lies, and statistics". Misuse of statistics can be both inadvertent and intentional, and the book *How to Lie with Statistics* outlines a range of considerations. In an attempt to shed light on the use and misuse of statistics, reviews of statistical techniques used in particular fields are conducted (e.g. Warne, Lazo, Ramos, and Ritter (2012)).

Ways to avoid misuse of statistics include using proper diagrams and avoiding bias. Misuse can occur when conclusions are overgeneralized and claimed to be representative of more than they really are, often by either deliberately or unconsciously overlooking sampling bias. Bar graphs are arguably the easiest diagrams to use and understand, and they can be made either by hand or with simple computer programs. Unfortunately, most people do not look for bias or errors, so they are not noticed. Thus, people may often believe that something is true even if it is not well represented. To make data gathered from statistics believable and accurate, the sample taken must be representative of the whole. According to Huff, "The dependability of a sample can be destroyed by [bias]... allow yourself some degree of skepticism."

To assist in the understanding of statistics Huff proposed a series of questions to be asked in each case:

- Who says so? (Does he/she have an axe to grind?)

- How does he/she know? (Does he/she have the resources to know the facts?)

- What's missing? (Does he/she give us a complete picture?)

- Did someone change the subject? (Does he/she offer us the right answer to the wrong problem?)

- Does it make sense? (Is his/her conclusion logical and consistent with what we already know?)

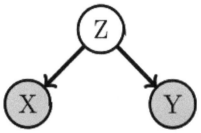

The confounding variable problem: *X* and *Y* may be correlated, not because there is causal relationship between them, but because both depend on a third variable *Z*. *Z* is called a confounding factor.

Misinterpretation: Correlation

The concept of correlation is particularly noteworthy for the potential confusion it can cause. Statistical analysis of a data set often reveals that two variables (properties) of the population under consideration tend to vary together, as if they were connected. For example, a study of annual income that also looks at age of death might find that poor people tend to have shorter lives than affluent people. The two variables are said to be correlated; however, they may or may not be the cause of one another. The correlation phenomena could be caused by a third, previously unconsidered phenomenon, called a lurking variable or confounding variable. For this reason, there is no way to immediately infer the existence of a causal relationship between the two variables.

History of Statistical Science

Gerolamo Cardano, the earliest pioneer on the mathematics of probability.

Statistical methods date back at least to the 5th century BC.

Some scholars pinpoint the origin of statistics to 1663, with the publication of *Natural and Political Observations upon the Bills of Mortality* by John Graunt. Early applications of statistical thinking revolved around the needs of states to base policy on demographic and economic data, hence its *stat-* etymology. The scope of the discipline of statistics broadened in the early 19th century to include the collection and analysis of data in general. Today, statistics is widely employed in government, business, and natural and social sciences.

Its mathematical foundations were laid in the 17th century with the development of the probability theory by Gerolamo Cardano, Blaise Pascal and Pierre de Fermat. Mathematical probability theory arose from the study of games of chance, although the concept of probability was already examined in medieval law and by philosophers such as Juan Caramuel. The method of least squares was first described by Adrien-Marie Legendre in 1805.

The modern field of statistics emerged in the late 19th and early 20th century in three stages. The first wave, at the turn of the century, was led by the work of Francis Galton and Karl Pearson, who transformed statistics into a rigorous mathematical discipline used for analysis, not just in science, but in industry and politics as well. Galton's contributions included introducing the concepts of standard deviation, correlation, regression analysis and the application of these methods to the study of the variety of human characteristics – height, weight, eyelash length among others. Pearson developed the Pearson product-moment correlation coefficient, defined as a product-moment, the method of moments for the fitting of distributions to samples and the Pearson distribution, among many other things. Galton and Pearson founded *Biometrika* as the first journal of mathematical statistics and biostatistics (then called biometry), and the latter founded the world's first university statistics department at University College London.

Karl Pearson, a founder of mathematical statistics.

Ronald Fisher coined the term null hypothesis during the Lady tasting tea experiment, which "is never proved or established, but is possibly disproved, in the course of experimentation".

The second wave of the 1910s and 20s was initiated by William Gosset, and reached its culmination in the insights of Ronald Fisher, who wrote the textbooks that were to define the academic discipline in universities around the world. Fisher's most important publications were his 1918 seminal paper *The Correlation between Relatives on the Supposition of Mendelian Inheritance*, which was the first to use the statistical term, variance, his classic 1925 work *Statistical Methods for Research Workers* and his 1935 *The Design of Experiments*, where he developed rigorous design of experiments models. He originated the concepts of sufficiency, ancillary statistics, Fisher's linear discriminator and Fisher information. In his 1930 book *The Genetical Theory of Natural Selection* he applied statistics to various biological concepts such as Fisher's principle). Nevertheless, A. W. F. Edwards has remarked that it is "probably the most celebrated argument in evolutionary biology". (about the sex ratio), the Fisherian runaway, a concept in sexual selection about a positive feedback runaway affect found in evolution.

The final wave, which mainly saw the refinement and expansion of earlier developments, emerged from the collaborative work between Egon Pearson and Jerzy Neyman in the 1930s. They introduced the concepts of "Type II" error, power of a test and confidence intervals. Jerzy Neyman in 1934 showed that stratified random sampling was in general a better method of estimation than purposive (quota) sampling.

Today, statistical methods are applied in all fields that involve decision making, for making accurate inferences from a collated body of data and for making decisions in the face of uncertainty based on statistical methodology. The use of modern computers has expedited large-scale statistical computations, and has also made possible new methods that are impractical to perform manually. Statistics continues to be an area of active research, for example on the problem of how to analyze Big data.

Applications

Applied Statistics, Theoretical Statistics and Mathematical Statistics

"Applied statistics" comprises descriptive statistics and the application of inferential statistics.

Theoretical statistics concerns both the logical arguments underlying justification of approaches to statistical inference, as well encompassing *mathematical statistics*. Mathematical statistics includes not only the manipulation of probability distributions necessary for deriving results related to methods of estimation and inference, but also various aspects of computational statistics and the design of experiments.

Machine Learning and Data Mining

There are two applications for machine learning and data mining: data management and data analysis. Statistics tools are necessary for the data analysis.

Statistics in Society

Statistics is applicable to a wide variety of academic disciplines, including natural and social sciences, government, and business. Statistical consultants can help organizations and companies that don't have in-house expertise relevant to their particular questions.

Statistical Computing

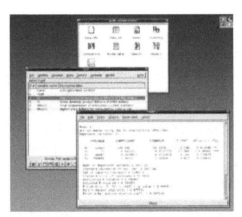

gretl, an example of an open source statistical package

The rapid and sustained increases in computing power starting from the second half of the 20th century have had a substantial impact on the practice of statistical science. Early statistical models were almost always from the class of linear models, but powerful computers, coupled with suitable numerical algorithms, caused an increased interest in nonlinear models (such as neural networks) as well as the creation of new types, such as generalized linear models and multilevel models.

Increased computing power has also led to the growing popularity of computationally intensive methods based on resampling, such as permutation tests and the bootstrap, while techniques such as Gibbs sampling have made use of Bayesian models more feasible. The computer revolution has implications for the future of statistics with new emphasis on "experimental" and "empirical" statistics. A large number of both general and special purpose statistical software are now available.

Statistics Applied to Mathematics or the Arts

Traditionally, statistics was concerned with drawing inferences using a semi-standardized methodology that was "required learning" in most sciences. This has changed with use of statistics in non-inferential contexts. What was once considered a dry subject, taken in many fields as a degree-requirement, is now viewed enthusiastically. Initially derided by some mathematical purists, it is now considered essential methodology in certain areas.

- In number theory, scatter plots of data generated by a distribution function may be transformed with familiar tools used in statistics to reveal underlying patterns, which may then lead to hypotheses.

- Methods of statistics including predictive methods in forecasting are combined with chaos theory and fractal geometry to create video works that are considered to have great beauty.

- The process art of Jackson Pollock relied on artistic experiments whereby underlying distributions in nature were artistically revealed. With the advent of computers, statistical methods were applied to formalize such distribution-driven natural processes to make and analyze moving video art.

- Methods of statistics may be used predicatively in performance art, as in a card trick based on a Markov process that only works some of the time, the occasion of which can be predicted using statistical methodology.

- Statistics can be used to predicatively create art, as in the statistical or stochastic music invented by Iannis Xenakis, where the music is performance-specific. Though this type of artistry does not always come out as expected, it does behave in ways that are predictable and tunable using statistics.

Specialized Disciplines

Statistical techniques are used in a wide range of types of scientific and social research, including: biostatistics, computational biology, computational sociology, network biology, social science, sociology and social research. Some fields of inquiry use applied statistics so extensively that they have specialized terminology. These disciplines include:

- Actuarial science (assesses risk in the insurance and finance industries)

- Applied information economics

- Astrostatistics (statistical evaluation of astronomical data)

- Biostatistics

- Business statistics

- Chemometrics (for analysis of data from chemistry)

- Data mining (applying statistics and pattern recognition to discover knowledge from data)

- Data science

- Demography

- Econometrics (statistical analysis of economic data)

- Energy statistics

- Engineering statistics

- Epidemiology (statistical analysis of disease)

- Geography and Geographic Information Systems, specifically in Spatial analysis

- Image processing

- Medical Statistics

- Political Science

- Psychological statistics

- Reliability engineering

- Social statistics

- Statistical Mechanics

In addition, there are particular types of statistical analysis that have also developed their own specialised terminology and methodology:

- Bootstrap / Jackknife resampling

- Multivariate statistics

- Statistical classification

- Structured data analysis (statistics)

- Structural equation modelling

- Survey methodology

- Survival analysis

- Statistics in various sports, particularly baseball - known as Sabermetrics - and cricket

Statistics form a key basis tool in business and manufacturing as well. It is used to understand measurement systems variability, control processes (as in statistical process control or SPC), for summarizing data, and to make data-driven decisions. In these roles, it is a key tool, and perhaps the only reliable tool.

Database

A database is an organized collection of data. It is the collection of schemas, tables, queries, reports, views, and other objects. The data are typically organized to model aspects of reality in a way that supports processes requiring information, such as modelling the availability of rooms in hotels in a way that supports finding a hotel with vacancies.

A database management system (DBMS) is a computer software application that interacts with the user, other applications, and the database itself to capture and analyze data. A general-purpose DBMS is designed to allow the definition, creation, querying, update, and administration of databases. Well-known DBMSs include MySQL, PostgreSQL, MongoDB, Microsoft SQL Server, Oracle, Sybase, SAP HANA, and IBM DB2. A database is not generally portable across different DBMSs, but different DBMS can interoperate by using standards such as SQL and ODBC or JDBC to allow a single application to work with more than one DBMS. Database management systems are often classified according to the database model that they support; the most popular database systems since the 1980s have all supported the relational model as represented by the SQL language. Sometimes a DBMS is loosely referred to as a 'database'.

Terminology and Overview

Formally, a "database" refers to a set of related data and the way it is organized. Access to this data is usually provided by a "database management system" (DBMS) consisting of an integrated set of computer software that allows users to interact with one or more databases and provides access to all of the data contained in the database (although restrictions may exist that limit access to particular data). The DBMS provides various functions that allow entry, storage and retrieval of large quantities of information and provides ways to manage how that information is organized.

Because of the close relationship between them, the term "database" is often used casually to refer to both a database and the DBMS used to manipulate it.

Outside the world of professional information technology, the term *database* is often used to refer to any collection of related data (such as a spreadsheet or a card index). This article is concerned only with databases where the size and usage requirements necessitate use of a database management system.

Existing DBMSs provide various functions that allow management of a database and its data which can be classified into four main functional groups:

- Data definition – Creation, modification and removal of definitions that define the organization of the data.

- Update – Insertion, modification, and deletion of the actual data.

- Retrieval – Providing information in a form directly usable or for further processing by other applications. The retrieved data may be made available in a form basically the same as it is stored in the database or in a new form obtained by altering or combining existing data from the database.

- Administration – Registering and monitoring users, enforcing data security, monitoring performance, maintaining data integrity, dealing with concurrency control, and recovering information that has been corrupted by some event such as an unexpected system failure.

Both a database and its DBMS conform to the principles of a particular database model. "Database system" refers collectively to the database model, database management system, and database.

Physically, database servers are dedicated computers that hold the actual databases and run only the DBMS and related software. Database servers are usually multiprocessor computers, with generous memory and RAID disk arrays used for stable storage. RAID is used for recovery of data if any of the disks fail. Hardware database accelerators, connected to one or more servers via a high-speed channel, are also used in large volume transaction processing environments. DBMSs are found at the heart of most database applications. DBMSs may be built around a custom multitasking kernel with built-in networking support, but modern DBMSs typically rely on a standard operating system to provide these functions from databases before the inception of Structured Query Language (SQL). The data recovered was disparate, redundant and disorderly, since there was no proper method to fetch it and arrange it in a concrete structure.

Since DBMSs comprise a significant economical market, computer and storage vendors often take into account DBMS requirements in their own development plans.

Databases and DBMSs can be categorized according to the database model(s) that they support (such as relational or XML), the type(s) of computer they run on (from a server cluster to a mobile phone), the query language(s) used to access the database (such as SQL or XQuery), and their internal engineering, which affects performance, scalability, resilience, and security.

Applications

Databases are used to support internal operations of organizations and to underpin online interactions with customers and suppliers.

Databases are used to hold administrative information and more specialized data, such as engineering data or economic models. Examples of database applications include computerized library systems, flight reservation systems, computerized parts inventory systems, and many content management systems that store websites as collections of webpages in a database.

General-purpose and Special-purpose DBMSs

A DBMS has evolved into a complex software system and its development typically requires thousands of human years of development effort.[a] Some general-purpose DBMSs such as Adabas, Oracle and DB2 have been undergoing upgrades since the 1970s. General-purpose DBMSs aim to meet the needs of as many applications as possible, which adds to the complexity. However, the fact that their development cost can be spread over a large number of users means that they are often the most cost-effective approach. However, a general-purpose DBMS is not always the optimal solution: in some cases a general-purpose DBMS may introduce unnecessary overhead. Therefore, there are many examples of systems that use special-purpose databases. A common example is an email system that performs many of the functions of a general-purpose DBMS such as the insertion and deletion of messages composed of various items of data or associating messages with a particular email address; but these functions are limited to what is required to handle email and don't provide the user with all of the functionality that would be available using a general-purpose DBMS.

Many other databases have application software that accesses the database on behalf of end-users, without exposing the DBMS interface directly. Application programmers may use a wire protocol directly, or more likely through an application programming interface. Database designers and database administrators interact with the DBMS through dedicated interfaces to build and maintain the applications' databases, and thus need some more knowledge and understanding about how DBMSs operate and the DBMSs' external interfaces and tuning parameters.

History

Following the technology progress in the areas of processors, computer memory, computer storage, and computer networks, the sizes, capabilities, and performance of databases and their respective DBMSs have grown in orders of magnitude. The development of database technology can be divided into three eras based on data model or structure: navigational, SQL/relational, and post-relational.

The two main early navigational data models were the hierarchical model, epitomized by IBM's IMS system, and the CODASYL model (network model), implemented in a number of products such as IDMS.

The relational model, first proposed in 1970 by Edgar F. Codd, departed from this tradition by insisting that applications should search for data by content, rather than by following links. The relational model employs sets of ledger-style tables, each used for a different type of entity. Only in the mid-1980s did computing hardware become powerful enough to allow the wide deployment of relational systems (DBMSs plus applications). By the early 1990s, however, relational systems dominated in all large-scale data processing applications, and as of 2015 they remain dominant : IBM DB2, Oracle, MySQL, and Microsoft SQL Server are the top DBMS. The dominant database language, standardised SQL for the relational model, has influenced database languages for other data models.

Object databases were developed in the 1980s to overcome the inconvenience of object-relational impedance mismatch, which led to the coining of the term "post-relational" and also the development of hybrid object-relational databases.

The next generation of post-relational databases in the late 2000s became known as NoSQL databases, introducing fast key-value stores and document-oriented databases. A competing "next generation" known as NewSQL databases attempted new implementations that retained the relational/SQL model while aiming to match the high performance of NoSQL compared to commercially available relational DBMSs.

1960s, Navigational DBMS

The introduction of the term *database* coincided with the availability of direct-access storage (disks and drums) from the mid-1960s onwards. The term represented a contrast with the tape-based systems of the past, allowing shared interactive use rather than daily batch processing. The Oxford English Dictionary cites a 1962 report by the System Development Corporation of California as the first to use the term "data-base" in a specific technical sense.

As computers grew in speed and capability, a number of general-purpose database systems emerged; by the mid-1960s a number of such systems had come into commercial use. Interest in a standard began to grow, and Charles Bachman, author of one such product, the Integrated Data Store (IDS), founded the "Database Task Group" within CODASYL, the group responsible for the creation and standardization of COBOL. In 1971, the Database Task Group delivered their standard, which generally became known as the "CODASYL approach", and soon a number of commercial products based on this approach entered the market.

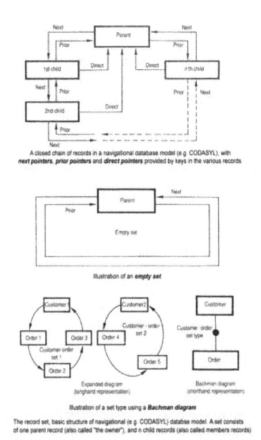

A closed chain of records in a navigational database model (e.g. CODASYL), with **next pointers**, **prior pointers** and **direct pointers** provided by keys in the various records.

Illustration of an **empty set**

Illustration of a set type using a **Bachman diagram**

The record set, basic structure of navigational (e.g. CODASYL) database model. A set consists of one parent record (also called "the owner"), and n child records (also called members records).

Basic structure of navigational CODASYL database model

The CODASYL approach relied on the "manual" navigation of a linked data set which was formed into a large network. Applications could find records by one of three methods:

1.   Use of a primary key (known as a CALC key, typically implemented by hashing)

2.   Navigating relationships (called sets) from one record to another

3.   Scanning all the records in a sequential order

Later systems added B-trees to provide alternate access paths. Many CODASYL databases also added a very straightforward query language. However, in the final tally, CODASYL was very complex and required significant training and effort to produce useful applications.

IBM also had their own DBMS in 1966, known as Information Management System (IMS). IMS was a development of software written for the Apollo program on the System/360. IMS was generally similar in concept to CODASYL, but used a strict hierarchy for its model of data navigation instead of CODASYL's network model. Both concepts later became known as navigational databases due to the way data was accessed, and Bachman's 1973 Turing Award presentation was *The Programmer as Navigator*. IMS is classified as a hierarchical database. IDMS and Cincom Systems' TOTAL database are classified as network databases. IMS remains in use as of 2014.

1970s, Relational DBMS

Edgar Codd worked at IBM in San Jose, California, in one of their offshoot offices that was primarily involved in the development of hard disk systems. He was unhappy with the navigational model of the CODASYL approach, notably the lack of a "search" facility. In 1970, he wrote a number of papers that outlined a new approach to database construction that eventually culminated in the groundbreaking *A Relational Model of Data for Large Shared Data Banks.*

In this paper, he described a new system for storing and working with large databases. Instead of records being stored in some sort of linked list of free-form records as in CODASYL, Codd's idea was to use a "table" of fixed-length records, with each table used for a different type of entity. A linked-list system would be very inefficient when storing "sparse" databases where some of the data for any one record could be left empty. The relational model solved this by splitting the data into a series of normalized tables (or *relations*), with optional elements being moved out of the main table to where they would take up room only if needed. Data may be freely inserted, deleted and edited in these tables, with the DBMS doing whatever maintenance needed to present a table view to the application/user.

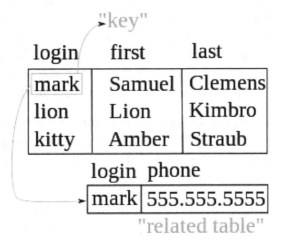

In the relational model, records are "linked" using virtual keys not stored in the database but defined as needed between the data contained in the records.

The relational model also allowed the content of the database to evolve without constant rewriting of links and pointers. The relational part comes from entities referencing other entities in what is known as one-to-many relationship, like a traditional hierarchical model, and many-to-many relationship, like a navigational (network) model. Thus, a relational model can express both hierarchical and navigational models, as well as its native tabular model, allowing for pure or combined modeling in terms of these three models, as the application requires.

For instance, a common use of a database system is to track information about users, their name, login information, various addresses and phone numbers. In the navigational approach, all of this data would be placed in a single record, and unused items would simply not be placed in the database. In the relational approach, the data would be *normalized* into a user table, an address table and a phone number table (for instance). Records would be created in these optional tables only if the address or phone numbers were actually provided.

Linking the information back together is the key to this system. In the relational model, some bit of information was used as a "key", uniquely defining a particular record. When information was being collected about a user, information stored in the optional tables would be found by searching for this key. For instance, if the login name of a user is unique, addresses and phone numbers for that user would be recorded with the login name as its key. This simple "re-linking" of related data back into a single collection is something that traditional computer languages are not designed for.

Just as the navigational approach would require programs to loop in order to collect records, the relational approach would require loops to collect information about any *one* record. Codd's solution to the necessary looping was a set-oriented language, a suggestion that would later spawn the ubiquitous SQL. Using a branch of mathematics known as tuple calculus, he demonstrated that such a system could support all the operations of normal databases (inserting, updating etc.) as well as providing a simple system for finding and returning *sets* of data in a single operation.

Codd's paper was picked up by two people at Berkeley, Eugene Wong and Michael Stonebraker. They started a project known as INGRES using funding that had already been allocated for a geographical database project and student programmers to produce code. Beginning in 1973, INGRES delivered its first test products which were generally ready for widespread use in 1979. INGRES was similar to System R in a number of ways, including the use of a "language" for data access, known as QUEL. Over time, INGRES moved to the emerging SQL standard.

IBM itself did one test implementation of the relational model, PRTV, and a production one, Business System 12, both now discontinued. Honeywell wrote MRDS for Multics, and now there are two new implementations: Alphora Dataphor and Rel. Most other DBMS implementations usually called *relational* are actually SQL DBMSs.

In 1970, the University of Michigan began development of the MICRO Information Management System based on D.L. Childs' Set-Theoretic Data model. MICRO was used to manage very large data sets by the US Department of Labor, the U.S. Environmental Protection Agency, and researchers from the University of Alberta, the University of Michigan, and Wayne State University. It ran on IBM mainframe computers using the Michigan Terminal System. The system remained in production until 1998.

Integrated Approach

In the 1970s and 1980s, attempts were made to build database systems with integrated hardware and software. The underlying philosophy was that such integration would provide higher performance at lower cost. Examples were IBM System/38, the early offering of Teradata, and the Britton Lee, Inc. database machine.

Another approach to hardware support for database management was ICL's CAFS accelerator, a hardware disk controller with programmable search capabilities. In the long term, these efforts were generally unsuccessful because specialized database machines could not keep pace with the rapid development and progress of general-purpose computers. Thus most database systems nowadays are software systems running on general-purpose hardware, using general-purpose computer data storage. However this idea is still pursued for certain applications by some companies like Netezza and Oracle (Exadata).

Late 1970s, SQL DBMS

IBM started working on a prototype system loosely based on Codd's concepts as *System R* in the early 1970s. The first version was ready in 1974/5, and work then started on multi-table systems in which the data could be split so that all of the data for a record (some of which is optional) did not have to be stored in a single large "chunk". Subsequent multi-user versions were tested by customers in 1978 and 1979, by which time a standardized query language – SQL – had been added. Codd's ideas were establishing themselves as both workable and superior to CODASYL, pushing IBM to develop a true production version of System R, known as *SQL/DS*, and, later, *Database 2* (DB2).

Larry Ellison's Oracle started from a different chain, based on IBM's papers on System R, and beat IBM to market when the first version was released in 1978.

Stonebraker went on to apply the lessons from INGRES to develop a new database, Postgres, which is now known as PostgreSQL. PostgreSQL is often used for global mission critical applications (the .org and .info domain name registries use it as their primary data store, as do many large companies and financial institutions).

In Sweden, Codd's paper was also read and Mimer SQL was developed from the mid-1970s at Uppsala University. In 1984, this project was consolidated into an independent enterprise. In the early 1980s, Mimer introduced transaction handling for high robustness in applications, an idea that was subsequently implemented on most other DBMSs.

Another data model, the entity–relationship model, emerged in 1976 and gained popularity for database design as it emphasized a more familiar description than the earlier relational model. Later on, entity–relationship constructs were retrofitted as a data modeling construct for the relational model, and the difference between the two have become irrelevant.

1980s, on the Desktop

The 1980s ushered in the age of desktop computing. The new computers empowered their users with spreadsheets like Lotus 1-2-3 and database software like dBASE. The dBASE product was lightweight and easy for any computer user to understand out of the box. C. Wayne Ratliff the creator of dBASE stated: "dBASE was different from programs like BASIC, C, FORTRAN, and COBOL in that a lot of the dirty work had already been done. The data manipulation is done by dBASE instead of by the user, so the user can concentrate on what he is doing, rather than having to mess with the dirty details of opening, reading, and closing files, and managing space allocation." dBASE was one of the top selling software titles in the 1980s and early 1990s.

1990s, Object-oriented

The 1990s, along with a rise in object-oriented programming, saw a growth in how data in various databases were handled. Programmers and designers began to treat the data in their databases as objects. That is to say that if a person's data were in a database, that person's attributes, such as their address, phone number, and age, were now considered to belong to that person instead of being extraneous data. This allows for relations between data to be relations to objects and their attributes and not to individual fields. The term "object-relational impedance mismatch" described the inconvenience of translating between programmed objects and database tables. Object databases and object-relational databases attempt to solve this problem by providing an object-oriented language (sometimes as extensions to SQL) that programmers can use as alternative to purely relational SQL. On the programming side, libraries known as object-relational mappings (ORMs) attempt to solve the same problem.

2000s, NoSQL and NewSQL

XML databases are a type of structured document-oriented database that allows querying based on XML document attributes. XML databases are mostly used in enterprise database management, where XML is being used as the machine-to-machine data interoperability standard. XML database management systems include commercial software MarkLogic and Oracle Berkeley DB XML, and a free use software Clusterpoint Distributed XML/JSON Database. All are enterprise software database platforms and support industry standard ACID-compliant transaction processing with strong database consistency characteristics and high level of database security.

NoSQL databases are often very fast, do not require fixed table schemas, avoid join operations by storing denormalized data, and are designed to scale horizontally. The most popular NoSQL systems include MongoDB, Couchbase, Riak, Memcached, Redis, CouchDB, Hazelcast, Apache Cassandra, and HBase, which are all open-source software products.

In recent years, there was a high demand for massively distributed databases with high partition tolerance but according to the CAP theorem it is impossible for a distributed system to simultaneously provide consistency, availability, and partition tolerance guarantees. A distributed system can satisfy any two of these guarantees at the same time, but not all three. For that reason, many NoSQL databases are using what is called eventual consistency to provide both availability and partition tolerance guarantees with a reduced level of data consistency.

NewSQL is a class of modern relational databases that aims to provide the same scalable performance of NoSQL systems for online transaction processing (read-write) workloads while still using SQL and maintaining the ACID guarantees of a traditional database system. Such databases include ScaleBase, Clustrix, EnterpriseDB, MemSQL, NuoDB, and VoltDB.

Research

Database technology has been an active research topic since the 1960s, both in academia and in the research and development groups of companies (for example IBM Research). Research activity includes theory and development of prototypes. Notable research topics have included models, the atomic transaction concept, and related concurrency control techniques, query languages and query optimization methods, RAID, and more.

The database research area has several dedicated academic journals (for example, *ACM Transactions on Database Systems*-TODS, *Data and Knowledge Engineering*-DKE) and annual conferences (e.g., ACM SIGMOD, ACM PODS, VLDB, IEEE ICDE).

Examples

One way to classify databases involves the type of their contents, for example: bibliographic, document-text, statistical, or multimedia objects. Another way is by their application area, for example: accounting, music compositions, movies, banking, manufacturing, or insurance. A third way is by some technical aspect, such as the database structure or interface type. This section lists a few of the adjectives used to characterize different kinds of databases.

- An in-memory database is a database that primarily resides in main memory, but is typically backed-up by non-volatile computer data storage. Main memory databases are faster than disk databases, and so are often used where response time is critical, such as in telecommunications network equipment. SAP HANA platform is a very hot topic for in-memory database. By May 2012, HANA was able to run on servers with 100TB main memory powered by IBM. The co founder of the company claimed that the system was big enough to run the 8 largest SAP customers.

- An active database includes an event-driven architecture which can respond to conditions both inside and outside the database. Possible uses include security monitoring, alerting, statistics gathering and authorization. Many databases provide active database features in the form of database triggers.

- A cloud database relies on cloud technology. Both the database and most of its DBMS reside remotely, "in the cloud", while its applications are both developed by programmers and later maintained and utilized by (application's) end-users through a web browser and Open APIs.

- Data warehouses archive data from operational databases and often from external sources such as market research firms. The warehouse becomes the central source of data for use by managers and other end-users who may not have access to operational data. For example, sales data might be aggregated to weekly totals and converted from internal product codes to use UPCs so that they can be compared with ACNielsen data. Some basic and essential components of data warehousing include extracting, analyzing, and mining data, transforming, loading, and managing data so as to make them available for further use.

- A deductive database combines logic programming with a relational database, for example by using the Datalog language.

- A distributed database is one in which both the data and the DBMS span multiple computers.

- A document-oriented database is designed for storing, retrieving, and managing document-oriented, or semi structured data, information. Document-oriented databases are one of the main categories of NoSQL databases.

- An embedded database system is a DBMS which is tightly integrated with an application software that requires access to stored data in such a way that the DBMS is hidden from the application's end-users and requires little or no ongoing maintenance.

- End-user databases consist of data developed by individual end-users. Examples of these are collections of documents, spreadsheets, presentations, multimedia, and other files. Several products exist to support such databases. Some of them are much simpler than full-fledged DBMSs, with more elementary DBMS functionality.

- A federated database system comprises several distinct databases, each with its own DBMS. It is handled as a single database by a federated database management system (FDBMS), which transparently integrates multiple autonomous DBMSs, possibly of different types (in which case it would also be a heterogeneous database system), and provides them with an integrated conceptual view.

- Sometimes the term *multi-database* is used as a synonym to federated database, though it may refer to a less integrated (e.g., without an FDBMS and a managed integrated schema) group of databases that cooperate in a single application. In this case, typically middleware is used for distribution, which typically includes an atomic commit protocol (ACP), e.g., the two-phase commit protocol, to allow distributed (global) transactions across the participating databases.

- A graph database is a kind of NoSQL database that uses graph structures with nodes, edges, and properties to represent and store information. General graph databases that can store any graph are distinct from specialized graph databases such as triplestores and network databases.

- An array DBMS is a kind of NoSQL DBMS that allows to model, store, and retrieve (usually large) multi-dimensional arrays such as satellite images and climate simulation output.

- In a hypertext or hypermedia database, any word or a piece of text representing an object, e.g., another piece of text, an article, a picture, or a film, can be hyperlinked to that object. Hypertext databases are particularly useful for organizing large amounts of disparate information. For example, they are useful for organizing online encyclopedias, where users can conveniently jump around the text. The World Wide Web is thus a large distributed hypertext database.

- A knowledge base (abbreviated KB, kb or Δ) is a special kind of database for knowledge management, providing the means for the computerized collection, organization, and retrieval of knowledge. Also a collection of data representing problems with their solutions and related experiences.

- A mobile database can be carried on or synchronized from a mobile computing device.

- Operational databases store detailed data about the operations of an organization. They typically process relatively high volumes of updates using transactions. Examples include customer databases that record contact, credit, and demographic information about a business' customers, personnel databases that hold information such as salary, benefits, skills data about employees, enterprise resource planning systems that record details about product components, parts inventory, and financial databases that keep track of the organization's money, accounting and financial dealings.

- A parallel database seeks to improve performance through parallelization for tasks such as loading data, building indexes and evaluating queries.

- The major parallel DBMS architectures which are induced by the underlying hardware architecture are:

- Shared memory architecture, where multiple processors share the main memory space, as well as other data storage.

- Shared disk architecture, where each processing unit (typically consisting of multiple processors) has its own main memory, but all units share the other storage.

- Shared nothing architecture, where each processing unit has its own main memory and other storage.

- Probabilistic databases employ fuzzy logic to draw inferences from imprecise data.

- Real-time databases process transactions fast enough for the result to come back and be acted on right away.

- A spatial database can store the data with multidimensional features. The queries on such data include location-based queries, like "Where is the closest hotel in my area?".

- A temporal database has built-in time aspects, for example a temporal data model and a temporal version of SQL. More specifically the temporal aspects usually include valid-time and transaction-time.

- A terminology-oriented database builds upon an object-oriented database, often customized for a specific field.

- An unstructured data database is intended to store in a manageable and protected way diverse objects that do not fit naturally and conveniently in common databases. It may include email messages, documents, journals, multimedia objects, etc. The name may be misleading since some objects can be highly structured. However, the entire possible object collection does not fit into a predefined structured framework. Most established DBMSs now support unstructured data in various ways, and new dedicated DBMSs are emerging.

Design and Modeling

The first task of a database designer is to produce a conceptual data model that reflects the structure of the information to be held in the database. A common approach to this is to develop an entity-relationship model, often with the aid of drawing tools. Another popular approach is the Unified Modeling Language. A successful data model will accurately reflect the possible state of the external world being modeled: for example, if people can have more than one phone number, it will allow this information to be captured. Designing a good conceptual data model requires a good understanding of the application domain; it typically involves asking deep questions about the things of interest to an organisation, like "can a customer also be a supplier?", or "if a product is sold with two different forms of packaging, are those the same product or different products?", or "if a plane flies from New York to Dubai via Frankfurt, is that one flight or two (or maybe even three)?". The answers to these questions establish definitions of the terminology used for entities (customers, products, flights, flight segments) and their relationships and attributes.

Producing the conceptual data model sometimes involves input from business processes, or the analysis of workflow in the organization. This can help to establish what information is needed in the database, and what can be left out. For example, it can help when deciding whether the database needs to hold historic data as well as current data.

Having produced a conceptual data model that users are happy with, the next stage is to translate this into a schema that implements the relevant data structures within the database. This process is often called logical database design, and the output is a logical data model expressed in the form of a schema. Whereas the conceptual data model is (in theory at least) independent of the choice of database technology, the logical data model will be expressed in terms of a particular database model supported by the chosen DBMS.

The most popular database model for general-purpose databases is the relational model, or more precisely, the relational model as represented by the SQL language. The process of creating a logical database design using this model uses a methodical approach known as normalization. The goal of normalization is to ensure that each elementary "fact" is only recorded in one place, so that insertions, updates, and deletions automatically maintain consistency.

The final stage of database design is to make the decisions that affect performance, scalability, recovery, security, and the like. This is often called *physical database design*. A key goal during this stage is data independence, meaning that the decisions made for performance optimization purposes should be invisible to end-users and applications. Physical design is driven mainly by performance requirements, and requires a good knowledge of the expected workload and access patterns, and a deep understanding of the features offered by the chosen DBMS.

Another aspect of physical database design is security. It involves both defining access control to database objects as well as defining security levels and methods for the data itself.

Models

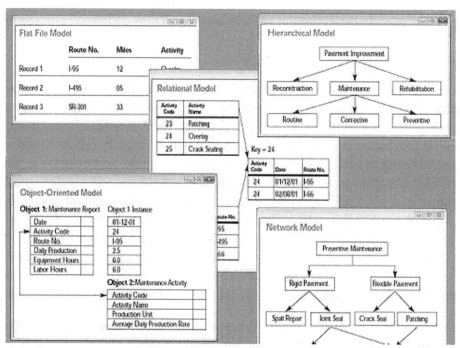

Collage of five types of database models

A database model is a type of data model that determines the logical structure of a database and fundamentally determines in which manner data can be stored, organized, and manipulated. The most popular example of a database model is the relational model (or the SQL approximation of relational), which uses a table-based format.

Common logical data models for databases include:

- Navigational databases
    - Hierarchical database model
    - Network model
    - Graph database
- Relational model
- Entity–relationship model
    - Enhanced entity–relationship model
- Object model
- Document model
- Entity–attribute–value model
- Star schema

An object-relational database combines the two related structures.

Physical data models include:

- Inverted index
- Flat file

Other models include:

- Associative model
- Multidimensional model
- Array model
- Multivalue model

Specialized models are optimized for particular types of data:

- XML database
- Semantic model
- Content store
- Event store
- Time series model

External, Conceptual, and Internal Views

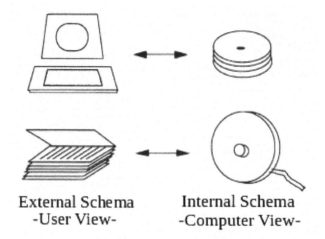

External Schema
-User View-

Internal Schema
-Computer View-

Traditional view of data

A database management system provides three views of the database data:

- The external level defines how each group of end-users sees the organization of data in the database. A single database can have any number of views at the external level.

- The conceptual level unifies the various external views into a compatible global view. It provides the synthesis of all the external views. It is out of the scope of the various database end-users, and is rather of interest to database application developers and database administrators.

- The internal level (or *physical level*) is the internal organization of data inside a DBMS. It is concerned with cost, performance, scalability and other operational matters. It deals with storage layout of the data, using storage structures such as indexes to enhance performance. Occasionally it stores data of individual views (materialized views), computed from generic data, if performance justification exists for such redundancy. It balances all the external views' performance requirements, possibly conflicting, in an attempt to optimize overall performance across all activities.

While there is typically only one conceptual (or logical) and physical (or internal) view of the data, there can be any number of different external views. This allows users to see database information in a more business-related way rather than from a technical, processing viewpoint. For example, a financial department of a company needs the payment details of all employees as part of the company's expenses, but does not need details about employees that are the interest of the human resources department. Thus different departments need different *views* of the company's database.

The three-level database architecture relates to the concept of *data independence* which was one of the major initial driving forces of the relational model. The idea is that changes made at a certain level do not affect the view at a higher level. For example, changes in the internal level do not affect application programs written using conceptual level interfaces, which reduces the impact of making physical changes to improve performance.

The conceptual view provides a level of indirection between internal and external. On one hand it provides a common view of the database, independent of different external view structures, and on the other hand it abstracts away details of how the data are stored or managed (internal level). In principle every level, and even every external view, can be presented by a different data model. In practice usually a given DBMS uses the same data model for both the external and the conceptual levels (e.g., relational model). The internal level, which is hidden inside the DBMS and depends on its implementation, requires a different level of detail and uses its own types of data structure types.

Separating the *external, conceptual* and *internal* levels was a major feature of the relational database model implementations that dominate 21st century databases.

Languages

Database languages are special-purpose languages, which do one or more of the following:

- Data definition language – defines data types and the relationships among them

- Data manipulation language – performs tasks such as inserting, updating, or deleting data occurrences

- Query language – allows searching for information and computing derived information

- Database languages are specific to a particular data model. Notable examples include:

- SQL combines the roles of data definition, data manipulation, and query in a single language. It was one of the first commercial languages for the relational model, although it departs in some respects from the relational model as described by Codd (for example, the rows and columns of a table can be ordered). SQL became a standard of the American National Standards Institute (ANSI) in 1986, and of the International Organization for Standardization (ISO) in 1987. The standards have been regularly enhanced since and is supported (with varying degrees of conformance) by all mainstream commercial relational DBMSs.

- OQL is an object model language standard (from the Object Data Management Group). It has influenced the design of some of the newer query languages like JDOQL and EJB QL.

- XQuery is a standard XML query language implemented by XML database systems such as MarkLogic and eXist, by relational databases with XML capability such as Oracle and DB2, and also by in-memory XML processors such as Saxon.

- SQL/XML combines XQuery with SQL.

- A database language may also incorporate features like:

- DBMS-specific Configuration and storage engine management

- Computations to modify query results, like counting, summing, averaging, sorting, grouping, and cross-referencing

- Constraint enforcement (e.g. in an automotive database, only allowing one engine type per car)

- Application programming interface version of the query language, for programmer convenience

Performance, Security, and Availability

Because of the critical importance of database technology to the smooth running of an enterprise, database systems include complex mechanisms to deliver the required performance, security, and availability, and allow database administrators to control the use of these features.

Storage

Database storage is the container of the physical materialization of a database. It comprises the *internal* (physical) *level* in the database architecture. It also contains all the information needed (e.g., metadata, "data about the data", and internal data structures) to reconstruct the *conceptual level* and *external level* from the internal level when needed. Putting data into permanent storage is generally the responsibility of the database engine a.k.a. "storage engine". Though typically accessed by a DBMS through the underlying operating system (and often utilizing the operating systems' file systems as intermediates for storage layout), storage properties and configuration setting are extremely important for the efficient operation of the DBMS, and thus are closely maintained by database administrators. A DBMS, while in operation, always has its database residing in several types of storage (e.g., memory and external storage). The database data and the additional needed information, possibly in very large amounts, are coded into bits. Data typically reside in the storage in structures that look completely different from the way the data look in the conceptual and external levels, but in ways that attempt to optimize (the best possible) these levels' reconstruction when needed by users and programs, as well as for computing additional types of needed information from the data (e.g., when querying the database).

Some DBMSs support specifying which character encoding was used to store data, so multiple encodings can be used in the same database.

Various low-level database storage structures are used by the storage engine to serialize the data model so it can be written to the medium of choice. Techniques such as indexing may be used to improve performance. Conventional storage is row-oriented, but there are also column-oriented and correlation databases.

Materialized Views

Often storage redundancy is employed to increase performance. A common example is storing *materialized views*, which consist of frequently needed *external views* or query results. Storing such views saves the expensive computing of them each time they are needed. The downsides of materialized views are the overhead incurred when updating them to keep them synchronized with their original updated database data, and the cost of storage redundancy.

Replication

Occasionally a database employs storage redundancy by database objects replication (with one or more copies) to increase data availability (both to improve performance of simultaneous multiple end-user accesses to a same database object, and to provide resiliency in a case of partial failure of a distributed database). Updates of a replicated object need to be synchronized across the object copies. In many cases, the entire database is replicated.

Security

Database security deals with all various aspects of protecting the database content, its owners, and its users. It ranges from protection from intentional unauthorized database uses to unintentional database accesses by unauthorized entities (e.g., a person or a computer program).

Database access control deals with controlling who (a person or a certain computer program) is allowed to access what information in the database. The information may comprise specific database objects (e.g., record types, specific records, data structures), certain computations over certain objects (e.g., query types, or specific queries), or utilizing specific access paths to the former (e.g., using specific indexes or other data structures to access information). Database access controls are set by special authorized (by the database owner) personnel that uses dedicated protected security DBMS interfaces.

This may be managed directly on an individual basis, or by the assignment of individuals and privileges to groups, or (in the most elaborate models) through the assignment of individuals and groups to roles which are then granted entitlements. Data security prevents unauthorized users from viewing or updating the database. Using passwords, users are allowed access to the entire database or subsets of it called "subschemas". For example, an employee database can contain all the data about an individual employee, but one group of users may be authorized to view only payroll data, while others are allowed access to only work history and medical data. If the DBMS provides a way to interactively enter and update the database, as well as interrogate it, this capability allows for managing personal databases.

Data security in general deals with protecting specific chunks of data, both physically (i.e., from corruption, or destruction, or remova), or the interpretation of them, or parts of them to meaningful information (e.g., by looking at the strings of bits that they comprise, concluding specific valid credit-card numbers).

Change and access logging records who accessed which attributes, what was changed, and when it was changed. Logging services allow for a forensic database audit later by keeping a record of access occurrences and changes. Sometimes application-level code is used to record changes rather than leaving this to the database. Monitoring can be set up to attempt to detect security breaches.

Transactions and Concurrency

Database transactions can be used to introduce some level of fault tolerance and data integrity after recovery from a crash. A database transaction is a unit of work, typically encapsulating a number of operations over a database (e.g., reading a database object, writing, acquiring lock, etc.), an abstraction supported in database and also other systems. Each transaction has well defined boundaries in terms of which program/code executions are included in that transaction (determined by the transaction's programmer via special transaction commands).

The acronym ACID describes some ideal properties of a database transaction: Atomicity, Consistency, Isolation, and Durability.

Migration

A database built with one DBMS is not portable to another DBMS (i.e., the other DBMS cannot run it). However, in some situations, it is desirable to move, migrate a database from one DBMS to another. The reasons are primarily economical (different DBMSs may have different total costs of ownership or TCOs), functional, and operational (different DBMSs may have different capabilities). The migration involves the database's transformation from one DBMS type to another. The transformation should maintain (if possible) the database related application (i.e., all related application programs) intact. Thus, the database's conceptual and external architectural levels should be maintained in the transformation. It may be desired that also some aspects of the architecture internal level are maintained. A complex or large database migration may be a complicated and costly (one-time) project by itself, which should be factored into the decision to migrate. This in spite of the fact that tools may exist to help migration between specific DBMSs. Typically, a DBMS vendor provides tools to help importing databases from other popular DBMSs.

Building, Maintaining, and Tuning

After designing a database for an application, the next stage is building the database. Typically, an appropriate general-purpose DBMS can be selected to be utilized for this purpose. A DBMS provides the needed user interfaces to be utilized by database administrators to define the needed application's data structures within the DBMS's respective data model. Other user interfaces are used to select needed DBMS parameters (like security related, storage allocation parameters, etc.).

When the database is ready (all its data structures and other needed components are defined), it is typically populated with initial application's data (database initialization, which is typically a distinct project; in many cases using specialized DBMS interfaces that support bulk insertion) before making it operational. In some cases, the database becomes operational while empty of application data, and data are accumulated during its operation.

After the database is created, initialised and populated it needs to be maintained. Various database parameters may need changing and the database may need to be tuned (tuning) for better performance; application's data structures may be changed or added, new related application programs may be written to add to the application's functionality, etc.

Backup and Restore

Sometimes it is desired to bring a database back to a previous state (for many reasons, e.g., cases when the database is found corrupted due to a software error, or if it has been updated with erroneous data). To achieve this, a backup operation is done occasionally or continuously, where each desired database state (i.e., the values of its data and their embedding in database's data structures) is kept within dedicated backup files (many techniques exist to do this effectively). When this state is needed, i.e., when it is decided by a database administrator to bring the database back to this state (e.g., by specifying this state by a desired point in time when the database was in this state), these files are utilized to restore that state.

Static Analysis

Static analysis techniques for software verification can be applied also in the scenario of query languages. In particular, the *Abstract interpretation framework has been extended to the field of query languages for relational databases as a way to support sound approximation techniques.

The semantics of query languages can be tuned according to suitable abstractions of the concrete domain of data. The abstraction of relational database system has many interesting applications, in particular, for security purposes, such as fine grained access control, watermarking, etc.

Other

Other DBMS features might include:

- Database logs

- Graphics component for producing graphs and charts, especially in a data warehouse system

- Query optimizer – Performs query optimization on every query to choose for it the most efficient *query plan* (a partial order (tree) of operations) to be executed to compute the query result. May be specific to a particular storage engine.

- Tools or hooks for database design, application programming, application program maintenance, database performance analysis and monitoring, database configuration monitoring, DBMS hardware configuration (a DBMS and related database may span computers, networks, and storage units) and related database mapping (especially for a distributed DBMS), storage allocation and database layout monitoring, storage migration, etc.

- Increasingly, there are calls for a single systems and methodology that incorporates all of these core functionalities into the same build, test, and deployment framework for database management and source control. Borrowing from other developments in the software industry, some are labeling such offerings "DevOps for Database". Packaged thusly, these database management solutions are supposed to be stable, secure, backed up, compliant, testable, and consistent between environments.

References

- Luger, George; Stubblefield, William (2004). Artificial Intelligence: Structures and Strategies for Complex Problem Solving (5th ed.). Benjamin/Cummings. ISBN 0-8053-4780-1.

- Russell, Stuart J.; Norvig, Peter (2003), Artificial Intelligence: A Modern Approach (2nd ed.), Upper Saddle River, New Jersey: Prentice Hall, ISBN 0-13-790395-2 .

- Poole, David; Mackworth, Alan; Goebel, Randy (1998). Computational Intelligence: A Logical Approach. New York: Oxford University Press. ISBN 0-19-510270-3.

- Bundy, Alan (1980). Artificial Intelligence: An Introductory Course (2nd ed.). Edinburgh University Press. ISBN 0-85224-410-X.

- Russell, Stuart; Norvig, Peter (2003) [1995]. Artificial Intelligence: A Modern Approach (2nd ed.). Prentice Hall. ISBN 978-0137903955.

- Mehryar Mohri, Afshin Rostamizadeh, Ameet Talwalkar (2012) Foundations of Machine Learning, MIT Press ISBN 978-0-262-01825-8.

- Moore, David (1992). "Teaching Statistics as a Respectable Subject". In F. Gordon and S. Gordon. Statistics for the Twenty-First Century. Washington, DC: The Mathematical Association of America. pp. 14–25. ISBN 978-0-88385-078-7.

- Chance, Beth L.; Rossman, Allan J. (2005). "Preface". Investigating Statistical Concepts, Applications, and

Methods (PDF). Duxbury Press. ISBN 978-0-495-05064-3.

- Lakshmikantham,, ed. by D. Kannan,... V. (2002). Handbook of stochastic analysis and applications. New York: M. Dekker. ISBN 0824706609.

- Everitt, Brian (1998). The Cambridge Dictionary of Statistics. Cambridge, UK New York: Cambridge University Press. ISBN 0521593468.

- Drennan, Robert D. (2008). "Statistics in archaeology". In Pearsall, Deborah M. Encyclopedia of Archaeology. Elsevier Inc. pp. 2093–2100. ISBN 978-0-12-373962-9.

- Anderson, D.R.; Sweeney, D.J.; Williams, T.A. (1994) Introduction to Statistics: Concepts and Applications, pp. 5–9. West Group. ISBN 978-0-314-03309-3

- A. M. Tillmann, "On the Computational Intractability of Exact and Approximate Dictionary Learning", IEEE Signal Processing Letters 22(1), 2015: 45–49.

- Cornell University Library. "Breiman : Statistical Modeling: The Two Cultures (with comments and a rejoinder by the author)". Retrieved 8 August 2015.

Permissions

Index